Parasites

The publisher gratefully acknowledges the generous support of the General Endowment Fund of the University of California Press Foundation.

Parasites

TALES OF HUMANITY'S MOST UNWELCOME GUESTS

Rosemary Drisdelle

UNIVERSITY OF CALIFORNIA PRESS

BERKELEY   LOS ANGELES   LONDON

University of California Press, one of the most
distinguished university presses in the United States,
enriches lives around the world by advancing scholarship
in the humanities, social sciences, and natural sciences.
Its activities are supported by the UC Press Foundation
and by philanthropic contributions from individuals
and institutions. For more information, visit
www.ucpress.edu.

University of California Press
Berkeley and Los Angeles, California

University of California Press, Ltd.
London, England

Library of Congress Cataloging-in-Publication Data
Drisdelle, Rosemary.
   Parasites : tales of humanity's most unwelcome guests /
Rosemary Drisdelle.
      p.   cm.
   Includes bibliographical references and index.
   ISBN 978-0-520-25938-6 (cloth : alk. paper)
   1. Parasites—Popular works.   I. Title.
QL757.D75   2010
591.6′5—dc22   2009026476

Manufactured in the United States of America
19 18 17 16 15 14 13 12 11 10
10 9 8 7 6 5 4 3 2 1

This book is printed on Cascades Enviro 100, a 100%
post consumer waste, recycled, de-inked fiber. FSC
recycled certified and processed chlorine free. It is acid
free, Ecologo certified, and manufactured by BioGas
energy.

To my husband, Vic, for giving me a new beginning and leaving me in peace to do something with it.

HOW PEOPLE GOT WORMS

In the beginning,
the Earth mother took a handful of clay
and rolled it between her palms,
rolled it and rolled it
    absently thinking
of calla lilies, fig blossoms, bull rushes.
It was long, and thin, and slippery
as entrails dangling from a buzzard's hooked beak.
She breathed on it thoughtlessly;
it wriggled and
      twisted
   like
    a serpent.
Now it had her attention,
and she saw that it was not good,
so she hid it
under Adam's rib.

ROSEMARY DRISDELLE
The Prairie Journal, 2006

CONTENTS

ILLUSTRATIONS

FIGURES

MAPS

ACKNOWLEDGMENTS

Many individuals contributed encouragement, suggestions, leads to new information, constructive criticism, and other assistance of various kinds to this work. My sincere thanks to all of them, in particular Judy Arbique, Russ Barton, William Campbell, Sally Colwell, David Cone, Geraldine Cooper Lesins, Kevin Forward, Clare Goulet, David Haldane, Todd Hatchette, Glen Lesins, Carolyn Swayze, my father, Martin Thomas, and the staff of microbiology at the QEII Health Sciences Centre in Halifax, Nova Scotia. Special thanks also to my agent, Michelle Tessler.

To my family, especially my husband, Victor Drisdelle, and my children, Beth McClelland, Kat McClelland, and Drew McClelland, thanks for your encouragement and for allowing me precious time to study and to write.

AUTHOR'S NOTE

A note about pseudonyms and fictitious characters: This is a work of nonfiction. In some accounts, pseudonyms are used when the real names are not known, or to protect the privacy of individuals whose identities are of no significance to this book. Where certain facts were not recorded, I have inferred details about cases from the available information. And in the rare instances in which I have created a character, I have aimed for a realistic composite of all those who have experienced the events under discussion. Again, I have done so only when an appropriate account of a single real individual was not available. In all cases, I have endeavored to make clear which details are fact and which are not.

Introduction

PARASITES ARE ALL AROUND US. Consider the ones that infect humans: hundreds of species live in human intestines, skin, lungs, muscle, brain, liver, blood, and everywhere else they can find a niche. Some of these parasites can live *only* in humans. When you realize that virtually every species of animal has a similarly large collection, and then acknowledge that plants have many as well, you begin to understand how numerous parasites really are. Even parasites have parasites.

Parasites are an odd and exceedingly diverse assortment of life forms that defy generalization: essentially their actions define them. The word *parasite* was first applied to humans, used to describe people who live by taking from others. The self-serving activities of such people are damaging to their hosts, whose resources they deplete. A *parasite* in the biological sense is similar: a parasite lives on, or in, another species, getting everything it needs from its host. In keeping with the cultural view that a parasite is a despicable creature, the strictest biological view holds that parasites damage their hosts.[1]

Curiously, however, the word *parasite* isn't used consistently to describe all life forms that live in this way. Bacteria, fungi, and viruses that multiply in the tissues of other species are traditionally excluded. Tiny predators, such as mosquitoes, are excluded as well because they feed on, but don't live on, their hosts. In a medical sense, at least, parasites include protozoa, worms, and certain things with legs, such as mites and insects—but only those that must spend at least part of their lives in or on the tissues of other living things.

We usually hear about parasites when they make people sick. Or we encounter them as a subject of revulsion—disgusting creatures to be annihilated as speedily as possible. Someone who unexpectedly discharges an intestinal worm is likely to grab the nearest makeshift weapon and pulverize it within seconds, despite the creature's utter inability to attack. If we discover an infestation of head lice, we quickly go on the attack, even if we have to douse ourselves with insecticides to win the battle. Even our enthusiasm for mistletoe, a traditional symbol of magic and affection, loses its luster when we learn that the plant is parasitic.

Our view of parasitism is a narrow one. Parasites not only have far-reaching and important impacts on the earth's ecology, but they have much broader effects on our daily lives than we realize. We humans believe that we orchestrate our own affairs, good or bad, and that events are steered by action and counteraction, turned by decisions of world leaders or collective will. We read history books and newspapers and seldom find parasites there. They are there, but we don't see them. In this book, I explore this wider world of parasites.

Many human experiences unfold after a chain of apparently insignificant events that make sense only when viewed in retrospect. Our encounters with parasites fit this category. A simple and innocent change in human behavior can open the door and let them in. On a personal level, you don't see parasites coming, yet before long you're boiling your drinking water, passing tapeworm segments into your underpants, or fighting a raging fever in a hospital bed. On a social level, parasites affect everything from exploration and war to food regulations and terrorist plots. They create an unpredictable ripple effect that can undermine many a human endeavor.

In this book, you'll meet some of the parasites that are hidden between the lines of history books and newspapers, and you'll learn about the things that people have done to them, or with them, and the collateral effects they've had on people. These parasites come from various taxonomic groups of animals and protozoa, and most are physically harmful to their hosts, though each has its place in the natural interactions of living things.

Parasites do not make value judgments about their hosts or take sides in the human conflicts they get involved in. They show up because an opportunity is an opportunity. In fact, they aren't unequivocally bad. They *can* be beneficial in unexpected ways. Parasites have shortened wars, protected ecosystems, and helped us craft standards for food and water that have made both infinitely safer. In the redeeming tradition of the silver lining, some of the parasites most dangerous to health have positive effects for someone when they get mixed up in human affairs. And, perhaps even more difficult to accept, a few intestinal companions may actually provide some health benefits.

In the pages that follow, I seize the parasites one by one, drag them into the light, and ask, "What are you and what are you up to?" To find them, I will take you to unfamiliar places: the woods and jungles of the world, desert oases, warm soil, bathroom plumbing, insect guts, and all the terrain of the human body, for this is where they lurk. And we'll have to be there at the right time: when something important is happening in people's lives.

Our questions will probe tantalizing mysteries. Examining each parasite in the context of the event uncovers the scientific pearl, the clue in the creature's natural history that pulls everything together. Scrutiny reveals, for instance, that domesticating a wild animal can unleash an epidemic of parasitic disease in people; that *Plasmodium* spp., agents of malaria, have a history of turning murderers and terrorists over to authorities; and that a tapeworm can hijack a personality and substitute a completely different, perhaps dangerous one.

We'll probe the human psyche as well, looking objectively at our fear of parasites and asking whether our revulsion makes sense and how far it can push us. To what lengths will people go to avoid parasites or get rid of them? Suicide? Child abuse? Murder? All of these. It's often difficult to predict or understand human reactions to parasites.

Our bad attitude springs partly from the fact that we're not used to seeing parasites. Hidden away within host tissues, most are invisible to us. They are all around us but we don't see them. It's relatively easy to pretend, even believe, that they exist only in other places. But parasites are thriving in the twenty-first century. In fact, people have left a lot of doors open in the past few thousand years, allowing more parasitic mayhem in human lives than ever before.

We are better at spotting parasites today than we were in the past, and better at understanding what they've been doing behind the scenes to change our lives. We know some ways to hinder them, but our victories are few. New ones appear even as we continue to battle the ones we've already got. Parasites can cause significant social chaos, even now, as they continue to slip between the lines of history.

This book can't retell the history of the world as it would have been without our uninvited guests: that's a history we will never know. We can shed light on the past, study all the facets of parasites, good and bad, and try to predict how the future might unfold if we were to take one course or another. In the end, however, we will encounter that familiar ripple effect, as random, small, unpredictable events accumulate and help shape great affairs.

ONE

Ambush

If I cause noisome beasts to pass through the land, and they spoil
it . . . , that no man may pass through because of the beasts . . . the
land shall be desolate.

EZEKIEL

14:15–16, Polyglott

THE DEGREE TO WHICH VARIOUS parasites have interfered in human
affairs cannot be overstated. Parasitic diseases such as schistosomiasis,
sleeping sickness, and malaria affect millions and muddle plans in everything from exploration to foreign aid. Others cast a more subtle shadow
but still wield enormous power. They wipe out populations; they topple
fragile ecosystems. The monsters hiding under our beds when we were
children grew up to be parasites. For those of us who grew up in the
cloistered "first world," they fill us with a distant dread, and rightly so;
for everyone else, the monsters have always had one cold and slippery foot
under the blanket.

Where did these monsters come from, and how did they gain such
power? Millennia ago, when humans were nomadic hunter-gatherers,
continually moving from place to place, the only really successful human
parasites were those that spent their entire lives on human hosts, moving
from one body to the next as opportunity arose. Lice, fleas, skin mites,
and pinworms are their contemporary equivalents. The rest, if they
infected humans at all, were probably either rare or responsible for relatively light infections.[1]

People who move about a lot tend to leave their parasitic troubles
behind them: by the time the malaria-carrying mosquito is ready to bite
again, or the worm egg has matured in warm moist soil, the potential

hosts have moved on. True, some worm eggs survive for years in the soil under the right conditions, and malaria can remain silent in the liver for years, but in prehistoric times, by the time a band of nomads returned to a favorite campsite, weather and animals would have dispersed eggs in feces, and blood levels of malaria parasites would likely have been minimal.[2] Levels of infection remained low.[3]

The big break for parasites came when humans began to stay in one place.[4] With the appearance of permanent settlements, mosquitoes had a food supply to which they could return again and again—and the malaria parasites they carried could complete their life cycles in continuous rhythm, at least where the climate was warm enough throughout the year. Meanwhile, trade between cultures helped parasites spread from one population to another.

Organic waste was an issue too. At best, sewage treatment amounted to spreading human and animal waste on cropland as fertilizer. The level of contamination of settled land and nearby water rose steadily. As food and drinking water became progressively more contaminated with feces, intestinal parasites boomed. Soon people domesticated animals and moved them into human spaces: the rate at which humans and animals passed pathogens back and forth accelerated. The stage was set for some real monsters to emerge as threats to human and animal health.

Thousands of years later, we have yet to figure out how to return our parasites to the margins. Like a creeping mist, they spread through communities, invading one body after another. Some parasitic diseases are quick and lethal; others bring slow decay, chipping away at daily life—but only the effects are visible.[5] Most of our parasites are well hidden: we can't see them, we don't understand them, and we are afraid that they, like the monsters under the bed, will "get us."

Trying to determine how many people parasites "got" in prehistoric, and even historic, times is a bit like looking for a needle in a blazing forge: almost no evidence remains. We find Egyptian mummies condemned to spend eternity with an intestinal tapeworm, fossilized human feces containing various worm eggs (if you don't want your intestinal contents analyzed thousands of years after your death, do not defecate in caves), and Ötzi, the enigmatic iceman who emerged from an Italian glacier after more than five thousand years with whipworm eggs still in his gut.

But how much trouble were these parasites to their collective hosts? The first tale for which we have credible evidence of a serious parasite menace took place more than three millennia ago in the Jordan Valley, where a young woman named Rahab catapulted herself to biblical infamy—and a parasitic worm may have made her do it.

—

Rahab lived on the site of perhaps the oldest permanent settlement on earth, home to humans for more than seven thousand years. Once, her village had been a much larger place, a walled town of several thousand people and a bustling center of agriculture and trade. Visitors brought trade goods and innovations from Egypt in the southwest and from the Mesopotamian cities in Syria and the Fertile Crescent in the northeast.

In Rahab's time, the village stood on a mound of old sun-dried brick, the remains of earlier buildings and protective walls now broken into rubble. Since the earliest settlers, the mound had grown, layer upon layer of dust and debris. New houses were built on top of the mound with the same adobe brick, made with mud and water from the nearby pond. This was Late Bronze Age Jericho, City of Palms.

Jericho was a lush haven, a green paradise in a harsh, arid land and an oasis of date palms, figs, and wheat, with a perpetual spring-fed pool. Where the green of the oasis faded, the deeply eroded limestone of the Judean hills climbed thousands of feet to the western horizon. Away to the south, a distant blue haze marked the Dead Sea, where the Jordan River ended. No river ran out to sea: under a baking sun, the water in the Dead Sea simply evaporated, leaving salts and minerals behind. The water was so salty that it could not be used.

Nobody lived by the Dead Sea, and without the oasis, no City of Palms could have taken root. The water in the oasis was clear and sweet, and it never ran out, but vital as it was to the Canaanites of Jericho, it may also have been the source of their ruin: unknown to them, scientists think, the precious springwater hid a deadly, invisible menace, one that had been imported from far away.

By Rahab's time, travelers and traders had been stopping at Jericho for thousands of years. At some point in that long past, and possibly on many occasions, visitors had arrived bearing more than items for trade. Some researchers believe they had arrived with a parasitic infection, a debilitating worm living in the blood. The theory is that when these visitors contaminated the oasis waters with their urine, *Schistosoma hematobium* came to Jericho, and it had been flourishing there ever since. Generation after generation, it made the people of Jericho sick.[6]

The village, in fact, was known for its dwindling population. Women had many miscarriages and few births. Too many of the children died in their teens, and even the adults were afflicted with a mysterious malady that drained them. Listless and weak, many lacked the energy to do a day's work. Some of the men had a grossly enlarged penis and were impotent. Rahab, a prostitute, probably knew this better than most. She likely knew, too, how much it hurt to urinate and saw that her own urine was cloudy and red with blood.

On the day her story begins, we can imagine that Rahab made her daily trip to the pool for water. Perhaps she paused to rest on the way back, feeling impossibly weary. The air was humid and still, a stillness made more noticeable by the lack of activity in the village. A small group of pallid, thin children played in the dust; others moved listlessly about in the street. A few adults were at work in the fields and orchards. Setting her vessel down and shading her eyes with one hand, Rahab gazed out past the village walls.

Rahab was not the only one watching the plain; others glanced nervously over their shoulders or simply stood and looked out. Despite the pall of lassitude, tension was growing in the village. To the east, the dry and dusty Jordan Valley stretched to the river, about five miles away, then across the Plains of Moab on the other side. An army had recently marched across those plains and forded the Jordan. Now Joshua and the Hebrews were camped on the inhospitable plain, preparing to attack. The villagers were far too few and far too tired. The fight wouldn't last long.

The microscopic eggs of the blood fluke *S. hematobium* are found in urine. When passed into freshwater, the larvae (miracidia) inside the eggs sense the change in environment and begin to move, flipping over and over until they burst out and swim freely. Like tiny revolving torpedoes, they spin briskly, searching for a welcoming species of snail. Quiet ponds like the one in Jericho, with stable water levels, relatively still water, and plant life around the shallow edge, are a perfect habitat for snails.

If a suitable snail is not available, the miracidia spin on like windup toys until they run out of energy and die, but if the right snail turns up, the larvae plunge in and begin a period of asexual multiplication. After about six weeks, the parasites (now called cercariae) emerge from the snails and hang about like jellyfish, slowly rising to the surface and then slowly sinking down again, waiting for humans to come to the water.

Figure 1. Male and female adult schistosomes. The slender female lies partially free from the male. Photo by the author.

In Jericho, the humans came every day. Unless the people walked across the parched valley to the banks of the Jordan, the oasis was virtually the only local source of water, and the villagers came in contact with it repeatedly. The infant Rahab, like all the babies of Jericho, was no doubt bathed in the springwater. From childhood on, she drank the water, cooked with it, and washed with it. Every time human skin came in contact with the water, cercariae that had recently emerged from snails had a chance to latch on. Each little parasite crept about briefly and then plunged its head through the skin, shedding its wriggling forked tail and disappearing in less than half a minute.

Cercariae that got through Rahab's skin would have set themselves adrift in her veins and traveled to her heart. From there they followed the bloodstream through lungs and intestines, eventually arriving in her liver, where they spent about three weeks maturing. Each adult male worm wrapped itself around a female like a thick, knobby blanket—two tiny worms that could easily curl up on the tip of Rahab's little finger. Theirs was a perpetual embrace that would last thirty years, if Rahab lived that long. Their final move took the worms, now young adults, to the blood vessels around Rahab's bladder.[7] The female worm soon began producing eggs.

Up to this point, baby Rahab probably felt fine, but as egg production began, she developed a fever and headache. She was tired and suffered chills, aching muscles, and pain in her abdomen, where the eggs, deposited in tiny vessels, were gradually moving through her bladder wall. Breaking through, the eggs mixed with blood and urine in the bladder, and Rahab began passing bloody urine.

Most of these symptoms passed, but the bleeding grew worse, and Rahab felt a burning sensation when she urinated. In time, bladder ulcers developed, and she suffered from painful bladder infections. Some eggs never reached the bladder and were swept away in the blood to lodge elsewhere, particularly in her liver and lungs. Rahab was probably always tired, and she was thin.

The story was likely the same for all the people of Jericho. Obliged to use water from a single source, they were continually exposed to the parasite, and they continually contaminated the oasis. Every one of the people of Jericho may have had the worms and suffered from various degrees of emaciation and fatigue. Some slowly wasted away and died from bladder cancer or heart disease. Others slipped helplessly into a state of chronic illness. The children suffered most.

Now Rahab looked up and down the almost deserted street in despair. The Hebrews were threatening, prepared for battle, and the worm was on their side. Rahab knew nothing of the parasite, but she knew of the sickness and understood what the outcome would be if the village were attacked. As she stooped to retrieve her water, she noticed two strangers in the street. As the book of Joshua reports, she guessed that they were Hebrew spies, come to scout the village and report back.

Rahab took a chance and approached the two men, quickly leading them away to her home at the edge of the village. Then, buying her life and the lives of her family, she told them about the poor state of the villagers. When searchers came knocking, she bought time, claiming the men had already left; then she helped the spies slip away, telling them where to hide to avoid detection.

The Hebrew scouts escaped the search parties, returning safely to Joshua in the plain. The biblical account relates that, after the ensuing battle, not a soul was left alive in Jericho except Rahab and her family, and that Joshua cursed the site: "Cursed be the man before the Lord, that riseth up and buildeth this city of Jericho" (Joshua 6:26). Thereafter, the dusty streets of Jericho were silent, and though the spring still flowed and filled the pool, only the breeze ruffled the waters where *S. hematobium* waited in vain.

Is any of this true? It may be true, for the remains of *Bulinus truncatus,* an intermediate snail host of *S. hematobium,* have been recovered from the mud brick used for construction in Bronze Age Jericho.[8] Other archaeological finds, including seashells and pottery, prove that the community traded with people from Egypt and Mesopotamia, areas where *S. hematobium* was well established. Biblical texts also suggest that Jericho was known for its low birthrate and that people suspected the water was tainted.[9]

Archaeological evidence indicates that, despite the city's attractiveness, no one lived in Jericho for about four hundred years after the Hebrews passed through in their quest for the Promised Land. In that time, with no infected humans to keep the cycle going, S. hematobium would have died out in the water. Droughts may have eradicated the snail as well. Today, Jericho is once again inhabited, and the parasite is absent.

Ironically, Joshua's act—destroying the village and leaving it deserted for generations—was the only thing that, at that time, could rid the lovely oasis of a lurking menace, making it once again a desirable place to live. Perhaps Joshua deserves some credit for being the first public health official, albeit inadvertently.

Because we now understand the life cycle of S. hematobium, we can indulge in "what if" considerations of this scenario of Jericho. What if the people had had more than one water source? What if they had troubled to keep the oasis waters free of urine? Levels of infection would have been much lower, if the worms thrived at all. An Old Testament Bible story might have turned out rather differently. In fact, the whole history of the place would probably have changed dramatically.

Humans do unwittingly clear the way for parasites, and in the case of schistosomes, we keep making the same mistake and getting the same results. In the past century, however, we're even better at making the mistake: we don't just contaminate the water supply; we also create the ideal habitat for the snail's intermediate hosts—a process innocently known as "water resources development." Because of this "development," the people who live on the shores of Lake Volta in Ghana have much in common with the Canaanites of Late Bronze Age Jericho.

⸺

The Akosombo Dam, on the Volta River in Ghana, was completed in 1964.[10] When the river was interrupted, an enormous fern-leaf–shaped lake formed, stretching more than three hundred miles into the heart of the country. The flooding created the largest artificial lake in the world and set off a chain of unintended consequences that, in hindsight, were completely predictable.

The relatively still, nutrient-rich water in the reservoir provided a perfect environment for aquatic plants, which soon flourished on and under the surface and at the edges of the lake. Snail species that live on aquatic plants increased along with their food supply. On the bottom, meanwhile, decaying organic matter fueled an increase in plankton, which in turn fueled an increase in fish.

Many of the people displaced by the rising water were unable to farm as they had in the past and turned to fishing instead. Others came from more distant regions, drawn to the lake by rumors of plentiful fish. Communities grew on the lake's shores. People bathed in the lake, used it for drinking water, and cooked with the water. The lake was the center of their world. They fished in it, swam in it, and contaminated it with their urine and feces.

In such a scenario, children and fishermen are at particularly serious risk of schistosomiasis because of their intense water contact; however, all of the people living by Lake Volta had frequent contact with the contaminated reservoir. Before the lake was created, between 5 and 10 percent of children in the region had adult worms of *S. hematobium* living in the blood vessels around their bladders. By 1969, 90 percent of children living in lakeside communities had them.

In 1981, Ghana built another dam downstream from Akosombo. The Kpong Dam created a headpond, which promptly became infested with aquatic plants, snails, *S. hematobium,* and *S. mansoni,* a second species of *Schistosoma.* Soon, more than half the people living near the headpond had *S. hematobium,* and a third had *S. mansoni.* In 1993, the World Health Organization reported that *S. hematobium* infested all of Ghana's water resource projects—hundreds of reservoirs frequented by people.[11] Most, if not all, are still infested today.

No massacre or biblical curse is likely to desolate the Lake Volta area for hundreds of years and wipe it clean of *Schistosoma* spp. Surveys of lakeside villages from the 1990s, more than thirty years after the problem was clearly understood, show that *S. hematobium* still infects almost all of the children. Untreated, both children and adults will eventually suffer the consequences of chronic schistosomiasis.

When the negative effects of the Akosombo Dam—environmental destruction, loss of biodiversity, displacement of people, and increase in various diseases—are tallied, it's fair to ask if the dam was worth this price. Kristina Zakhary, who studied the schistosomiasis situation around Lake Volta in the mid-1990s and summarized its causes and effects, wrote,

"From the public health point of view, while the Volta River Hydro Development Project helped to solve some problems, it has, in the meantime, created other serious health and sanitation problems which are still lingering."[12] Schistosomiasis was only the worst of these problems.

Terrifyingly, the large water impoundments in Ghana also increased other parasitic threats. Cases of malaria increased because the mosquitoes that carry the disease found new bodies of water in which to breed. River blindness, caused by a tissue-dwelling worm, was spread by black flies breeding in the rushing streams below the dams. People migrating from the north to Lake Volta brought trypanosomes, the parasites of sleeping sickness, to the tsetse flies (*Glossina* spp.) and to the people of the south—and like the rise of *S. hematobium,* the spread of this parasite was a replay of a human mistake.

Today, trypanosome species share a territory in Africa known as the tsetse belt, a broad stripe that bisects the continent from the southern margins of the Sahara Desert to about twenty degrees south latitude. Because trypanosomes cannot live without their tsetse hosts, they are confined to this belt where the tsetse flies live. Comprehending the complex interplay between the parasites, the flies, and the environment is a bit like fiddling with a three-dimensional puzzle that has multiple solutions.

To find a configuration that causes enough disease to decimate cultures and change history, we must juxtapose mammalian hosts, three subspecies of trypanosomes, various species of tsetse flies, and multiple ecosystems. Some combinations produce nagana, an infection deadly in animals. Some result in Gambian sleeping sickness, a slow but usually fatal infection in humans. Some produce Rhodesian sleeping sickness, a sporadic but rapidly fatal disease that affects both animals and humans.

First, let's look at the trypanosomes. A number of species exist, but in the African puzzle, the important ones are subspecies of *Trypanosoma brucei: T. brucei brucei, T. brucei gambiense*, and *T. brucei rhodesiense*. Like identical triplets, they look exactly alike but interact differently with life around them. *Trypanosoma b. brucei* causes nagana but does not cause disease in humans; *T. b. gambiense* infects *only* humans, causing the Gambian form of sleeping sickness; *T. b. rhodesiense* is an animal trypanosome, but it can infect people as well. All three have had an immeasurable impact on people living in the tsetse belt.

Trypanosoma b. brucei, transmitted by many species of *Glossina,* is perhaps the kindest of the lot, though it is hardly benevolent: it has little effect on most of Africa's native animals, though they carry the parasite. Nagana is deadly to introduced species, many of which die within two weeks of a tsetse bite. This might seem like a blessing given that introduced species are causing problems all over the world; the problem for people is that nagana kills domestic breeds and makes it impossible to raise domesticated animals in much of Africa's tsetse belt. Cattle, horses, sheep, goats, donkeys, camels, and even dogs can't live there. In practical terms, the inability to raise these animals means that humans tend not to live there either. If you dare go into nagana territory, don't take your animals with you.

Animals also suffer from *T. b. rhodesiense*, but when there are few animals around to bite, the tsetses—*G. morsitans, G. swynnertoni*, and *G. pallidipes*—bite humans instead. The pieces of the puzzle necessary for Rhodesian sleeping sickness to gain a foothold are open savannah where the appropriate tsetse species lurk, a lack of animals to keep the flies busy, humans, and the parasite. *Trypanosoma b. rhodesiense* can arrive in an infected mammalian host—either animal or human—or in an infected tsetse fly. Outbreaks in humans occur periodically, especially after a pathogen of cattle, such as rhinderpest, wipes out domestic herds. Human fatalities begin within a few months of the trypanosome's arrival.

Trypanosoma b. gambiense has a different story, one similar to the arrival of sleeping sickness at Lake Volta, and one that recalls the days when Africa was called the "dark continent." In the nineteenth and twentieth centuries, European explorers made their reputations by venturing into that darkness. American journalist Henry Morton Stanley was one of them, remembered for his recklessly adventurous treks through Africa in the late 1800s.

Stanley searched for missing explorer David Livingstone in east central Africa and famously found him ("Dr. Livingstone, I presume?"). Then he explored the Congo River and helped establish the Congo Free State for King Leopold II of Belgium. Later still, he led an expedition through unexplored African jungle to rescue the marooned Emin Pasha. Emin was governor of what was then Equatoria, territory abandoned by Egypt and surrounded by hostile native governments. Like a dam built in schistosome territory, Stanley had a dreadful ripple effect: he led both slavers and trypanosomes to new places where they could prey on the native people.

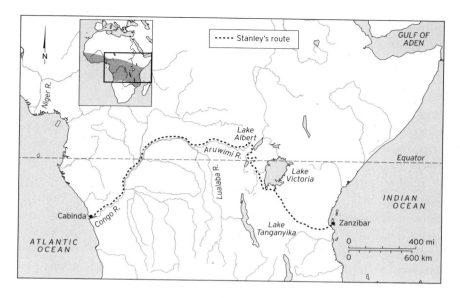

Map 1. Equatorial Africa, showing Stanley's route from west to east in 1887. Inset: the tsetse belt.

Before Stanley's Congo expeditions, sleeping sickness in humans was transmitted in only a few isolated pockets in western Africa. The disease was known in the Niger River region in the 1300s and in Liberia in the 1800s, and slave traders carrying captive natives from western Africa in the 1700s were familiar with its symptoms. But until the late 1800s, a general lack of travel and commerce between indigenous groups kept the parasite from spreading: the tsetse fly may have been widely distributed, but the disease was not. Stanley changed this status quo, beginning a flurry of exploration and exploitation by foreign adventurers and creating a widening zone of sleeping sickness that persists to this day.

The damage started in the Congo Basin, which Stanley first approached from the east in 1877. His journey to the mouth of the river got the attention of Leopold II, who was eager to exploit the region. Leopold soon employed Stanley to help him establish a Belgian territory in west central Africa. From 1879 to 1884, Stanley established stations along the Congo River to support foreign explorers and traders, and explorers, traders—and slavers—came in considerable numbers. Traffic increased significantly on the lower river.

In 1887, Stanley repeated his transect of the continent, following the Congo in the opposite direction. Beginning at the river mouth, he led a large expedition of hundreds east, a voyage officially undertaken to rescue Emin Pasha but sponsored by Leopold II and thus also a voyage of exploration. Diverging from his earlier route, when he had come from the east, Stanley slashed and paddled his way up the unexplored Aruwimi River, emerging from the jungle in the general vicinity of Lake Albert. On this trip, and frequently thereafter, people traveling from the west coast ventured deeper into the dense rainforest than they ever had before.

Stanley's group and those that followed in the next few years encountered cannibals and other hostile indigenous tribes; dense, wet jungle; poisonous snakes; and stinging ants, sand fleas, mosquitoes, gadflies, and tsetse flies. They died from violence, starvation, infection, snakebite, and malaria, but they did not die of sleeping sickness: perhaps the tsetses that bit them were the wrong species, but more likely, they just weren't carrying the parasite—yet.

Stanley's companions—officers, soldiers, and native carriers—were primarily from Europe, the Middle East, and eastern Africa, respectively: they wouldn't have brought western trypanosomes from any of these homelands, and sleeping sickness wasn't present in the Congo territory they traveled through.[13] They probably didn't bring the parasite into the heart of Africa, as some have claimed: they merely laid out the red carpet for it to track them east.

Some of those that came after Stanley may have been accompanied by infected tsetse flies (which tend to pursue dark-colored moving objects such as game animals, boats, and vehicles), and some of them doubtless already had the parasites circulating in their blood, having been infected elsewhere. One thing is certain: the forested banks of the Congo were ideal habitat for *G. palpalis* and *G. tachinoides,* the tsetse vectors of *T. b. gambiense,* and the bites of these flies were soon to indirectly cause the deaths of thousands. Not until the 1890s, however, did people living in the region really understand that something terrible had arrived.

The bite of the tsetse was familiar to the indigenous people of Africa in colonial times. Inflicted by a large brownish-gray fly, which drives its mouthparts through the skin and sucks out a blood meal, the bite may be red and itchy but is generally not too bothersome. Even in an area afflicted by sleeping sickness, nine out of ten tsetse flies play no part in the parasite's story; they are incapable of passing it on. The appearance of a small sore at the bite site, however, is a bad sign: it suggests that when the fly bit, its saliva carried thousands of tiny parasites to a new host.

The first people infected in the Congo Basin felt fine for weeks to months; some of them, a very few, fought off the infection.[14] The parasites multiplied in the bloodstreams of the rest. These organisms were trypomastigotes of *T. b. gambiense,* each resembling a whimsical undulating crescent moon with a long whiplike tail and a frill along the outer curve. Blood stages multiply by duplicating their genetic material and dividing into two trypomastigotes. Even if there were only a few to start with, there were soon abundant parasites circulating. They swam freely in the blood, dodging blood cells or bunting their way through the bloodstream like alligators in a river full of floating inner tubes.

Just having frilly crescent-shaped parasites in the bloodstream doesn't make you sick, and therein lies the danger: many people are unaware of their infection and thus provide a long-term pool of parasites for hungry tsetses to drink from and spread the infection. Following Stanley, infected travelers moved through regions where the parasite was absent, but the tsetse flies were as hungry as ever, and some of them fed on infected humans, taking in trypomastigotes with their blood meal.

In the susceptible fly, the parasites clustered in the midgut and multiplied. Thousands moved forward again to the fly's salivary glands and continued to multiply. After about two weeks, the infected human might have moved on, but the fly remained. At its next blood meal, and at every blood meal for the rest of its life, it delivered thousands of parasites to another host.[15]

Meanwhile, the asymptomatic stage came to an end for those with long-standing infection. Trypomastigotes invaded lymph nodes, setting off an uncomfortable period of intermittent fevers and headaches. A general feeling of illness and loss of appetite were not unusual, but a particular symptom, ominously known as Winterbottom's sign, separated this fever from the others common in the jungle: swelling of the cervical lymph nodes at the back of the neck portended a bad outcome.

The trypomastigotes were still multiplying. Swelling of the hands, feet, and face, and a rash, came and went like the fever. The liver and spleen enlarged. Parasites invaded almost every organ, making themselves at home in the tissue spaces between cells. Ultimately, they arrived in the brain, and the infection finally earned its name.

Invasion of the brain brought on confusion, apathy, terrible fatigue, loss of coordination, and a pervasive sleepiness. Sleep progressed to coma and coma to death; usually another organism caused a secondary infection that the weakened immune system could not fight off. For those who do not defeat trypanosomes in the early stages, death usually comes within a couple of years.

By the first years of the twentieth century, the worst had happened. Sleeping sickness had moved inexorably up the Congo River from the west, killing thousands. It had traveled 1,200 miles (1,931 kilometers) to Stanley Falls, where the Congo River becomes the Lualaba River. It had spread up many of the rivers that flow into the Congo. And then it had leapt to Lake Victoria, presumably carried once more by infected travelers.

In 1904, the *New York Times* reported that sleeping sickness had emptied whole villages around Lake Victoria in east central Africa. Over thirty thousand people had already died. The publication reported, "It is no exaggeration to say that the civilized nations find themselves today in the presence of a terrible evil that is beginning to oppose a powerful barrier to their colonial enterprises in tropical Africa."[16]

To be fair to Stanley, if he hadn't opened the way for Gambian sleeping sickness to blanket the western two-thirds of the tsetse belt, someone else would have. In fact David Livingstone probably contributed significantly to a similar spread of nagana to new territory as he moved through Africa for some twenty-four years as an explorer, missionary, and doctor. Together, the two men offered a case study of how to turn the tsetse belt—one-third of the African continent—into the trypanosome belt. The irony is that as they determinedly shed light on the "dark continent," they made much of it virtually uninhabitable.

The 1904 *New York Times* article predicted that trypanosomiasis was "likely to be ended by [the] investigation of experts," but this proved a false hope.[17] Millions died in the succeeding century, and Africans and experts still battle the parasite in the tsetse belt. "Colonial enterprises" may have been thwarted, but their legacy continues.

The impact of trypanosomiasis is multidimensional, like the disease itself. Although the tsetse belt has certainly killed millions, it has also been instrumental in preventing other countries from colonizing much of Africa. It hobbled invading armies, who were reduced to foot soldiers when trypanosomes claimed their horses. It prevented exploitation of the indigenous animals and other natural resources, saving the ecosystem from much of the environmental degradation that damaged other parts of the continent.

Trypanosomes have also directed countless careers and financial resources to the "tsetse fly problem." In 1973, John J. McKelvey, Jr., wrote that more time and money had been expended on trypanosomiasis than on malaria—a curious statistic when one considers that malaria is much more widespread, has interfered in many more endeavors, and has killed many more people.[18] And McKelvey wrote at a time when malaria research was surging.

—

Stanley suffered bouts of malaria during his mission to rescue Emin Pasha. David Livingstone had it as well; in fact, he nursed his entire family through it. Both men were lucky: the disease didn't kill them. Entire expeditions of explorers succumbed to it. Malaria, caused by *Plasmodium* spp., another blood parasite, is the consummate killer. It is spread by mosquitoes, and close to a million people die from it each year, even today.

Four species of *Plasmodium* infect humans: *P. falciparum, P. vivax, P. malariae,* and *P. ovale. Plasmodium falciparum* is the worst of the lot, accounting for half of all cases of malaria and the majority of deaths. We tend to think of malaria as a tropical disease, but in the past, *Plasmodium* spp. have made themselves at home in England, the United States, southern Canada, and even Siberia. In Stanley's day, Africa was a hot spot for malaria, as it is today. So was Southeast Asia.

Various scholars have credited malaria with bringing down the Roman Empire, ending the conquests of Alexander the Great, and even killing more than half the people who have ever lived. These grand statements are hard to prove, of course, though they may well be true: proof requires medical test results and statistics that don't exist. We do know, however, that *Plasmodium* spp. have been a formidable force in many wars, including the American Civil War, both world wars, and more recent conflicts, taking out more combatants than conventional weapons. In the Vietnam War of the 1960s and 1970s, malaria was an invisible enemy that struck hard on both sides of the conflict—and there are some solid statistics to prove it.

Almost all of Vietnam is a high-risk area for malaria, even today; in the first years of the Vietnam War, an antimalaria campaign was under way in the country. In a shrewd act of indirect biological warfare, the Viet Cong (People's Liberation Armed Forces) recognized the potential of the parasite to undermine its enemy and successfully compromised the campaign. Simply targeting personnel in the field made malaria eradication a very high risk, and therefore undesirable, occupation. Malaria surged in South Vietnam: mostly the milder *P. vivax* in the low-lying coastal areas and the dreadful *P. falciparum* in the western highlands and jungles.

The typical American soldier arriving in Vietnam was issued antimalarials, and he had to take them or face severe discipline. He was also required to sleep under mosquito netting because the mosquitoes that carry malaria typically fly, and bite, at night. If you've ever slept under mosquito netting, you know that no matter how carefully you tuck the edges in, you need only press an arm or a foot against the netting while you sleep to invite the mosquitoes to have their way. And in Vietnam, nights were hot and American sleepers were restless.

Forcing down the bitter antimalarial chloroquine pill and tucking in the bed netting failed to prevent thousands of mosquito bites from transmitting malaria to American troops: everyone stood a good chance of contracting the parasite within days of arriving in Vietnam. Whole divisions were put out of action.

However, Americans weren't the only ones to suffer. In suppressing the antimalaria campaign, the Viet Cong, operating in the western jungles, trod the slippery slope navigated by anyone who tries to use an infectious agent against an enemy: the weapon can turn on the wielder. Some of the Viet Cong had a degree of immunity to the parasite; all of them had that immunity tested. In fact, they faced the parasite before ever arriving in South Vietnam.

Many Viet Cong troops, the *bo dois*, entered South Vietnam after spending eight weeks or more on foot, walking a network of trails, roads, and rivers through the dense jungles of western Vietnam and eastern Laos and Cambodia. This territory was rife with mosquitoes and *Plasmodium*—the Ho Chi Minh Trail. The trail was a lifeline of the Viet Cong, bringing troops and supplies south in a steady stream.

Most of the trail was so well hidden from the air that American military pilots could not locate it, but this was scant comfort for Viet Cong troops trained in the arts of ambush and camouflage: there were dozens of other ways to die on the trail, and malaria was one of them. Like the tsetse fly in Africa, mosquitoes were unavoidable. The mosquito that infected each traveler was a female *Anopheles* sp., a mosquito that had previously sucked the *Plasmodium*-infested blood of another human.

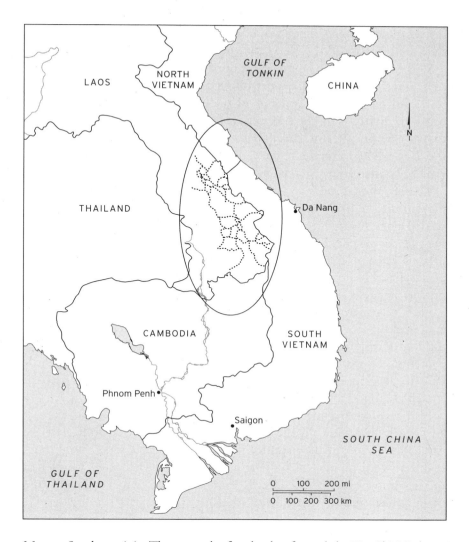

Map 2. Southeast Asia. The network of paths that formed the Ho Chi Minh
Trail in Laos, bridging North and South Vietnam, is circled.

When the mosquito jabbed her thin, needlelike proboscis into a soldier's blood vessel, she injected saliva into the wound to prevent blood
from clotting while she obtained her meal. Mixed with her saliva were
microscopic sporozoites of the parasite, wisps of life so tiny that four
hundred of them laid end to end would stretch about a quarter of an inch

(fifteen micrometers). They would have been on the move immediately: they don't remain in the blood for long.

Within twenty-four hours, the sporozoites could be found inside liver cells, transforming into plumper forms called trophozoites. The trophozoites fed on the liquid contents of the liver cells and grew. Soon, they began to multiply. By the end of a week, each trophozoite had given rise to many new organisms, called merozoites, which packed the space inside the liver cell and eventually burst out through damaged and broken cell walls. The merozoites left the liver and went back to the blood.

Though the typical Viet Cong recruit was doubtless well aware of the mosquitoes, he likely felt no ill effects from the parasite at first and proceeded along the trail from one campsite to the next for almost two weeks. He carried weapons, a hammock, food, antimalarials, and vitamin pills, or, if he was a porter, he pushed a bicycle loaded with hundreds of pounds of supplies. He advanced about eighty miles, while trying to avoid falling prey to air raids, intestinal diseases, and wild animals.[19]

Each tiny merozoite attached itself to the outside of a red blood cell and, pushing its way through the cell wall, floated free inside. Transforming into a trophozoite again, it began to feed. Taking in the cell's fluid contents, the trophozoite rounded up until it resembled a plump little balloon floating inside the red cell, its body—cytoplasm and nucleus—stretched around a liquid food vacuole.

Had there been a medical clinic equipped with a good microscope at any of the campsites on the trail, which there wasn't, a drop of blood would have exposed the parasites, the so-called signet rings—tiny rings, each one with its nucleus bulging at the edge. If you could forget that they're eating your red blood cells from the inside out, you might find them quite beautiful: stained with conventional dyes, the cytoplasm—the body of the parasite—is blue, delicate, and wispy, like a bit of evening sky, while the nucleus is a large red dot at the edge. Whoever described these forms as signet rings—a description that stuck—missed the mark: it should have been gemstone rings—solitaires—and the stone is a ruby.

But these rings were not to be treasured. Feeding on the nutrients in the food vacuole, ring-shaped trophozoites grew larger in the *bo doi's* red blood cells and lost their spherical shape, spreading out to look more like amoebae. As they grew, they produced waste products—golden brown pigment that was recognized as a flag for malaria before anyone knew what caused the disease. After just a few hours, there was enough pigment in the blood to be easily visible through a microscope.

The infected *bo doi* was likely feeling a bit under the weather at this point: he may have suspected he had a touch of the flu, suffering fatigue, headache, and aching joints, or he may have known exactly what was happening, having seen others succumb. Either way, his health was about to deteriorate frighteningly. In the next stage of development, trophozoites multiply inside red blood cells, producing a dozen or more merozoites, and then destroy the cell as they burst into the surrounding blood plasma. Millions of infected red blood cells disintegrate simultaneously. Then each merozoite invades a new red blood cell and begins the process all over again. Eventually, some merozoites mature into gametocytes, the stage that can infect another mosquito.

When legions of red blood cells break down at once, the stricken human suffers a malarial attack, or paroxysm. Each time a paroxysm strikes, the victim suddenly feels bitterly cold. He shivers with chill as his body temperature shoots up past 40°C. In the relative comforts of home, a *bo doi* might retire to bed with chattering teeth, wrapping himself in blankets, or huddle by the stove in chilled misery, but none of these comforts were available along the Ho Chi Minh Trail, and nights could be cool. In any case, neither would have helped.

Within an hour, everything would change: a terrible headache would set in, and the *bo doi* would be roaring hot and incoherent, collapsing on the trail or lying helpless in a hammock at one of the campsites. Several hours would pass before his fever eased; then he would find himself soaked with sweat and utterly exhausted. Afterward, perhaps, he could sleep, but like a recurring nightmare, the paroxysm would return with a vengeance every twenty-four to forty-eight hours as the next generation of sporozoites spilled out of decimated red blood cells and invaded new ones.

For both Viet Cong and American soldiers, the disease sometimes took a frightening turn, causing the victim to slide into unconsciousness, with involuntary flailing of limbs, muscle spasms, and grinding of teeth. In the brain, red blood cells infested with parasites crowded small blood vessels and lined the walls of larger ones, casting a strange plum-colored pall over the brain tissue. Deprived of oxygen, the brain faltered. Without swift and competent medical treatment, the patient died.

The Viet Cong suffered severe losses from malaria just like the Americans. The *bo dois* carried antimalarials, but not enough, and like the American pills, the drugs were not always effective against the parasite. *Plasmodium falciparum* had seen the drug before, and it had evolved a way to evade the medicine.

Chloroquine was the best drug anyone had against malaria at the time, but chloroquine-resistant *P. falciparum* had emerged from the remote border areas between Thailand and Burma in the early 1960s. This resistant strain spread quickly, and it didn't have far to go to reach the jungles along and around the Ho Chi Minh Trail. The Vietnam War happened at just the right time, and in just the right place, to put this dangerous parasite on everybody's hit list.

For malaria to wreak such havoc on the Ho Chi Minh Trail, a group of circumstances had to come together. First, there had to be mosquitoes, and not just any mosquitoes but a species in which the parasite could reproduce successfully. Fortunately, in many mosquito species, *Plasmodium* simply dies, but in mosquitoes belonging to the genus *Anopheles,* it reproduces and can be passed forward.

The thumb of land that includes Cambodia and southern Laos and Vietnam lies at low elevations hospitable to mosquitoes and has its fair share of *Anopheles* spp. Various species have been there for centuries, breeding in the abundant wetlands and feeding on both people and animals. Some rest outdoors during the day; some prefer to rest indoors, in human shelters. Some breed in shade, some in sunshine, some aren't fussy. The foreign soldiers and the Vietnamese on the trail had nowhere to hide.

Second, there had to be a reservoir of *Plasmodium.* Again, the parasite had such a long history in the area that a pool of infected local people— some ill, some carrying the parasite without symptoms—was assured, and the resistant *P. falciparum* had arrived and was already in that pool. Steady traffic on the trail merely increased the pool, providing the last requirement for heightened transmission of the disease: an endless stream of new potential hosts with little or no immunity to malaria. *Plasmodium* thrived on the Ho Chi Minh Trail.

Those *bo dois* who arrived at their destination, however, had a weapon that was stowed in their bloodstream rather than their packs. Whereas many Vietnamese had some resistance to the disease, having shared the land with it all their lives, American troops fighting in the hills and jungles of South Vietnam had no resistance at all, and their antimalarials weren't working. They succumbed in great numbers.

To what degree *Plasmodium* affected the outcome of the Vietnam War is impossible to say, and no one knows how events would have unfolded had the parasite not been at work. Estimates suggest that between 2 and 10 percent of Viet Cong who walked the Ho Chi Minh Trail died from disease on the journey, with higher losses in the early years. Meanwhile, over sixty-five thousand cases of malaria occurred in American troops (U.S. Army, Navy, and Marine Corps) between 1962 and 1970, resulting in over a million sick days and taking whole divisions out of action for weeks.[20] U.S. troops suffered more casualties from the parasite than from combat.[21]

Ironically, a major impact came *after* the war. Chloroquine resistance was relatively new to the medical world going into the Vietnam War, and both the Americans and the Viet Cong were soon searching desperately for new and better drugs. The resulting expenditure of resources produced antimalarials that have saved countless lives since, and arguably the best of them came from the Chinese work that aided the Viet Cong. Some historians believe that by the end of the conflict, the parasite, on one hand, and superior antimalarials, on the other, gave the Viet Cong a decided edge.

Chinese research produced artesunate, a derivative of the medicinal plant *Artemisia annua*.[22] The American side produced mefloquine. Resistance to mefloquine soon appeared, as it has with virtually every antimalarial before it. *Artemisia* derivatives, meanwhile, proved to be the most powerful antimalarials ever discovered, and they are now used in combination with mefloquine and other drugs: when these drug cocktails are administered, the cure rate is higher, the treatment works more quickly, and the parasites don't have time to develop resistance to drugs.

The indirect impact of malaria in the Vietnam War will ultimately be far greater than its direct impact was: it may have indirectly contributed to its own defeat. But history has not yet recorded such a statistic, and we will never grasp the full impact. We can only say that if *A. annua* helps us finally to push *P. falciparum* back into the shadows it inhabited thousands of years ago, innumerable things in our world will change.

———

Trypanosoma spp. need the tsetse fly, *Plasmodium* spp. need the mosquito, and *Schistosoma* spp. need the snail. They can spread to new places, and they do, but only to places where their other hosts can also survive. They are unlikely to infiltrate every human population. Not all human parasites face such barriers, however: many need only the human host and can be transmitted almost everywhere. The majority use efficient vehicles that

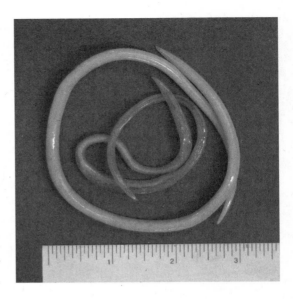

Figure 2. *Ascaris lumbricoides* worms. Photo by the author.

bring them in daily contact with their hosts: food and water. *Ascaris lumbricoides* is a common example.

Ascaris lumbricoides, the large intestinal roundworm, is second only to pinworm, *Enterobius vermicularis,* as the most cosmopolitan roundworm of humans. *Ascaris lumbricoides* is large not only in comparison to other roundworms that are parasitic in humans, but it is literally large: mature females can be well over a foot (30.5 centimeters) long. They bear considerable resemblance to really big night crawlers, or dew worms, but the two are not related. The earthworm is not parasitic, whereas *A. lumbricoides* worms are found in the small intestines of a quarter of the earth's human inhabitants.

Eggs of *A. lumbricoides* are found in human stool, and they have been found in coprolites—preserved human stool—at archaeological sites in North and South America, Europe, Africa, the Middle East, and New Zealand. The oldest of these finds dates from more than twenty-four thousand years ago.[23] *A. lumbricoides* has indeed been with us for a very long time, and it exists almost everywhere on earth. Today, it is relatively uncommon in countries with good sanitation and very common in places where sanitation is lacking.

What personal and global mischief has *A. lumbricoides* been perpetrating in human societies for two dozen millennia or more? Joshua and many of the Hebrews may have had large intestinal worms, Henry Morton Stanley probably had them, and the slavers who plied the Atlantic probably had them. In fact, a respected medical authority has suggested that a Gordian knot of ascaris worms brought down none other than explorer Captain James Cook.

If the tale of Rahab, Jericho, and the schistosomes is based on fragmentary scientific evidence, the theory of Captain Cook and his roundworms is even more speculative. Still, the tantalizing possibility exists that *A. lumbricoides* changed the course of history by taking out one of the most famous explorers of all time, and the medical authority who proposed the scenario, Vice-Admiral Sir James Watt, former medical director-general of the British Royal Navy, is not to be lightly dismissed.[24] Watt's accusation against *A. lumbricoides* came in 1979, two hundred years after Cook's death.

On all three of Cook's voyages, a number of crew members kept journals and gave detailed accounts of life with Cook, at sea and in indigenous societies. The sailors were required to surrender these journals at the end of each voyage, and most of the texts are still in existence today. Thus, a great deal is known about Captain James Cook from both his own records and from the journals of his crew members: the bulk of Watt's evidence comes from firsthand accounts of events.[25]

The explorers were not always welcome in new lands, but Cook, known for his fair and humane treatment both of his crew members and of native people, characteristically sought peaceful solutions. Avoiding bloodshed and attempting to make amends with natives when events took a bad turn, he chastised crew members if they resorted to violence or destruction to settle disagreements. He was well liked by his crews, even looked upon as a father figure.

However, Cook suffered from unpleasant and unexplained personality changes on his last voyage, ordering harsh, even brutal treatment of his crew and natives. A number of the crew members were so confused and dismayed by events during the last voyage that they made detailed entries in their journals.

In Tonga, Cook ordered that natives who were throwing stones be flogged and mutilated with knives. In Moorea, the drama started when a crew member took something from a native. The native, in turn, snatched a goat as it grazed on the shore. Cook angrily demanded the goat, but as soon as it was returned, a second goat was stolen. The second animal turned out to be a high-priced goat: when demands and then threats failed to restore it, Cook raged across the island, torching homes and smashing canoes until he and his men had caused destruction sufficient to keep islanders busy rebuilding for years.

A few days later, a native was apprehended on Cook's ship in possession of items stolen on board. An enraged Cook ordered the ship's barber to shave the man's head and cut off his ears. Only the intervention of a lieutenant prevented the barber from complying. The thief was lucky to be cast overboard near an island with just part of one ear missing. Soon another native was caught stealing, and this one did lose both his hair and his ears.

Reports of sporadic cruelty and cold rages, so uncharacteristic of the younger Cook, punctuate the journals of his men for the remainder of his command. In the North Pacific, he would allow only bread to men who refused to eat walrus and was apparently willing to let them starve if necessary. In Hawaii, he cut off the men's brandy ration when they turned up their noses at sugarcane beer. He accused them of mutinous behavior. Crew members were lashed for spreading venereal diseases to native women, and natives were lashed for theft.

At other times, Cook seemed to lose interest in the voyage and to forget his passion for exploring and discovering new things, and he was some-times careless with navigation. In December 1778, after arriving at the Hawaiian Islands and taking on fresh supplies, he forgot to increase the rations of his hungry men. In Hawaii, he was described as passive, inde-cisive, and distant. What was wrong with James Cook? Was he suffering from stress, or was there a deeper problem? James Watt suggests the problem was *A. lumbricoides.*

The female *A. lumbricoides,* like many parasitic worms, is a prolific egg producer, depositing two hundred thousand microscopic eggs in the host's feces every day. In tropical climates where humans, especially chil-dren, often defecate outside on the ground, the soil can contain enormous numbers of these infective eggs. They remain alive and infective for years, even in cold or dry conditions, and many eventually make their way into human hosts via dirty hands, unwashed fruits and vegetables, and contaminated water.

Fertile eggs are golden brown, slightly oval, and lumpy all over, like a walnut in the shell. If the shell were transparent, you would see a larva developing, curled in the egg's hollow center. After only a few weeks in warm damp soil, the larva is ready to hatch should it be swallowed by a human.

The sturdy eggshell protects the larva until it reaches the small intestine; then the juvenile breaks out, threads its way through the wall of the gut, and enters the bloodstream to ride the current. If it doesn't get lost on the way—and many do—the larva travels through the heart and crosses another tissue barrier into the airspace of the lungs. Larvae are coughed up into the throat and then swallowed, or they make the trip on their own, crawling up the airways like microscopic eels. If they have matured sufficiently, they will survive the harsh acid conditions in the stomach and pass through to the small intestine where, home at last, they grow into large mature roundworms.

Ascaris lumbricoides adults lie side by side along the small intestine, suspended in a liquid environment like long slender submarines holding position. They are slightly shiny, quite smooth, and pale pink; sometimes the delicate tracings of their internal structures are visible through the skin. Curiously, they have an odor reminiscent of latex paint.

The worms take in nutrients from the surrounding liquid through delicate mouths with three lips arranged around a central opening like the leaves of a three-leaf clover. About three months pass between the moment a person swallows the egg and the day the first egg from a newly adult worm passes out in the feces—about a quarter of the average *A. lumbricoides* worm's life span.

The things that *A. lumbricoides* is known for, however, do not tend to come out in a straightforward play-by-play of its life cycle. This worm sometimes goes wandering and, leaving the intestine, causes panic by crawling out through the mouth or nose of an appalled host. Immature ones can even crawl up the tiny tube that drains tears from the eye. More dangerously, they may crawl up the bile duct to the liver, or thrash until they break through the intestinal wall into the abdominal cavity. Adults in the small intestine, meanwhile, interfere with absorption of nutrients.

Large numbers of these big worms can be a serious problem, especially if they start tying themselves in collective knots, which can quickly result in intestinal blockage. Intriguingly, the worms' tendencies both to wander and to form hopeless tangles are increased by drugs or fever in the human host. Thus, the migration of worms or a sudden intestinal blockage during an illness is more likely to be the result of a fever than the cause of it.

For Watt, the story of Cook and his worms began not on the captain's third and final voyage, but on his second, in January 1774. Cook and his men on the *Resolution* explored the southern latitudes of the Pacific below the Antarctic Circle, searching for a southern continent no one had ever seen. Cook was determined to go as far south as was physically possible and to venture farther than anyone had done before. He and his men proceeded until they were halted by a vast expanse of ice.

This moment was historic, but the exhilaration of adventure and discovery were dimmed for the captain: he was not feeling at all well. A man who prided himself on his health and on the health of his crew, he was forced to give control of the ship to his first officer and retire to bed with bilious colic.[26] It was not Cook's first sign of illness—he had been suffering from constipation and vomiting for several months—and it was not his last. He got back on his feet but felt worse and worse as the ship sailed north to warmer climates. He hid his illness until, at the end of February, he suffered an acute intestinal obstruction.

Watt suggests that "it is . . . likely, since Cook was anything but fastidious about eating native foods, that this was a heavy ascaris (roundworm) infestation of the intestine, a condition that can cause acute obstruction and which . . . was often associated in the army with bilious fever, worms sometimes escaping from the patient's mouth." This proposed mass of *A. lumbricoides* worms would have been maturing in Cook's intestines in the approximately three months since the ship left Tahiti. Fortunately, he survived the obstruction, but the journals make no mention of the appearance of any worms.

As for the curious and gradual changes in Cook's personality during the third voyage, which began in 1776, we cannot directly attribute them to roundworms. These worms were not migrating to his brain and affecting his behavior, though other parasitic worm larvae may do so. There might be an indirect connection, however. Watt points out that Cook's symptoms parallel those of vitamin B deficiency: loss of appetite, weight loss, irritability, personality deterioration, confusion, loss of the ability to concentrate, and even psychosis.

Nutritional deficiencies, particularly scurvy, which results from a lack of vitamin C, were well-known problems on long sea voyages in Cook's time. Before leaving any port, Cook took on board as many fruits and vegetables as he could get; nevertheless, the diet on board between stops was unquestionably very poor. After several years at sea, the expedition was totally dependent on whatever food supplies the men could take on when they stopped, and on the fish and seabirds they could catch at sea.

When food supplies spoiled or ran out, crew members were hungry and miserable.

Ascaris lumbricoides and other intestinal worms impair the nutritional health of their hosts in various ways. If nothing else, loss of appetite has a negative effect. Could an intestinal worm infection combined with long-term, if intermittent, malnutrition have produced a vitamin deficiency in James Cook? Sir James Watt thought that it could.

Watt's theory has one obvious kink: if James Cook had an intestine full of healthy *A. lumbricoides* in 1778 and 1779, agitating an already malnourished condition, the worms could not have been the ones accused of causing intestinal obstruction in 1776. *Ascaris lumbricoides* simply doesn't live that long. Cook's worms would have died of old age and been passed or digested before the third voyage set sail. Cook would have had to be repeatedly reinfected from new sources on his journeys and at home to maintain an infestation for that long.

It would be no surprise if James Cook had intestinal worms, or, for that matter, if all of his crew had them most of the time. *Ascaris lumbricoides* was present not only on the tropical Pacific islands where Cook and his crews spent so much time but also in Europe. Because the connection between human feces and intestinal worms was not understood, contamination of food and water was commonplace, and in tropical places, even if crops were not fertilized with human waste, the activities of insects, worms, and animals could spread eggs far and wide. Everyone on board probably had *A. lumbricoides* and other intestinal worms as well, and some evidence exists that certain individuals have a predisposition to heavy infestations. If Cook was one of them, he might have had a lot of worms.

In fact, some intestinal worms cause vitamin deficiencies. The fish tapeworms, *Diphyllobothrium* spp., cause vitamin B12 deficiency in some people and still live in about nine million human intestines today. However, scientists have so far not found a direct connection between *A. lumbricoides* and a specific vitamin deficiency.

In January 1779, Cook and his crew on the *Resolution* and the *Discovery*, captained by Charles Clerke, limped into Kealakekua Bay, Hawaii. They had been at the island recently and had not intended to return so soon, but a storm had damaged the ships and repairs were needed. It would be the last port of call for Cook.

The explorers got less respect than they were accustomed to from the Hawaiian people at Kealakekua Bay and endured even more theft than usual. Tension mounted, and Cook uncharacteristically ordered sentries to load their muskets with ball instead of shot. The theft of a boat on February 14, 1779, was the final insult for Cook. With little apparent thought of the possible consequences, Cook loaded his own musket with ball and went ashore with a handful of armed marines—a menacing-looking shore party. He then attempted to kidnap one of the Hawaiian chiefs.

Cook's group was vastly outnumbered by the Hawaiians, who gathered with stones, spears, and daggers. No one has ever been able to explain why Cook would place himself in such a position or abandon the peaceful methods he had habitually used when dealing with native people. The situation escalated suddenly. Cook shot one man dead before being overwhelmed and repeatedly stabbed by the angry crowd. Four marines died with him.

Cook's body was briefly deserted at the water's edge, and by the time the crew gathered themselves together to collect him, the Hawaiians had already taken his remains. The body was carried inland, and that night the grieving sailors on the *Resolution* and the *Discovery* saw the light of distant fires. The next day, when they asked that the body be returned, they learned what the natives had done.

Cook and the other dead had been cut up and burned, a Hawaiian custom for treatment of the remains of great men. The bones had then been distributed to various people on the island. After continued demands, a collection of bones, a piece of Cook's thigh, his scalp, his hands and feet, and a few personal items were finally returned to the ship. These remains were consigned to the sea in Kealakekua Bay.

In the end, Cook's story raises more questions than answers. The connection between Cook's potential parasites and his psychotic behavior near the end of his life remains a fascinating mystery. Did he have a heavy intestinal load of worms? Perhaps the Hawaiian natives who prepared his remains for the fire knew the answer, if we could only ask them.

An even more provocative question is not what effect *A. lumbricoides* had on the exploration of the world (after all, we've probably discovered by now everything that Cook missed) but whether the worm is affecting human progress in other ways. People who have the worm in their intestines, particularly children, don't seem to do as well in school as those who are not infected. Moreover, the more worms a child harbors, the more scholastic difficulty he or she is likely to have.

Ascaris lumbricoides is such a common worm—in some populations, more than 90 percent of children are infected—that these effects suggest a vast loss of human potential. What has the worm cost us as a species? What is it still costing us? To make matters worse, research on other intestinal worms suggests that they also sabotage learning.[27]

The only reason that most of our intestinal parasites are able to do their damage is that we are still incapable of preventing what comes out of our intestines from getting mixed up with what goes into our mouths. Insect-borne parasites such as *Plasmodium* spp. and *Trypanosoma* spp. and skin penetrators such as *Schistosoma* spp. are the exceptions: most parasites, like *A. lumbricoides,* are swallowed. We put great effort into making our food and water safe, but this effort frequently fails. Behind each food- and waterborne parasite is a natural and a human history that makes it a formidable opponent.

TWO

Market of Peril

The history of food safety regulation is filled with government
watchdogs chasing the horses after they have left the barn.

DAVID A. KESSLER
Commissioner, U.S. Food and Drug Administration, 1994

IF YOU WANT TO AVOID foodborne illness, don't eat.

The problem with food, usually, is what we can't see: while lions,
wolves, and crocodiles are wilderness predators, parasites, bacteria, and
even viruses prowl the grocery store. Because most are microscopic, we
have no idea we're stalked until it's too late, and typically, we know
nothing about the patch of earth or water that a plant or animal product
has come from, so we can't predict the likelihood of trouble if we eat it.
In the realm of food safety, however, ignorance is not bliss: most of our
parasites are swallowed. What better way to get inside a human body?

Would you accept food from a complete stranger? Something raw,
unwrapped, passed from hands that might be dirty; something that might
have been irrigated or washed with contaminated water, walked on by
flies, fertilized with untreated sewage, reared or slaughtered in unsanitary
conditions? You do this every day when you consume food you have not
produced yourself. Why? Well, because you're hungry and, if you live in
a developed country, because you have faith in the regulations that protect
your food supply.

Parasites have inspired more than a few of those regulations, vastly
complicating the lives of farmers, fishers, food handlers, processors, and
vendors—and forcing the wary to cook everything well. Parasites close
restaurants, spoil traditional recipes, and make people pick at their food.

Parasites inflate fly-swatter sales. Our obsessive behavior only gets worse as we gain an understanding of the foe. We've learned that humans cooperate with parasites—spreading them, unintentionally concentrating them in human communities and domestic animals, giving them what they need out of habit and ignorance. Indeed, the more we learn about the ease with which parasites get into, or onto, our food, the more we come to consider fresh foods with a suspicious eye.

Our efforts have not eliminated parasites. They still work behind the scenes wreaking havoc in our lives. In many ways, regulation has made things better than they were, but the food safety that we enjoy is new, hard won, and still fragile. To see how both the risks and attitudes have changed, we needn't go back very far.

In 1942, a woman in Ontario, Canada, discovered that lunch can be a risky affair. For Edith Beckett (a pseudonym), it began at the meat peddler's counter when she purchased plump sausages made with fresh pork by the peddler himself.[1] As always, he had purchased pork from a local meatpacking company, grinding it with his own equipment. As Beckett left with her pound of sausages, the two likely wished each other a pleasant day. Beckett had no idea that she had just been targeted by a potentially deadly parasite.

Late on Saturday morning, Beckett slapped the sausages into a frying pan and turned on the heat. At some point during the first half hour or so, she tasted a pinch of sausage to judge whether the dish needed seasoning. Satisfied, she covered the pan and let the meat simmer for another ninety minutes.

The Beckett family enjoyed the sausage lunch, but by Sunday evening, Edith Beckett probably suspected she was coming down with something. If her case was typical, she was a little feverish, and she felt sweaty and nauseated. Soon, she started vomiting; then came bouts of diarrhea. Her belly hurt. Initially, her illness was typical of food poisoning or a stomach virus.

Thinking she had an ordinary stomach bug, Beckett likely waited stoically for it to run its course, but the trouble didn't pass as expected: most stomach viruses clear up within a couple of days, but at the end of the week, Beckett was still plagued with vomiting and diarrhea. We know from the report of the lawsuit that followed that she was soon to be seriously ill.

In the second week, Beckett ran a fever. Her muscles ached, and she had a peculiar puffiness around her eyes. The disease was already bad, but it would get still worse: in the third week after the sausage lunch, Beckett's fever soared. Her muscles hurt so much she could hardly move about, and she was pitifully tired and weak. Swollen glands in her throat made swallowing difficult. Just drawing a breath was a physical challenge. Now, Beckett's heartbeat was weak and faltering. As the week drew to a close, it was possible she could die.

———

In ancient Greek, *parasite* meant a person who dined at another's expense, a mooch, like the friend who always seems to show up exactly at dinnertime. We can easily see why the creatures that live in us and on us have acquired the same label: they flourish at our expense. All too often, parasites are able to dine on us because we have dined on them. Arriving at the table unannounced and unseen, they are not just *at* dinner, they *are* dinner.

How do parasites get into our mouths so adeptly? They do so through a common chain of events with a multitude of variations: a parasite infests food and goes undetected. We go to the market (or more often, the supermarket), make a purchase, and, completely oblivious to the parasite hitching a ride, we bring the food to the table. Having done nothing to render the parasite harmless, we eat. Once again, we have unwittingly cleared the way. The rest is up to the parasite.

Fortunately, we can alter this sequence of events: once we truly understand how a parasite wangles an invitation into our bodies, we can work out ways to bar the intruder from our dining rooms. A personal solution is to make sure the organism is good and dead before we eat it. Alternatively, we can try to remove it from food, or we can interrupt its life cycle so that it doesn't get into our food in the first place. The first solution was the only one available to Edith Beckett, but given human nature, the last one is the only one with significant chance of widespread success.

The pork in Beckett's sausage came from a pig infested with a tiny tissue parasite—*Trichinella spiralis,* a worm so small that its young live tucked inside the cells of its host. When Beckett made her purchase, parasitic larvae coiled inside the pig's muscle cells were still very much alive, even after the animal had been slaughtered and the pork had been ground. When Beckett swallowed that small amount of raw pork as she tasted the undercooked sausage, *T. spiralis* larvae went with it to her stomach. By the time the family sat down to lunch that day, all the larvae in the cooked sausage were quite dead, but the ones that Beckett had swallowed were beginning a new phase.

Beckett had made a serious mistake. *Trichinella spiralis* larvae are so small that a single gram of meat can contain more than a thousand of them: swallowing even a pinch of infested pork may result in a fatal infection. Beckett's digestive enzymes released larvae from the pork muscle and they rapidly invaded the tissues in her small intestine. Oblivious, at first, to the drama unfolding in her belly, she would soon look back on the day with deep regret. We know her story because of the lawsuit that resulted when she suffered long-term health problems.

In 1942, Canada had meat inspection, but inspectors limited their investigation to a few problem areas. People knew that pigs carried a deadly parasite, and they knew that eating undercooked pork was dangerous; in fact, the worm's life cycle had been figured out in 1860. *Trichinella spiralis* larvae in pork, however, could not be detected by veterinary surgeons who inspected the pig carcass because the larvae were too tiny to detect and because at that time, no commercially viable test was available. They simply lacked the means to check every part of every pig for larvae. Fresh pork was a case of *caveat emptor:* buyer beware.

The fresh-pork problem had a long and contentious history. In the late nineteenth century, almost a dozen European countries imposed an embargo on pork imported from the United States, causing uproar in the American pork industry. American pork was infested with *trichinae* (*T. spiralis* larvae), the Europeans said, and people were getting trichinosis.[2] In response, the U.S. government sought a process to ensure that exported pork was not infected.

After ten years of negotiations, inspection regulations requiring microscopic screening of pork were finally in place to detect *T. spiralis* larvae. This method simply could not inspect the whole pig, however, and if the entire animal were inspected, no pork would be left to sell. The export of trichinae-infested pork continued, and by 1910, the regulations were abandoned.[3] Cases of local and exported trichinosis persisted in people like Edith Beckett who ate undercooked pork.

—

Twenty-four hours after Beckett swallowed the *T. spiralis* larvae, they were damaging her small intestine. They invaded the delicate lining, piercing cells one after another like mobile needles. Hour after hour, they fed and matured, damaging tissue and excreting toxic waste products. In less than two days, their growth spurt ended.

If Beckett could have peered through a microscope at her irritated intestinal tissue, she would have seen the adult females, about a tenth of an inch (three millimeters) long, slender and pale—typically wormlike. Each was threaded through more than four hundred cells in a wiggly row. Now fully grown, the females sought out the smaller males. If an experienced parasitologist had peered through the microscope, a diagnosis would have been possible, for these invaders were recognizable: Edith Beckett had trichinosis.

After mating, the female worms produced eggs that hatched before being released. Through a microscope, focusing on a female worm, Beckett would have seen hundreds of tiny larvae wriggling inside. If she had watched long enough—about three days—she would have seen them leave; by the sixth day after she ate the sausage, larvae were migrating throughout her intestinal tissues and into her lymphatic system, headed for her bloodstream.

Meanwhile, the adult females in Beckett's intestines were still alive and producing more larvae, which followed the first ones in a continuous migrational parade. Newborn larvae entered her blood circulation and traveled throughout her body. Leaving the blood again, they damaged vessel walls and other tissues as they burrowed through. As armies of larvae migrated through her heart and other organs, they caused serious problems.

By the third week, the larvae had done enough muscle and organ damage to cause Beckett's breathing troubles and fluttering heartbeat. Arriving in a steady stream from her intestine, thousands of larvae invaded muscles, entering individual muscle cells, their final destination.

A small piece of muscle—ideally a biopsy from around the eyes or from the tongue or jaw where the parasites were particularly numerous—would have revealed many larvae curled up within living cells. We don't know the details of Beckett's medical treatment, but at this stage, if her doctor had guessed the diagnosis, he could have confirmed it with just such a biopsy, looking at a very thin sample of tissue on a microscope slide. If he saw larvae, he would have had no doubt.

Unfortunately, even with a diagnosis, little could have been done for Beckett. The infection ran its course, however, and her condition slowly started to improve. At the end of a month, the crisis had passed. Vomiting and diarrhea gradually tapered off, fever subsided, and the puffiness in her face faded.

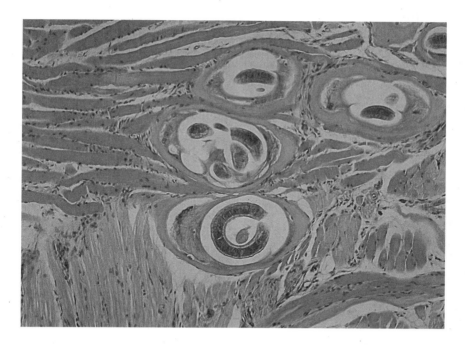

Figure 3. Larvae of *Trichinella spiralis* inside nurse cells in muscle. Photo by the author.

During Beckett's acute illness, each tiny larva settled inside a muscle cell and took control of cell functions like a commander in a hostile takeover. With the cells to serve the larvae's every need, they grew until they were about four one-hundredths of an inch (one millimeter) long, wrapped in a tight coil so they still fit inside their tiny homes. Each occupied cell, now called a nurse cell, continued to change and adapt to its new job for nearly two months, developing an increased blood supply and a thicker wall.

Eventually all changes stopped and the little parasitic time capsules became dormant, with larvae curled up inside nurse cells like sleeping serpents, waiting to be eaten by the next host. Though this was unlikely to happen, the larvae could wait: they were equipped to survive for more than thirty years.

Prolific though they were, the adult worms finally grew old. After a few months, they were all dead and larvae ceased migrating through Beckett's body to invade her muscles. Only the dormant larvae remained, and the lingering debilitating aftereffects of their attack: the pain in Beckett's muscles persisted, and damage to her internal organs was agonizingly slow to heal. The malady that had at first appeared to be ordinary flu had become a chronic illness. Beckett worried that her health was ruined, that she would never again feel well.

We can hardly fault Beckett for looking for someone to blame for her misery. Predictably, she turned her wrath on the peddler who had sold her sausages infested with parasites, the only fresh pork Beckett had eaten before becoming ill. She and her husband claimed that the pork was unfit for human consumption, being infested with trichinae. They sued both the meatpacking company where the pig was slaughtered and the meat peddler.

The judge in the case, however, was well aware of the history of trichinosis and the limitations of pork inspection: the truth was that neither the meat packer nor the meat peddler could have known that the pork sold to Edith Beckett contained parasites. In his remarks, the judge said, "A hog with trichinae in it in the encysted form is not an unhealthy or diseased animal, nor is it unfit for food after being properly cooked. . . . The normal use of fresh pork is to eat it after cooking."[4] Edith Beckett, he judged, bore full responsibility for her illness.

The judge, the meat packer, the meat peddler, and Beckett's contemporaries held the same opinion: people who do not want trichinosis should cook their pork well. But as long as thorough cooking was the only solution, the risk of catching the parasite would remain high. A lot has changed since 1942: the transatlantic fuss over *T. spiralis* set in motion a trend toward preventive farming practices and screening of farm produce that would make food much safer in general for consumers. By that token, we might consider *T. spiralis* the patron parasite of meat inspection.

People soon found better ways to outwit *T. spiralis:* farmers, who had inadvertently created a chain of events that worked to the advantage of the worm, could also break that chain. Pigs acquire *T. spiralis* in the same manner that humans do—by eating the larvae in raw animal tissue. Pigs get it from other pigs when they nip off each other's tails or cannibalize farmyard fatalities. They get it from eating garbage: at one time, it was common practice to feed raw garbage, containing bits and pieces of raw meat and other animal remains, to pigs. And they get it from rats, which also commonly carry the parasite, a fact that has probably escaped most of us because we don't customarily eat rats, undercooked or otherwise. Pigs, however, enjoy a nice plump rat, dead or alive, and rats are available because they, too, like garbage.

Behind Beckett's suffering, then, farther back than the peddler and the meat packer, was a tale of pigs, rats, and raw garbage thrown together by people. The solution was a simple and sensible law that drastically reduced the number of people who would share Beckett's experience. Many countries passed laws against feeding raw garbage to pigs.[5]

Obviously such laws imposed an onerous responsibility on livestock farmers, who now had no cheap and easy way to dispose of farm waste, including the remains of animals that died or were slaughtered on the farm. What were they to do with the remains?[6]

Some farmers set aside a little unused corner somewhere on the property that no one spoke of and few visited. Typically, they selected a secluded meadow some distance from the farmhouse, hidden behind a thick screen of evergreen trees, or a shady patch within the clump of trees itself—the farm's gruesome little secret. A few such secrets doubtless still exist. On a hot, still summer day, the only sound in the meadow was the drone of flies, drawn to the area in large numbers because of the scattered remains of farm animals in various stages of decomposition, from freshly dead to graying bones.

Farmers initially didn't understand why they should not leave dead livestock to decompose in the open. But there are very good reasons. The multitudes of flies are a problem—we'll return to them shortly—but other animals feeding on carcasses create a problem as well. We already know this practice can spread *T. spiralis:* it can also spread other disease-causing organisms, among them a dangerous tapeworm, *Echinococcus granulosus,* or hydatid worm. For *E. granulosus,* people typically provide the links by keeping herds of sheep and sheepdogs.

Echinococcus granulosus usually spreads to farm dogs when they feed on dead sheep infested with the parasite. Like other intestinal tapeworms, *E. granulosus* attaches to the intestinal wall—in this case, the dog's intestinal wall—and absorbs nutrients through its skin. It's small, less than a quarter of an inch (three to six millimeters) long, and it latches on with its scolex, a head equipped with a double row of hooks and a ring of suckers.

As the hydatid worm matures, it produces three segments, or proglottids, the oldest and largest of which is full of infective eggs. The eggs are released when the proglottid drops off the end of the worm and bursts like a balloon filled with pea gravel. The worm makes up for its small size with vast numbers: one dog's gut can host thousands of the worms and pass on hundreds of thousands of eggs to the outside world with a single bowel movement. When eggs are deposited in the pasture, they may be swallowed by grazing animals, which then become the next hosts. When eggs are swallowed by humans, humans become the hosts—accidental sheep.

Dogs transfer eggs to their mouths and fur when they clean themselves, and they contaminate the environment with their droppings. Even when the dog does not leave its feces in the vegetable garden or in a field of cabbages, eggs can easily contaminate food. They are distributed by runoff from rainfall; the activities of birds, flies, and other insects; the wanderings of earthworms; and even the spreading of farm manure on the fields as a fertilizer.

In the usual way of tapeworms, an egg of *E. granulosus* hatches in the intestine of an animal or human, and a larva, or onchosphere, emerges. The onchosphere migrates into the host's tissues; its destination is usually the liver, but it may go to other places such as the lung, bone, or brain. Indeed, it may end up virtually anywhere. Wherever it settles, it encases itself in a fluid-filled cyst, or hydatid cyst, that grows larger and larger as years pass, its size restricted only by the space around it. A hydatid cyst can grow until it exceeds the available space and causes problems. Eventually its sheer bulk can cause liver failure, bone fracture, symptoms of a brain tumor, or other disease, depending on its location. If it ruptures, the escaping fluid can cause an overwhelming, often fatal, allergic reaction.

Inside the cyst, the parasite doesn't rest—it multiplies. Soon, the cyst contains thousands of hooked protoscolices, forming like patches of ripe berries, singly or in clusters inside daughter cysts. Breaking free, they fall to the bottom of the cavity, sloshing around in the liquid there. This accumulating drift of tapeworm offspring is called hydatid sand.

Wherever intensive sheep rearing takes place, hydatid disease is a problem, thanks in large part to the domestic sheepdog, an animal that continually interacts with sheep as well as people.[7] When a dog lunches on a dead sheep, the hydatid sand and the other protoscolices in the cyst deliver huge numbers of worms to the dog's intestines. About two months later, the dog starts passing *E. granulosus* eggs—usually around human dwellings and food crops.

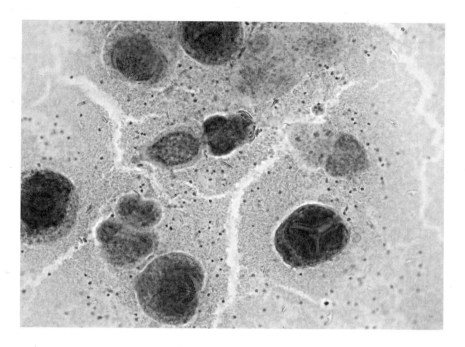

Figure 4. Hydatid sand. Protoscolices of *Echinococcus granulosis* wait to be swallowed. The one in the center has unfolded, hooklets ready to latch on. Photo by the author.

Hydatid disease has been a scourge of humanity for thousands of years: wherever dead animals are improperly disposed of or animal viscera are thrown into garbage bins or into waterways where both domestic and feral dogs can feed on them, the incidence of hydatid disease remains high.

We can almost imagine *T. spiralis* and *E. granulosus* as supervillains, subtly growing in strength as the centuries passed, laughing with maniacal glee as humans domesticated both dogs and sheep and then put them together; and as we domesticated pigs, fed them meat scraps, and housed them with rats. The setup was just too perfect. Most infections in humans were, and still are, dead ends for the villains, because we aren't usually eaten by other animals these days, but the worms did well nonetheless.

Now we understand how we have aided them and are struggling to undo the damage: food safety measures are expensive, inconvenient, and almost impossible to apply everywhere indefinitely, but they do make a difference: they can send the worms back to the wild. Where control measures for *E. granulosus* have been implemented—proper disposal of animal remains, with screening, treatment, and immunization of dogs—the incidence has dropped dramatically. Iceland, New Zealand, and Tasmania have virtually eliminated the worm, but these nations are island environments; banishing it from larger land masses will not be so easy, particularly where wild animals are infected.

Legislation now requires that pork, other than any intended for sale as fresh pork, should be frozen, cooked, or cured to kill *T. spiralis* larvae. Pork producers pay more attention to rodent control, and methods are available to test animals sent for slaughter. In the United States, reported cases have dropped from more than four hundred per year in the 1950s to about a dozen per year today, with most of the current ones stemming from wild game rather than pork.

The responsibility for ensuring that pork products are safe to eat and that dogs don't pass on hydatid disease has shifted from the consumer to the producer, food inspection agencies, and public health officials. Today, Edith Beckett's lawsuit would unfold differently: as soon as her illness was diagnosed, someone would be tracking down the source, identifying other cases, and doing whatever is necessary to prevent any new ones.

But as the saying goes, when one door closes, another opens. If regulations have changed, so has the marketplace: today it's bigger. We enjoy unprecedented access to foods from around the globe. Attractively displayed, many are still fresh even after traveling from distant lands. In fact, more and more of our food is grown thousands of miles from where it's consumed, and in increasingly multicultural societies, we enjoy trying international dishes. Even a local market, more like the one Edith Beckett probably shopped at, may offer a variety of imported goods, especially if it is open all year round.

—

The typical Western farmer's market is no more likely to be the source of a dangerous parasite than is a large chain grocery store; in fact, the large-scale production and distribution favored by big stores allow a parasite in food to reach far more people than ever before. But for many of us, "the farmer's market" conjures up an earthy image. At the market, we feel somehow closer to our food, closer to the source of the products we buy and the people who produce them. We understand where and how the plants grew and the animals were reared. For this reason, the farmer's market is a good place to explore the unseen, not-so-wholesome possibilities in food.

Every kind of food is there: the goat cheese is just around the corner from the Middle Eastern dishes, and the smoked mackerel is just a few steps from the tofu and farm-fresh eggs. Local, organic, or imported fruits and vegetables, grains for sprouting, fair-trade coffee, Gouda cheese, fresh meat and seafood, fresh-baked goods, and a vast selection of homemade pickles and jams are all on offer at the market.

In the northern winter months, imported fruits and vegetables are particularly appealing to palates longing for spring. We dream of asparagus, strawberry shortcake, perhaps fruit salad. A luscious display of plump fresh raspberries at a produce stall can evoke daydreams of raspberries with vanilla ice cream, or cheesecake. Raspberries, irresistible nuggets of tangy flavor, don't usually make us think of parasites.

Imported fruit may not be as wholesome as it looks, however. Where are the raspberries from? In the United States and Canada, importation of raspberries and blackberries from Guatemala is restricted during some parts of the year and is allowed only under strict conditions at other times. A parasite dictated these restrictions—*Cyclospora cayetanensis.*

Cyclospora cayetanensis, recognized in the 1990s, is a relative newcomer to our list of disease-causing parasites. Spherical oocysts of *C. cayetanensis,* the things that we swallow, are so small that seven hundred of them laid out in a straight line would stretch about a quarter of an inch (6.4 millimeters). Not only are they impossible to see, tucked away in the clefts and crevices of a plump raspberry or blackberry, they are also impossible to get rid of. If oocysts are on the berry, the chances are good that thorough washing will not remove them all.

Once past your lips, the parasite usually takes about a week to make its presence known. During this time, banana-shaped sporozoites emerge from the oocysts, invade cells in the intestinal wall, and begin to multiply. At first they divide asexually; eventually male and female forms appear. These reproduce sexually, resulting in innumerable oocysts that, when released, are passed in the feces.

The unfortunate victim, meanwhile, endures severe abdominal cramps, loss of appetite, explosive watery diarrhea, and occasionally fever and vomiting. Diarrhea may seem to be clearing up and then return with a vengeance in a bout of cyclical suffering that continues for many days.

The next stage of the life cycle of *C. cayetanensis* is still something of a mystery. Where does the parasite go between attacks on humans? Oocysts are immature when they're passed. Dull glassy spheres with a cluster of smaller spheres inside, they need time to develop, or sporulate, before they can make anyone else sick. Sporulation happens somewhere in the environment, probably in warm lakes and ponds. Then, when water containing oocysts of *C. cayetanensis* is sprayed on crops, the oocysts are on board food and ready to go.

In the spring of 1996, sporulated oocysts crashed business meetings, company parties, luncheons, and bridal parties and invaded private homes and restaurants in North America. Roughly fifteen hundred people met the parasite, and many of those who fell sick had one recent indulgence in common: Guatemalan raspberries.[8]

Guatemala is a beautiful mountainous country in the middle of Central America. The soil quality in much of the country is poor, and farmers have traditionally cleared land, used it for two or three years, and moved on. Nevertheless, half of Guatemala's labor force is employed in agriculture, and the country exports huge amounts of produce, much of it to the United States. A prevalent problem in Guatemala, as in many tropical countries, is a lack of clean water. In these conditions, *C. cayetanensis* can flourish, but the exact source of the contamination was not identified in 1996.

Cyclosporiasis erupted again in the spring of 1997; again Guatemala was implicated. Growers stopped exporting the berries while they and government departments struggled with the problem. In 1999, the Guatemalan Berry Commission and the Guatemalan government implemented the Model Plan of Excellence. Guatemalan raspberry growers could export again, as long as they followed the plan, a detailed and strict set of regulations that imposed safety practices, inspections, and audits by the U.S. Food and Drug Administration (FDA). Under the plan, every container was marked so that it could be traced back to the farm where the berries had ripened on the cane.[9]

Despite these efforts, more outbreaks of cyclosporiasis occurred in the spring of 2000. Conclusive proof that raspberries were truly to blame finally came when DNA of *C. cayetanensis*—its unique genetic code—was recovered from the raspberry cream filling of a wedding cake in Philadelphia.[10] By this time, very few raspberries were coming out of Guatemala: the parasite had taken a devastating toll on the industry as well as on its victims, and in 2002, only three of an estimated eighty-five raspberry growers were still exporting the berries.[11]

Today, if you find Guatemalan raspberries or blackberries in North American markets, they may indeed be safe, thanks to the vigilance of the Canadian Food Inspection Agency and the FDA in the United States. But *C. cayetanensis* has popped up in tropical countries other than Guatemala; focusing on raspberries and blackberries from that country alone could be a mistake. And what are we to make of the cyclosporiasis outbreak in Pennsylvania in 2004? Apparently this time the parasite traveled on imported snow peas, a good vehicle for the successful parasite because snow peas are often eaten raw.[12]

Standing in the chill that *C. cayetanensis* has cast over raspberries and the unfortunate Guatemalan berry growers, some of us may pass on the raspberry cheesecake that was once so appealing. We may give snow peas a miss too, if we see any. But other farmers' tables still offer fresh greens and other vegetables to spark the appetite. Fresh watercress, for instance, is a familiar product at farmer's markets in France. This crisp, leafy plant is delicious in salads and sandwiches; nothing can substitute for its unique spicy taste.

As the name suggests, watercress is traditionally grown in running water. The plant likes cool, wet conditions and flourishes in the water-holes, springs, and swampy meadows of rainy springtime Europe. It has also long been cultivated there in watercress beds. But a problem has plagued European watercress lovers for as long as they've been harvesting the plant: the environment that is so perfect for watercress is also perfect for snails, and the snails often carry with them another watercress lover that poses a hidden threat to animals and humans. This threat, another parasitic worm, is the reason why commercial watercress growers in France are required to keep their irrigation ditches clean and to prevent water from running off animal pastures into watercress beds.

The liver fluke *Fasciola hepatica* is the cause of "sheep liver rot." The worm is a little over an inch (three centimeters) long and looks like a large flattened leech. It makes itself at home in the bile ducts, the tubes that drain bile from the liver to the gallbladder and small intestine. Feeding on the tissues there, adult worms produce golden brown eggs that are washed down into the intestine with bile. Each egg has a little trapdoor, or operculum, at one end: imagine a brown chicken's egg with a small domed snap cap at the pointy end.

Eggs passed by sheep and other grazing animals wash into waterways during rainstorms. They hatch after about a week and a half, each trap-door releasing a miracidium similar to the *Schistosoma hematobium* mira-

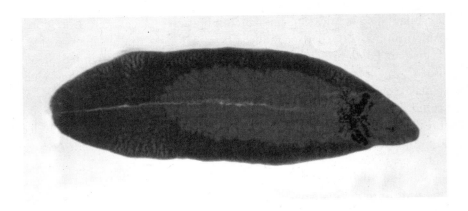

Figure 5. A *Fasciola hepatica* adult fluke. Actual size: 1.2 inches (3 centimeters). Photo by Martin Thomas.

cidia in Jericho's spring. And like those other miracidia, these are looking for a suitable snail. If they find their snail, they burrow in through the mollusk's spreading foot and begin to reproduce.

If the snail remains in the water, cercariae emerge, and when they find themselves in a watercress bed where the snails are enjoying the crisp greens, the cercariae shed their tails, transforming into metacercariae, and attach to watercress leaves, building transparent shields. There, they wait. If a grazing animal does not come along and help itself to the crop, the metacercariae will be harvested, bundled up with the watercress, and taken to the supermarket or the farmer's market. From there, they may well finish up in your sandwich.

In the spring of 2002, eighteen people in Nord-Pas-de-Calais, the French region bordering Belgium in the northeast, were found to have flukes of *F. hepatica* residing in their livers.[13] When investigators asked about watercress, because that plant and *F. hepatica* have often traveled together in the past, they discovered that seventeen of the eighteen infected people had eaten watercress purchased at local supermarkets.

Metacercariae on the greens had been released from their capsules and had crawled through the intestinal wall, inched their way across the abdominal cavity to the liver, and then plunged inside. In people who had eaten watercress more recently, the juvenile worms were spending several weeks wandering around in the liver, a trail of tissue damage in their wake. These destructive wanderings in sheep explain the name "sheep liver rot," and a human liver fares no better. Older worms had already settled down in bile ducts and were maturing there, causing inflammation, swelling, and ultimately, permanent restriction of the flow of bile.

Though some infections go unnoticed, fever and an enlarged liver are hallmarks of fascioliasis. Anemia (a decrease in red blood cells) is also common. Eleven of the human victims of this epidemic were hospitalized with fatigue, fever, pain in their muscles and abdomens, and for some, itching skin. Some may have had the worms for long enough that golden brown eggs with snap caps were already appearing in their feces.

Investigators learned that fifteen of the seventeen victims who ate watercress had bought plants produced by the same commercial grower. Knowing the life cycle of the parasite, we can predict the situation at the farm. Sure enough, irrigation ditches had not been cleared, and rainwater was running off pastures where animals grazed, a violation of regulations. When word of this unfortunate chain of events got out, many more people than this commercial producer had cause to reflect on the tremendous power wielded by one little worm.

The story affects us today as well: a mental image of what sheep liver rot might look and feel like hangs over the mound of innocent watercress beckoning at the market—and causes the informed and the paranoid alike to walk away. We leave the watercress for other market shoppers. Is *anything* here at the market safe to eat? Tables stretch ahead: fruits, vegetables, meats, seafood, pickles. Ah, pickled herring; raw fish.

Different regions often have their own variations of pickled herring. The version in Maritime Canada is called Solomon Gundy and usually contains lots of onions and whole peppercorns; in Jamaica, Solomon Gundy is very spicy; in Germany, it is often called *rollmops,* with the herring wrapped around a bit of pickle. A typical recipe calls for raw, lightly salted herring, dilute vinegar, pickling spice, onion, and dried chili. The brine is brought to a boil and cooled, then poured over the herring. Six days later, it's ready to eat. And it's good: the firm texture of the raw pickled fish is as addictive as the tangy, peppery taste. Pickled herring is safe, surely. What parasite would survive in such a hostile acid environment?

In 2000, Dieter Jansen (a pseudonym), a German man, began feeling ill about four hours after eating homemade rollmops.[14] Stricken suddenly, he was incapacitated by diarrhea, abdominal cramps, and severe chest pain. Jansen's symptoms were so bad that he soon sought medical help. When he was asked what he had eaten, he mentioned the pickled herring. Warning bells went off for German doctors. They had an immediate presumptive diagnosis, but they needed an endoscope to confirm it: they wanted to have a look inside Jansen's stomach.

An endoscope is a long, thin optical fiber with a remote video camera and a light on the end. Doctors use it to look inside the throat, stomach, and intestine without having to resort to surgery. Jansen's throat was sprayed with numbing medication, and he then swallowed the lighted end of the endoscope. Next, air blown in through the tube expanded Jansen's stomach like a balloon and flattened out the folds of his stomach lining, while the light illuminated a busy interior space.

The camera transmitted an image of the activity in Jansen's stomach: doctors saw what looked like live worms, long and slender, like pale tendrils, twisting and wriggling. The worms were burrowing into the stomach wall, which explained Jansen's suffering. The parasites had been in the herring, and neither salting nor pickling had killed them; now they were making themselves comfortable in a new host.

German doctors already knew what the invaders were: they were not worms but larvae of the parasitic worm *Anisakis simplex,* also known as herring worm or whale worm. They recognized the worms because this sort of illness had happened before: the parasite had gained notoriety in the Netherlands more than forty years earlier, and again in the 1980s. On its first documented appearance, it had turned up in a group of Dutch people who had eaten a traditional meal of lightly salted fish.

It was not really surprising that *A. simplex* infestations in humans emerged first in the Netherlands. The country is bordered in the north by the North Sea, with its abundance of fish and marine mammals, and fishing has been a mainstay of the Dutch economy since medieval times. The herring fishery is the largest part of this industry, and as fishers of herring, the Dutch have been leaders in innovation and efficiency. They know and love their herring.

When an unrecognized worm was found in one of the stricken Dutch, and subsequently identified as a parasite from herring, the Netherlands government was quick to realize what the parasite could do to consumers, and to the fishery. The government soon made changes aimed at the larvae, creating new laws that came into force in the 1960s: all fish to be eaten raw, marinated, or lightly preserved were first to be frozen at −4°F (−20°C) for at least twenty-four hours to kill the parasite.

The worm has a complicated life cycle that evolved utterly without humans. A herring allowed to live out its days in the ocean acquires more and more of the larvae as it ages. The larvae, well over an inch (more than two and a half centimeters) long, have a boring tooth on the head, useful for battering through host tissue. Each larva lies tightly coiled in the flesh of the fish, mostly among the internal organs, but if the herring is eaten by a porpoise or whale, the larvae move out of the fish and bore into the stomach wall of the mammal, where they grow to adults. When humans acquire the larvae, they are accidental hosts, understudies for sea mammals: the wriggling larvae act just as if they had been swallowed by a whale.

Worm eggs pass out of the sea mammal in feces and, dispersing in the surrounding waters, they sink slowly toward the ocean floor. On the way down, many are eaten by krill, tiny shrimplike creatures that are breakfast, lunch, and dinner for numerous fish and mammals in the ocean. When krill eat the parasite eggs, and are then eaten by herring or other fish, the larvae are back in a fish host. Many species of fish can harbor the larvae, and a similar worm, *Pseudoterranova decipiens,* follows a parallel life cycle through seals and cod, and unfortunately sometimes through people.

Although these larvae, coiled in fish tissue, are easily visible to the naked eye, people often eat them accidentally—and for the well informed, this prospect can be a huge deterrent to eating raw fish. In the late 1980s, a sudden rise in public awareness followed an anisakid larval guest appearance on a German television program; suddenly, everyone knew about the worm, and no one wanted it. In a bid to calm panicked fish lovers, European food regulators attempted to control larvae in imported fish, but this task is not easy: fish and parasites have never agreed to international borders.[15] Inspectors can stop an infected fish at the border when it arrives in a truck, but no government can prevent it from swimming into coastal waters and getting caught in local nets. Every country with an ocean fishery has its own anisakid to contend with.

Laws similar to the freezing laws in the Netherlands, to assure that the larvae are dead when they are eaten, have been adopted by both the European Union and by the FDA in the United States, but in some places, laws that stand in the way of obtaining truly fresh fish are not at all popular. What would freezing laws do, for instance, to Japanese sushi, a delicious rice dish often served with raw fish? On the heels of the Dutch discovery, Japanese doctors realized they had been handed an answer to their own public health mystery, but without an easy solution. The Japanese love raw fish, and a law requiring freezing would defy long tradition. The love of sushi outweighs any fear of the worm. Freezing, sushi connoisseurs insist, changes both the texture and flavor of fish; if it isn't fresh, it isn't right.

To market shoppers who don't see raw fish as a delicacy, however, the fear prevails. Sadly, the thought of probing each morsel of pickled herring looking for coiled-up larvae is not very appealing. We skip the pickled herring. Though the risk is small, the herring will taste much better when we've forgotten the story. We'll skip the sushi too. And the ceviche. No raw fish! Today's supper will be thoroughly cooked.

A butcher with a refrigerated display case offers other animal products: fresh chicken and farm-fresh eggs; ground beef, ribs, and tenderloin; venison; pig's feet and fresh pork sausage. Is it okay to indulge? The meat supply is safer now, but we still can't be absolutely certain that nothing is hidden within the products we buy. Between 1997 and 2001, seventy-two cases of human trichinosis were reported to the U.S. Centers for Disease Control. Eight were associated with the consumption of commercial pork. Nine appeared to have come from noncommercial pork—raised at home or sold direct from the farm.[16]

We know the frightening history of rare pork, but what about rare beef? An old story of a farmer, a herd of cows, and a tapeworm illustrates why we can't be too sure. This story is hearsay, but it is entirely plausible.[17] The farmer—so the story goes—was a Prince Edward Island beef producer who ran afoul of the law because of another business he was running on the side. You might say he was his own worst enemy, but that is often the case when parasites are involved. This farmer made his big mistake in the outhouse.

In rural areas of North America in the 1950s and 1960s, the outhouse was still a common sight. Indeed, the small building, a little bigger than a phone booth, with a roll of toilet paper (if you're lucky) or an old catalogue and one or two round holes cut in a bench, is still found at summer cottages and in parks and camping grounds. A common teenage prank in rural Prince Edward Island at the time was to pick up an outhouse and move it back a few feet under the cover of darkness, making the path to the toilet a path of peril for the inattentive.

But people sometimes move outhouses for other reasons. When the pit under your outhouse starts to fill up, you basically have two choices. You can dig a new pit and move the outhouse over, fill in the old hole, and pretend you don't know why the grass grows so green, or you can hire someone to pump out the cesspool so that the outhouse remains usable where it sits. The latter option was the farmer's gold mine and his downfall: he cleaned out outhouse cesspools in his spare time.

For the farmer, this sideline offered a double benefit: he was paid for the pumping, and he didn't have to pay to dump the stuff. Instead, he obtained free fertilizer via the age-old practice of using night soil (human excrement) on his fields. The problem with the plan was something meat inspectors have long known: the practice of fertilizing crops with untreated human feces puts infective eggs of human intestinal worms, not to mention other things, where they are highly likely to come in contact with a human. In this case, they were virtually certain to come in contact with cattle.

Unknown to the resourceful farmer, at least one of his outhouse customers had a prolific intestinal companion, a beef farmer's nemesis—*Taenia saginata*, the beef tapeworm. The worm was releasing proglottids—segments that look remarkably like large cucumber seeds—and thousands of microscopic eggs into the feces of its host and thence into the outhouse cesspool. Transported from there and spread on the fields, these tough little brown spherical eggs were just where they needed to be. The larval onchospheres within would be viable for months. They need only wait long enough for cattle to come grazing and swallow them.

Inside a steer, the hatching oncosphere travels away from the intestine: eggs hatch, and the larvae migrate to the steer's muscle tissue, where they form tiny pearly cysts, barely visible to the naked eye. When the steer is slaughtered and turned into ground beef and tenderloin, larvae are alive and well, and waiting to be eaten. If the problem is not noticed when the animal is slaughtered, some of the larvae will likely live to infect humans, considering the number of people who enjoy their steak or burger rare. The larvae escape their cysts, attach to the human intestinal wall, and begin to grow.

Attached in the small intestine, the adult worm can grow amazingly large, forming a ribbon of thousands of proglottids long enough to wrap around the outside of a basic outhouse four or five times. The scolex attaches to the intestinal wall solely with suckers. Although symptoms of an intestinal tapeworm are typically mild, a beef tapeworm is still to be avoided—at the least, the appearance of proglottids, often very much alive, in your toilet bowl or boxers is enough to ruin your day.

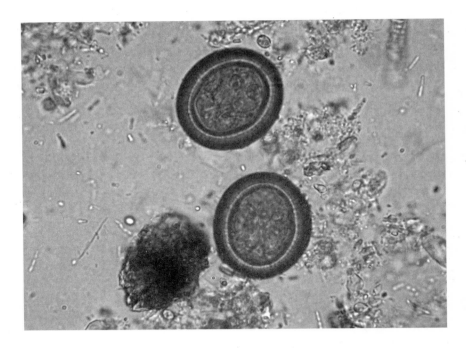

Figure 6. Eggs of *Taenia* sp. Photo by the author.

Molecular methods, which detect the unique genetic code of *T. saginata*, now allow effective screening of beef in developed countries; however, in the 1960s, as many as a quarter of *T. saginata* infections in steers were missed by meat-inspection procedures.[18] Ultimately, however, meat inspectors did notice the parasites in the farmer's cattle. Thus, the story came to light, the herd was condemned, and the contaminated pastures were declared unsuitable for grazing until all the onchospheres had died, waiting for cattle that never came. One can only speculate as to whether any meat from the infected animals reached consumers with rare beef in their dinner plans.

What is the likelihood of such a set of circumstances happening today? At least in the West, laws governing the disposal of sewage, greatly improved sanitation, and refined meat-inspection procedures make us feel quite secure. Still, a thread runs through these examples: food safety routines break down, regulations aren't followed, people make mistakes. Such imperfections in the regulatory scheme will always exist.

We inspect the meat at the market critically and try not to think about tapeworms. The butcher slaps our ground beef onto the scale. We see a large gray fly alight on it briefly and then buzz on at the wave of the butcher's beefy hand. Wait a minute. Flies around food are a health hazard. They are hard to control, especially outdoors, but food vendors must ensure that flies cannot contaminate food.

Guarding against flies and other insects can be a challenge, especially in warm climates, and many people are casual about this task. For example, when health inspectors in New Delhi, India, closed a brand-new Kentucky Fried Chicken restaurant after observing two flies in the same room as thawing chickens, many viewed the closure as ludicrous.[19] Two flies in the kitchen? In New Delhi, just two flies in the kitchen might well be an indication of cleanliness, not negligence.

The restaurant marked the advent of Kentucky Fried Chicken in New Delhi, and it had been in operation for just twenty-three days. The media were quick to pick up on the story, and in general, depicted the closure of the Kentucky Fried Chicken as a political event: an act of resistance to the arrival of fast food from the West. These flies, perhaps, were pawns (though that doesn't make them innocent of carrying disease).

A trio of flies in New York achieved a greater consensus of public opinion. The New York restaurant Rocco's was the set for a reality television production, *The Restaurant,* in which cameras invaded the kitchen, spied on tables, and eavesdropped on the staff. But the exploits and intrigues of staff and patrons were not the main focus of the show; the chef was the star. Starting up a restaurant is a risky venture, and the tribulations of chef Rocco DiSpirito formed the main story line.

DiSpirito had plenty of challenges right from the start, including troubles with his staff and bad reviews of his food—all entertainment for avid viewers of reality television. In reality television, though, the restaurant is real. The food, the patrons, and the flies are real. So are the health inspectors. At the end of July 2003, inspectors from the New York Department of Health and Mental Hygiene paid a surprise visit to Rocco's, and by the time they finished their inspection, DiSpirito had a notice citing six different violations. Flies were first on the list.

"Evidence of live flies in facility in that three live flies observed in rear kitchen food preparation area," read the damning notice.[20] In short order, this bad news had spread and directed many an appetite elsewhere.

Flies shouldn't be in the same sentence with *food,* especially at an upscale restaurant.

The flies didn't bring down Rocco's on their own but added weight to a host of other problems that did. The restaurant doesn't exist anymore. A new establishment flourishes where Rocco's once stood, and we trust that management doesn't allow flies in the kitchen. Whereas the motives of certain health inspectors in India might be suspect, health inspectors in North America take flies and other insects in the kitchen very seriously. We'll pursue the market fly to find out why.

Imagine immobilizing the busy insect in midflight. It hangs in the hot summer air. Let's take a good look. Why is it so vilified? We'll begin by blowing it up to about five hundred times its natural size. It levitates above the ground like a small blimp more than sixteen feet (five meters) long, a hairy monster with two glassy wings and six bristly, bent, sticklike legs. Its eyes are enormous, multifaceted, and red, like the surface of a ripe raspberry.

Our fly has three bold black stripes on its thorax, which break into a checkered pattern on its abdomen farther back. These markings reveal that it is probably a flesh fly, a fly that deposits its maggots, already hatched from eggs, on the remains of dead animals. This one was probably investigating our ground beef as a potential place to deposit maggots where there would be abundant food. For the adult fly, food is any dead and decaying organic matter—dead animals, rotting vegetation, and human and animal excrement.

Our market stroll is becoming reminiscent of a scene in a horror film; giant flies are not for the faint of heart. At five hundred times its actual size, this fly is frightening, bulky enough to block all the pedestrian traffic between the market stalls and to put its sticky feet down in the area behind them like the supports of a carnival tent. It's not the monster, however, or even its plump white maggots that concern us here; it's the fellow travelers that the fly has carried from other places.

Like a pair of nylon stockings on a crisp winter day, the fly's body has electrostatic charges. It pulls in tiny objects from all around. If we get close enough to its hairy underside, we will find it adorned like a Christmas tree, peppered with organisms and litter from the human feces it walked and fed on by an exposed sewer outflow, as well as from the decaying body of a dead sheep in a nearby field and the garbage dumped in the woods or alley behind the market. Innumerable objects are caught in the fly's bristly hairs. Like garlands of Christmas lights, other debris is stuck along its crooked legs, now splayed above the market stalls.

One of the larger items is a spherical object, golden brown and about the size of a marble. Held up to the light, it reveals a pocked texture around its outer edge, as though myriad tiny channels lead toward the center. The insides of marbles are often fascinating—starbursts of striped color like pennants flapping in the breeze or constellations of tiny bubbles—and this one is no less intriguing. In its murky brown depths, we see a fan of delicate hooks, like shark teeth dangling from a necklace. This marble is a tapeworm egg. It might be a pork or beef tapeworm egg from human feces, or an *E. granulosus* egg from a dog, or an egg of another species; many look similar. It stuck to the fly when the insect walked on feces.

Peering more closely into the underworld of the fly, we see smaller objects stuck in the forest of hairs. There are a few glittering balls that look like large, slightly flattened grains of cooked tapioca. Inside each ball, smaller shiny flattened balls are visible. They can only have come from cat feces: they are *Toxoplasma gondii* oocysts—a protozoan relative of *C. cayetanensis*—and they are infective to us and other vertebrates.

We jump back as a snakelike creature thrusts out suddenly from a cranny on the fly's belly. It is between four and five inches (eleven to twelve centimeters) long and as thick as a pencil. It's a larva, probably newly hatched from another egg caught in the fly's hairy undercoating. It might be a harmless plant nematode (roundworm) larva, picked up from the soil, but knowing where the fly prefers to loiter, it is more likely to be a parasitic larva from human or animal feces.

If this larva is a human hookworm larva, it's harmless at this stage: it requires a couple of days in warm, moist soil before it can plunge through human skin and travel through the lungs, up the trachea, and down to the intestine, to mature there and start producing eggs of its own. As we watch, the larva's thrashing frees it and it drops to the ground, wriggling in the moist soil. Soon it disappears below the surface.

If we keep looking, we may find other parasites on the fly: worm eggs, protozoan cysts, and, so tiny that we can discern only a shimmering film of life, billions of bacteria and viruses.[21] But let's leave the beast's belly, where more unpleasant things may drop on us if we linger, and look the fly in the face.

Flies have a long, thin strawlike proboscis, with a hairy mouth at the end like a sponge mop designed to draw up liquids. When a fly lands on a potential food source, it produces a vomit drop and proceeds to suck up the mess—and with it, new food.

We toss the purchased hamburger to our fly, having abruptly decided against any supper at all tonight, and the insect obligingly produces a gush of rich soup. In it, a collection of bacteria, viruses, and protozoa that the fly has swallowed in its previous exploits slosh around. Drifting in the puddle are more of the same small things we saw stuck to the fly's body, and others we don't recognize. Some shiny little spheres are rising slowly to the surface like tiny bubbles. They are about as big as grains of pickling salt, so small, even at five hundred times their usual size, that no internal detail is visible.

Despite their small size, these little globes do have smaller things inside: curved against the inside wall of each one, like a bunch of bananas, four sporozoites wait to emerge in a human intestine. Whether they are deposited on food in a vomit drop, or pass through the fly to emerge, unscathed, from the other end, they are highly infectious: swallow just ten of them, and you will quite likely become ill.

Of course, we wouldn't think of swallowing these bits of flotsam, bobbing in a pool of fly vomit. Remember, however, that at their true size of about one five-thousandth of an inch (three to five micrometers), they would be utterly invisible. These are oocysts of *Cryptosporidium parvum,* notorious for contaminating water supplies and issuing from our kitchen taps. They and their sort have made water supplies and water utilities another battleground between people and parasite. If our stroll through the farmer's market was disturbing, try a trip through a water utility.

THREE

Drinking-Water Advisory

> Throughout the history of literature, the guy who poisons the well
> has been the worst of all villains.
>
> AUTHOR UNKNOWN

THE TRUCK DRIVER SAYS IT'S "a Cambodian journey."

A haze of fine dust hangs in the air as about thirty travelers, tourists, and locals coated with the red stuff climb out of a couple of half-ton trucks and scramble down a steep riverbank. Single file, we step courageously across the gap to the listing bow of a covered passenger boat. About two-thirds go below; the rest of us arrange ourselves on the flat roof, tucked between bags, packages, and backpacks in the hot Cambodian sun. It is late February, the dry season. There will be no rain today.

In the dry season, boats traveling the Stoeng Sangke from Batdambang to Tonle Sap, the largest lake in Cambodia, must cast off a considerable distance downriver from Batdambang. Even at this mooring, the craft repeatedly becomes mired in muddy shallows. The enterprising crew coaxes it along, sometimes jumping into the river to free up the propeller and to remove plastic bags and other items jamming the blades. Gradually the water gets deeper, but its murky brown color, reminiscent of strong milky coffee, never thins.

The Stoeng Sangke runs through northwestern Cambodia like a winding snake. In the dry season, dense vegetation still grows right down to the water's edge in many places, but in others a continuous row of flimsy huts stands atop high banks or a long, narrow floating village clings to the shore. As the motorboat proceeds up the widening waterway, we wave at

Figure 7. Life along the Stoeng Sangke. Photo by the author.

happy children playing and bathing in river water. Adults wash dishes or do laundry in the river; some fish; some tend pigs whose floating sties appear ready to slip beneath the dark surface at any moment.

These industrious Cambodian people get everything from the river. They're primarily fishers, but they have other occupations as well: many process fish, some farm fish, crocodiles, ducks, or livestock. A few poach birds and birds' eggs; a few manage a little farming on land that floods when the rains come; a handful run shops, selling supplies and food, mostly to travelers like those on the boat.

The boat trip to Siem Reap takes all day, and the nearer to Tonle Sap Lake the motorboat comes, the more people, fishing operations, and floating villages slip by. At length, the crew pulls up to a floating building and announces that passengers can buy food and visit the washroom. For many, the food items on offer are mysterious, but the bathroom facilities are starkly simple: one follows a tortuous floating path around the corners of buildings, sometimes with the brown water lapping gently just inches away, to reach a tiny cubicle with walls about five feet high and a corrugated iron door. Inside is a square hole in the floor, opening directly into the water below.

Now the truth dawns on even the least deductive tourist. This river is indeed everything to the people who live on it. It is their water supply, their food source, the basis of all livelihood, a transportation route, an address—and a sewer. Doubtless, it is the source of many an intestinal illness.

—

It's worlds away from Cambodia's Stoeng Sangke. Or is it? The North Saskatchewan River roars down from its headwaters in Canada's Rocky Mountains through the foothills and across the prairie, as predictable as spring thaw. By March, the river is growing as temperatures rise, swollen by melting snow and ice. It will be at its mightiest in June and July, pushing hundreds of cubic meters of water per second past the city of Edmonton, across the Saskatchewan border just north of Lloydminster, and on past the stretch where the Battlefords—the city of North Battleford and the smaller town of Battleford—face each other across the river. Edmonton, Lloydminster, and North Battleford all depend on the river for their water supply.

With the melting snow and the runoff from spring rain, the land near the river's banks gets a good rinse, and abundant surface material washes into the current. Animal wastes from pastureland account for a lot of this material; debris that has built up in frozen layers over the winter is stirred and carried away, laden with parasites and bacteria. Smaller watercourses joining the river bring debris from distant parts of the watershed as well, where wild animals contribute their own intestinal organisms. Like the Stoeng Sangke, the North Saskatchewan River is contaminated.

Clean drinking water is a hallmark of a developed country, an earnest goal of developing countries, and a preoccupation of organizations such as the United Nations. But ensuring a clean water supply is not easy. The best approach to water treatment is typically multipronged. First, protect the watershed, the geographical area from which the drinking water is drawn. Second, try to remove particles suspended in the water. Finally, disinfect and test the water. The amount of human effort that has been spent applying these principles is staggering. But like the Stoeng Sangke and the North Saskatchewan River, virtually all surface water on earth is contaminated, and we still fall victim to waterborne diseases. In developed countries today, the majority of outbreaks of diarrhea linked to contaminated water are caused by protozoan parasites.

Chemicals that kill dangerous bacteria and viruses in drinking water do not kill parasites, at least at the concentrations routinely used. The usual way to get rid of parasites in water is to filter them out. In the United States, the Safe Drinking Water Act requires water treatment plants to filter surface water unless the water source meets stringent requirements for purity and protection from contaminants—which means parasites don't get into the water in the first place.

Initial purity is a good idea but hard to achieve in practice; even a pristine water supply can be contaminated, and there often isn't any way of knowing—except in hindsight—when parasites are in the water. A water utility in British Columbia, Canada, discovered this fact the hard way in 1995, when something unique and unpredictable happened to a reservoir on Vancouver Island.

The first sign of trouble was a sudden unexplained increase in human cases of the parasitic disease toxoplasmosis in and around the city of Victoria on Vancouver Island. When the British Columbia Centre for Disease Control and the Capital Regional District Health Department began investigating the outbreak in March 1995, the city had already seen fifteen cases since the beginning of the year, in a population that normally saw between one and four cases annually. A lot more people than usual were infected with the parasite, but where were they being exposed?

Toxoplasmosis is caused by *Toxoplasma gondii,* a parasite related to *Cyclospora cayetanensis* and *Cryptosporidium* spp. Oval oocysts of *Toxoplasma gondii,* found in cat feces and in soil where cats have defecated, are infective to humans and other animals. The crescent-shaped tachyzoites and bradyzoites, *T. gondii* stages that live in animal tissue, are infective as well: people typically get toxoplasmosis either by accidentally swallowing fecal material from cats or by eating undercooked meat.

The source of the Victoria outbreak proved elusive. Investigators knew they were looking for a common source, something to which all of the infected people had been exposed. They ruled out direct exposure to cat feces, raw meat, food or beverages consumed by all the patients, and unpasteurized milk and goat's milk—all sources previously linked to toxoplasmosis outbreaks. And they concluded that none of the patients had become infected while traveling abroad.

However, when investigators plotted patients' homes on a map, a pattern emerged. Almost all lived in a particular geographic area—the area served by the Humpback Reservoir, one of two main water sources for greater Victoria. The Humpback lay in a pristine watershed that delivered water to over two hundred thousand people. Water from the Humpback was chemically treated but was not filtered before arriving in faucets and water fountains.

If toxoplasmosis is transmitted in water, the infective stage has to be oocysts. Like the oocysts of *C. cayetanensis,* but a tiny bit larger, these tough little oval parasites can survive in cool water, waiting to release their sporozoites until they are safe inside the intestine of a human.[1] When the time is right, eight crescent-shaped sporozoites emerge from each oocyst.

Once liberated, sporozoites invade body cells, including white blood cells and macrophages—cells of the immune system. They become tachyzoites (meaning fast zoites). Baggy crescent moons with a scrap of nuclear material near the middle, the delicate invaders rapidly duplicate their genes and split apart to double in number, and double again, and again. When the cell is crammed full, it bursts, its violent death releasing a flood of parasites. They rush to invade new cells and start the process over again.

Eventually, the immune system successfully isolates the parasites and builds a barricade around them, forming cysts. Now called bradyzoites (or slow zoites), they multiply very slowly and usually stay isolated in their tissue prisons. Symptoms, if any, subside. Though the parasites may live for many years, a healthy immune system keeps them in check indefinitely.

Toxoplasma gondii, spread around the globe primarily by cats and rodents, is so common that many people worldwide have been infected at some time in their lives. Most don't know that they have the parasite because typical cases are mild or go completely unnoticed. Typical symptoms mimic a mild case of flu, sometimes with swollen lymph nodes, muscle aches, and fatigue. The infection can be much more serious in people whose immune systems aren't working properly and in unborn babies.

If a woman is infected with *T. gondii* for the first time while she is pregnant, the parasite often invades the growing fetus, probably by traveling in the blood. When the infection does not kill the fetus, resulting in spontaneous abortion or stillbirth, it is a major cause of birth defects, including brain damage and blindness. Forty-two of the diagnosed cases in Victoria were pregnant women. Eleven of them gave birth to infected infants, many of whom have probably suffered immediate or delayed health problems as a result.

By the time the Victoria toxoplasmosis outbreak was over in the summer of 1995, 110 people had been diagnosed with the disease, but because many cases either have no symptoms or remain undiagnosed, this group was just the tip of the toxoplasmosis iceberg. An epidemiological analysis of the outbreak concluded that the actual number of infected people was between 2,900 and 7,700.[2]

This epidemic was the first time a municipal water supply was suspected as the source of a toxoplasmosis outbreak. No standard methods exist for testing a water supply for the parasite, but when investigators went looking for the usual suspects—cats—they found them. The reservoir lay close to populated areas and was frequented not only by domestic and feral cats but also by wild cougars. When some of the cats were trapped and tested, they had antibodies to *T. gondii,* which confirmed that they had been infected with the parasite.

A look at rainfall patterns and turbidity (cloudiness indicating suspended material) in the water provided more evidence. The area had seen two recent periods of heavy rainfall, the first in November 1994 and the second in February 1995. Records at the reservoir showed high water turbidity during these periods: heavy rainfall had increased the runoff from the watershed into the reservoir and washed debris off land into the water. Given the cat population around the reservoir, the debris was sure to have included cat feces.

Investigators reasoned that if cat feces in the environment around the reservoir were the source of the parasite, the water should have contained more oocysts in the water at times of heavy rainfall and runoff, and consequently more cases of infection. Sure enough, clusters of toxoplasmosis cases had been diagnosed in December 1994 and March 1995, following the November and February rainfall peaks.

With the conclusion that the water from Humpback Reservoir was the source of the epidemic, the parasite dealt its final blow. Government regulation required that the Capital Regional District Water Department in Victoria follow the U.S. Environmental Protection Agency (EPA) requirements for unfiltered surface water. One of the EPA stipulations is that any water source that has ever been identified as the source of an outbreak of disease must be filtered—and the Humpback Reservoir now fell into this category.

Victoria chose a different solution. The Humpback was a relatively small reservoir, and authorities decided not to go to the expense of installing a filtration system. In 1995, the reservoir was disconnected from the water supply for greater Victoria, and in 1998, it was drained. It is now part of the Sooke Hills Wilderness Regional Park and is presumably still a haunt of cougars and smaller cats—and *T. gondii.*

Even for water treatment plants using filtration, a protected watershed is an important part of providing safe drinking water. Water treatment facilities usually seek to limit public access to the watershed area, prohibit the rearing of livestock in the watershed, and avoid contamination by human wastes, yet none of these measures prevented *T. gondii* from doing irreparable damage to both people and infrastructure in Victoria. In fact, the Victoria outbreak demonstrated how easily a watershed can become contaminated without anyone knowing until it is too late. At the time, about nine hundred other water treatment facilities in Canada were providing unfiltered water.[3]

Although keeping a watershed clean is desirable, it isn't always possible. The North Saskatchewan River basin, framing a river more than a thousand kilometers long, winding across two provinces past cropland, livestock operations, towns, and cities, is a perfect example. It simply can't be protected. As a result, the North Saskatchewan River is laden with bacteria and parasites.

In the spring, when the water is high and turbid, the river tends to have high numbers of cysts of *Giardia lamblia* and oocysts of *Cryptosporidium* spp., sometimes one hundred oocysts or more per liter.[4] Oocysts of *Cryptosporidium* spp. are light and buoyant, so they tend to stay suspended in the water, and they're built to survive in the chilly spring runoff. Swept along with other debris, they are carried downstream for vast distances. On their way across the Canadian prairies, they are carried past communities that draw a water supply from the river.

These organisms are *tiny.* If you could sit astride an oocyst and bob along in the stream, you'd have to be the size of a small bacterium, about six hundred-thousandths of an inch (one- or two-thousandths of a millimeter) long. A cyst of *G. lamblia,* drifting nearby in the current, would be larger than your oocyst watercraft: it would look about the size of a minibus to you. Much larger, a paper matchstick floating by would be seventeen thousand times your size: from the perspective of your actual dimensions, an object this much bigger than you would be a little over eighteen and a half miles (about thirty kilometers) long and would almost span the Strait of Dover, between England and France, at its narrowest point.

An oocyst of *Cryptosporidium* is spherical, with a slightly rough outside surface like the skin of an orange. Perched on top and groping for a

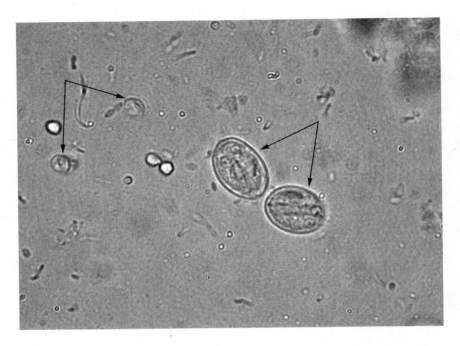

Figure 8. Cysts of *Giardia lamblia* and oocysts of *Cryptosporidium* sp. float side by side. Photo by the author.

handhold, you'll notice a thin groove, like a closed zipper. If you could unzip it and peel back the edges of the opening to peer inside, you might first notice a cluster of smaller spheres, bunched together on one side. Then, looking deeper, you'd spot the sporozoites—four long sausage-shaped bodies nestled against the curved inner wall like fat sleeping maggots. At least three times as long as you (remember, you are the size of a bacterium), they are formidable but harmless at the moment: they will not stir as long as the oocyst is in the water.

Cryptosporidium is so well dispersed in the environment that virtually all surface waters contain the oocysts.[5] Oocysts in the North Saskatchewan River are probably a mixed lot that come from various sources. Most have been shed in the feces of livestock and then washed into the river by spring rain. Cattle are infamous for carrying *Cryptosporidium parvum,* and newborn calves are often infected: within days of birth, they develop "scours" and pass millions of oocysts in watery diarrhea. Adult cattle often shed oocysts of *C. parvum* in their feces even when they are not ill, which explains why newborn calves catch it so frequently.

Canada geese spread oocysts as well, though the *Cryptosporidium* spp. that infect cows and humans don't make them sick.[6] These large birds habitually visit farm pastures and, wandering behind grazing cattle, peck kernels of undigested corn from cow patties. With the kernels come oocysts. The trip through a goose is simply a detour for *Cryptosporidium:* no harm is done to either bird or parasite. Oocysts hitch a ride for a while as they work their way through the bird's gut; then issuing from the other end, they are deposited on whatever land or in whatever body of water the goose visits next. Some oocysts in the North Saskatchewan River have doubtless arrived in this fashion, courtesy of migrating Canada geese or other waterbirds.

Some oocysts in the river come from people. Along the river, effluent from sewage systems is discharged into the waterway; the city of Edmonton discharges wastewater into the river after the water has passed through its sewage treatment plant, and in North Battleford in 2001, wastewater was discharged from a sewage treatment plant one and a quarter miles (two kilometers) *upstream* from the intake for the city's potable water supply. After treatment, no oocysts should remain in the discharged water, but discharge of untreated wastewater inevitably occurs from time to time.

One way to discharge untreated wastewater from a sewage treatment plant is through a process known as blending—blending, that is, of treated water with untreated water. When an extreme weather event occurs, such as very heavy rainfall, the volume of water entering a plant may exceed the plant's capacity, at which point water is diverted from the plant and discharged without full treatment. Blending is not rare. In November 2003, the EPA proposed a new policy that would allow sewage treatment plants to turn to blending any time it rains, instead of restricting the practice to heavy rainfall events.

Critics of the proposal, who regarded blending under any circumstances to be a violation of laws designed to protect water sources from contamination, were outraged. They envisioned, probably rightly so, that lakes and waterways would repeatedly be contaminated with untreated sewage. The proposal caused such contention that in 2005, the U.S. Congress waded into the fight, voting in an amendment to the Interior, Environment, and Related Agencies Appropriations bill to prevent the EPA from implementing the policy. Nonetheless, blending continues in extreme weather.

In 2001, the North Battleford sewage treatment plant had a built-in system for blending. If spring runoff and rains overflowed the storm-water system, causing flooding in the streets, storm water entered sewers through sewer manholes. When the water level in the sewage system rose high enough, wastewater overflowed through a weir in one of the manholes and was diverted around the plant, blended with treated water, and discharged into the North Saskatchewan River.

The only disinfection the diverted water received was the diluted chlorine in the treated water. Any parasitic cysts or oocysts would be unaffected by the low concentrations of chlorine and would enter the river untouched. With changing currents, the discharged water from the sewage treatment plant occasionally passed over the intake for the city's drinking-water supply downstream.

In late March 2001, the oocyst on which you are riding, whatever its origin, would have been carried over the intake for the North Battleford water treatment plant and drawn into the plant along with millions of other oocysts.[7] Cysts of *G. lamblia,* bacteria, sediment, and other fine debris would have gone through the intake as well. You are swept into a well and then sucked up through a sand separator, a centrifuge designed to remove large particles from water. Heavier things, like grains of sand, bits of rock, and scraps of plants, are dragged past you and thrown to the side by centrifugal force, while you and your oocyst, too small and light to be caught in the vortex, rise effortlessly up the middle like a shimmery hot-air balloon.

On the other side of the separator, chemicals blend with water: aluminum sulphate, an ionic polymer, and sometimes polyaluminum chloride, to make the remaining particles in the water clump together; potassium permanganate to oxidize and remove minerals; chlorine to disinfect; and lime to prevent the water from being too acid. In a good system, these chemicals mix vigorously with the water, but here in North Battleford, they would have blended in gradually. Bacteria in the water die because of the chlorine, but your oocyst, carrying its dormant sporozoites, sails calmly through this chemical brew and drops into the solids contact unit.

In the solids contact unit, you and the oocyst, cysts of *G. lamblia,* bacteria, dust, and all the other particles in the water should tangle up and get jammed together in a dense fluffy substance called floc. Floc forms when particles in water come together. In normal circumstances, chemicals ensure that the particles are attracted to one another, and floc particles already in the unit act as big foundation blocks that smaller particles are particularly attracted to, building bigger and bigger clumps. When clumps are big enough, they fall out of the water, forming a layer of sludge.

But not today. On March 20, 2001, the solids contact unit at the North Battleford surface-water treatment plant was shut down for servicing: the unit was cracked, and the plant operators needed to assess the damage and repair it, if necessary. To complete the repair, they needed to clean out all the accumulated sludge in the unit. The unit was up and running the same day, but after it returned to operation, no building blocks of sludge were left to help accelerate formation of floc in the unit, and particles in the water did not settle out. They would not settle out for more than a month.

Passing through the solids contact unit, you escape being cemented into a chemical snowflake because floc is not forming. You drift toward the filters—barricades of anthracite coal and sand meant to stop anything remaining in the water from passing into North Battleford's drinking-water supply. The filters are the city's last line of defense.

Because *Cryptosporidium* spp. and other waterborne protozoa are not affected by chlorine, filtration has become a standard for adequate treatment of surface water. Health Canada water-quality guidelines now recommend filtration for the removal of protozoa, and the U.S. Safe Drinking Water Act, which mandates filtration of surface water in most watersheds, is recognized as a leading piece of legislation by many other countries, which seek to model it.

The mere potential for an outbreak of waterborne disease can cause a major uproar: on April 24, 1997, the United States filed a lawsuit against New York City because the municipality was not filtering water from its Croton watershed, a water supply that provides drinking water to more than a million New Yorkers. Of more than 10,000 surface drinking-water sources in the United States at that time, only 135 could safely avoid filtering. The Croton water-supply system was not one of them.

Under pressure from the EPA and New York State, the city agreed to protect the Croton watershed from contamination and to filter the Croton water supply by September 2006.[8] The city was fined $1 million for its prior failure to filter the water. As of August 2009, however, the Croton water treatment plant was still under construction, overshadowed by strident opposition and massive cost overruns. A new deadline of October 31, 2011, is unlikely to be met. Somewhere in a comfortable intestine,

G. lamblia and *Cryptosporidium* must be toasting each other—with water, of course.

——

It's hard to believe that any unfiltered surface-water supply is safe. The toxoplasmosis outbreak in Victoria, British Columbia, proved how difficult it is to guarantee protection of a watershed. And if outbreaks linked to cats and drinking water are rare, the relationship between *G. lamblia,* beavers, and drinking water is legendary.

The question of whether humans first gave *G. lamblia* to beavers and other animals, or whether they gave it to us, is debatable. Regardless, the dangers of drinking from mountain streams have been rediscovered time and again by unfortunate outdoor enthusiasts. Water downstream from a beaver dam is to be avoided even if you are very thirsty, and humans and beavers alike have contaminated municipal water supplies on many occasions. The tiny cysts of *G. lamblia,* unaffected by chlorination, must be filtered out.

One of the best-documented outbreaks of giardiasis linked to beavers happened in 1990 in Canada, in Creston, British Columbia.[9] The town is in rugged country close to the border with Idaho: mountains to the north climb well over sixty-five hundred feet (two thousand meters) above sea level. Roads and communities in the area are nestled in river valleys. Creston is just south of the lower tip of Kootenay Lake, in the wedge formed by Kootenay River in the west and Goat River in the east.

In the late 1980s, about forty-two hundred people lived in Creston. The town drew an untreated, unfiltered water supply from Arrow Creek, a stream that rushed down from mountainous country to the northwest. No other communities lay upstream on Arrow Creek; in fact, the terrain was so formidable that there was little human activity upstream of any kind, particularly in winter. Arrow Creek was as pristine a water supply as you could imagine.

In the fall of 1989, a beaver migrated to Arrow Creek, probably from a larger beaver colony on nearby Goat River. The wanderer was discovered living downstream from the town's water-supply intake. It could do little damage downstream, but residents worried that the animal might move again, to a new location farther up the creek: if it moved above the intake, it might contaminate the town's water supply. Though removing the beaver seemed advisable, the animal remained undisturbed because it was living on private land, and the landowner would not give permission to go in and remove it.

In the winter of 1990, an outbreak of diarrhea hit residents of Creston and nearby Erickson, which shared the Arrow Creek water supply. Some sought medical advice and submitted stool samples. Indeed, the samples tested positive for giardiasis—beaver fever. In short order, the investigators focused on water as a probable source of the problem.

When the tiny oval cysts of *G. lamblia* get into a beverage glass and are swallowed, they transform to the next stage of their life cycle in the small intestine. Cyst walls break down, releasing two flattened teardrop-shaped trophozoites. Each trophozoite has two googly-eye nuclei at the rounded end, a suction cup on the bottom, and several streaming tentacle-like flagellae.

In the intestine, trophozoites latch onto the wall with the suction cup and cling there, feeding on the liquid bowel contents and mucus that surround them. Soon they start dividing: each one into two, and each of these into two more, until millions of teardrop parasites lie side by side, covering the intestinal surface like plastic wrap.

This coating of the intestinal wall blocks the host's absorption of nutrients and water, causing severe watery diarrhea accompanied by abdominal pain, gas, weight loss, and dehydration. The incapacitated victim passes millions of parasites in liquid stool.

Though the worst of the illness generally lasts only a few days, giardiasis has a habit of hanging on, with symptoms returning after they've abated, and returning again. Even when diarrhea ends, the infected host continues to pass parasites in stool.

Trophozoites die quickly outside the body, but on the trip through the intestine, some prepare for the hostile outside world by wrapping themselves in a protective cyst wall. At the same time, each organism divides once more, making each oval cyst a microscopic time capsule with two organisms tucked inside. The cysts are tough: they survive winter water temperatures and the usual water treatment chemicals. If they are lucky, they eventually end up in water destined, once again, for the kitchen tap.

In Creston, what went down the toilet couldn't come back through the kitchen tap because the town treated its sewage, discharging treated wastewater into the Kootenay River on the opposite side of the town from Arrow Creek. Even cysts of *G. lamblia* from human waste that survived sewage treatment had no chance of entering the town's water supply. Where, then, were residents picking up *G. lamblia*?

The answer is that the beaver had moved and was now about two-thirds of a mile (one kilometer) *above* the water intake, safely tucked away inside a new dam and blanketed by more than a meter of snow. The creek was completely frozen over, and winter weather made the dam a virtual fortress. For the present, the beaver was irremovable, and the people of Creston were stuck with an order to boil water from the British Columbia Ministry of Health that was to last a long time.

By the time the outbreak was over, 124 people had stool samples that tested positive for *G. lamblia*—again, just the tip of the iceberg: many more went undiagnosed. Samples of tap water in Creston, from the town's water distribution system and from Arrow Creek downstream of the intake, all contained cysts of *G. lamblia.*

On March 15, 1990, the beaver was finally ousted from its dam and tested for *Giardia.* Its feces, not surprisingly, contained many cysts of the parasite, providing strong evidence that the creature was the source of the problem. Even stronger evidence came soon thereafter: after the beaver was evicted, water samples in the creek and in the town water system were negative for cysts of *G. lamblia,* and further testing proved the cysts excreted by the beaver were the same strain as the ones obtained from sick patients in Creston.

Many beavers ply the waterways of southern British Columbia, and nearly half of them shed cysts of *G. lamblia* in their feces.[10] Presumably the Creston beaver paid for its unfortunate parasitic infestation with its life, although its demise is not documented, but the parasite wasn't finished with Creston yet: it became the launching pad for a lengthy and heated debate between area residents and the Ministry of Health.

The Ministry of Health sought to impose water treatment, including chlorination, on the Arrow Creek water supply, whereas residents opposed chlorination for health and environmental reasons. Ultimately, the two sides agreed to filtration and ultraviolet disinfection of the water, with minimal chlorination. The new Arrow Creek Water Treatment Plant began treating water in October 2005.

———

Back in North Battleford in 2001, filters were already in place, and they should have been removing any small bits of floc that escaped the solids contact unit. Filters vary, but the ones in this treatment plant were composed of a layer of anthracite coal on top of a layer of sand. As particles are carried into this type of filter, they become stuck at the surface or trapped somewhere within the filter's labyrinth. They lodge there and accumulate, building up gradually. Literally becoming part of the filter, they help catch particles coming through after them. As more and more material is trapped in the filter, the size of particles able to wash through to the other side gets smaller and smaller.

Eventually the flow of water through such a filter is impeded because there is too much debris caught inside: this debris has to be cleared out. The filters are cleaned by backwashing, first with air and then with water, forcing everything back through the filter in the direction from which it has come. Of course, after backwashing, the filters let larger particles through until debris builds up in them again.

The water used for backwashing should be discarded because of the material suspended in it, but North Battleford had no way to discharge it. Backwashed water was recycled, so that any material flushed out of the filter, including oocysts, went back in and had another chance to get through to the other side. At a minimum, the filters in North Battleford were cleaned about every three days.

You and the oocyst, having made your way through the solids contact unit, arrive at the North Battleford filters shortly after a backwash has been performed. Because you are so tiny, you are able to run the gauntlet, twisting and winding your way through the anthracite and sand—boulders to you at your present size—like a veteran whitewater rafter on a giant beach ball. Millions of other oocysts slip through around you. Soon you are on the far side, rushing on to the clearwell, a holding tank where another dousing of chlorine awaits you; then you're off to the city's water mains.

The operators at the water treatment plant in North Battleford did not know enough about *Cryptosporidium* and the importance of good filtration. They did not know that chlorine would not kill the parasite, nor did they understand that having zero settling in the solids contact unit would allow oocysts to pass through. If they had known, they would have realized that zero settling and recently backwashed filters were a free pass for the parasite.

They should have known, not only because water safety was their responsibility but because contamination of a municipal water supply with *Cryptosporidium* had happened before. Eight years earlier, at exactly the same time of year, the city of Milwaukee, Wisconsin, suffered a similar misfortune. Operators at Milwaukee's southern water treatment plant, which draws its water supply from Lake Michigan, noted increased turbidity in the water, beginning around March 21. They tried adjusting the chemical mix that they were adding but still had difficulty controlling turbidity, partly because a monitor that would have helped them was installed incorrectly and was not working. The plant was shut down—too late—on April 9.

Like the plant in North Battleford, the Milwaukee plant failed to treat water effectively because of inadequate formation of floc and inadequate filtration. Oocysts of *Cryptosporidium* entered the city's water distribution system, and some 403,000 people became sick.[11] More than 100 died.

The source of the oocysts in the Milwaukee outbreak will never be known for certain—at the time, people pointed fingers variously at spring runoff from agricultural land, offal from slaughterhouses around the lake, or human waste from sewer outfalls. A storm of lawsuits followed the outbreak, with the city of Milwaukee and General Chemical Corporation, the supplier of water treatment chemicals to the plant, eventually paying out millions of dollars in individual and class action settlements.[12] An assessment of the medical costs and productivity losses arising from this outbreak produced a conservative estimated cost of about $96 million, two-thirds of which resulted from lost productivity.[13]

The shocking magnitude of the outbreak in Milwaukee made *Cryptosporidium* highly visible to the public and to anyone connected with water treatment. Knowledge acquired from the investigation of that outbreak prompted vigilant water regulators everywhere to take a close look at existing standards and regulations. Turbidity of water became a much bigger issue for water treatment plants.

One thing we haven't learned, though, is how to detect oocysts efficiently. Tests for *Cryptosporidium* spp. and *G. lamblia* require filtration and testing of huge volumes of water. Even then, when the parasites are found in a water sample, it's difficult to tell whether they are still alive and capable of causing disease. The testing is time-consuming and expensive to perform; continuous testing is far beyond the capabilities of the average drinking-water utility.

Because of these limitations, water treatment plants typically test for *Cryptosporidium* spp. and *G. lamblia* only periodically. At other times, they try to avoid the problem by watching turbidity, testing for bacteria, ensuring good filtration, and protecting the watershed area from contamination. Indeed, they have a legal responsibility to do so: when they fail, and protozoa slip through water treatment systems and make people sick, operators and regulators are held accountable.

In North Battleford, you and your oocyst have evaded every obstacle designed to remove you. The chemical baths, the solids contact unit, and the filters lie far behind. Tumbling through the water mains, oocysts disperse like commuter traffic in morning rush hour. You thread your way from larger mains to smaller ones and into the plumbing of a North Battleford building. Nobody knows you are there.

A thirsty boy turns a tap—or perhaps hits a button—on a water fountain and you burst from the spout in a rush of clear, cold water. You are swallowed by the boy. Sliding down the boy's throat, you drop into his stomach, and before long, you move into his small intestine. Here, your ride on the oocyst ends as the zipperlike suture in its wall opens.

Maggotlike sporozoites inside the oocyst come to life and begin to worm their way out through the opening. Dangling from the suspended oocyst, long and crescent shaped, they emerge slowly. By the time all of the sporozoites are completely free, you are being dragged through the ileum, the third part of the small intestine. Now your oocyst is just an empty sac like a discarded plastic bag; you are swept away with it in the intestinal undertow.

The sporozoites, meanwhile, head for cells lining the ileum and burrow into the outer cell membrane. They don't go all the way inside the cell but remain in a little pocket within the cell membrane, as though they have settled down between the layers of the outside wall of a house. They multiply, each producing eight crescent-shaped merozoites. The merozoites burst out of the pocket and invade new cells, each merozoite making a new pocket. Multiplication begins anew, and again merozoites burst out and invade a new group of cells, creating a cycle of asexual multiplication that can go on and on, resulting in vast numbers of parasites.

Some of the merozoites develop differently, producing male and female stages—gametocytes—that reproduce sexually, resulting in oocysts. Oocysts grow in the same space within the cell membrane, bulging out like fat bubbles that are about to break free and float away. Some open and sporozoites emerge like groping fingers, wriggling free and invading new cells to start the cycle again. Millions of intact oocysts do break away, floating free in the intestine.

—

Some 5,800 to 7,100 residents of the Battlefords and about 400 visitors from outside the area acquired cryptosporidiosis in March and April 2001 after drinking from fountains and taps in North Battleford. In a typical case, symptoms began about five days after infection. The destruction of intestinal cells caused abdominal pain and fever, and bowel contents flushed out in profuse, watery diarrhea that went on for days. Millions of oocysts were released to the outside world with each trip to the toilet.

Fourteen days after operators cleaned the solids contact unit at the water treatment plant, the first diagnosed case of cryptosporidiosis was reported to the Battlefords Health District. The patient was a child who lived on a farm about eight miles (thirteen kilometers) outside North Battleford. A history of contact with farm livestock and the time of year fit a typical scenario, and the public health inspector who spoke with the child's mother had no reason to suspect the North Battleford water supply.

The second case came a day later, on April 5, but the public health nurse was out of the office and didn't see the report until April 10. Meanwhile, on April 9, the operators at the water treatment plant had given up on getting the solids contact unit to produce floc spontaneously. As a substitute for sludge, missing since they cleaned out the unit, they ordered some bentonite, absorbent clay formed when volcanic ash breaks down. No one thought to alert the public health authorities to the problem in the plant.

The second patient was another child, a resident of Battleford, across the river from North Battleford, and a student at the same school as the first case. This child's mother commented that she had heard many students at the school had diarrhea. Shortly, a younger sibling of this second child developed symptoms.

Geoffrey Lipsett, family doctor for the second patient, telephoned the local Wal-Mart pharmacy to investigate antidiarrheal medications for the younger child. The pharmacist told him that over-the-counter diarrhea remedies were disappearing from store shelves so fast that the store couldn't keep up with demand. With this information, Dr. Lipsett was the first to suspect that something big was going on. He called Gerhard Benadé, medical health officer for the Battlefords Health District.

The peak of the epidemic was April 13, but on that day, officials were still not sure whether they *had* an epidemic. A survey of pharmacies on April 14 confirmed that Wal-Mart's pharmacy was not the only outlet experiencing high sales of diarrhea medications, yet hospital emergency departments were not seeing an increase in patients with diarrhea. Most people were not going to their physicians, or to hospital emergency departments, so authorities still had no solid evidence of a problem.

On April 17, another confirmed case turned up—a teenager who lived in Battleford but attended John Paul II School in North Battleford. The next case, reported on April 19, came from Turtleford, a town about fifty-six miles (ninety kilometers) outside the city. Three family members of the Turtleford case subsequently became ill. As the medical officer of health for the area, Dr. Benadé was aware of all these cases, but he didn't yet know all the facts, one of which was that the family from Turtleford had recently attended a hockey tournament in North Battleford.

Four more cases were reported on April 23. Three of these patients lived in North Battleford, finally casting the spotlight on the city. Dr. Benadé's suspicions were now thoroughly aroused: he knew he might be dealing with an outbreak of cryptosporidiosis—a cluster of cases with a common source. But what, and where, was the source? It might be a swimming pool, something served at a social event, or animals on a farm; it might be in Turtleford, Battleford, or North Battleford, or somewhere that hadn't been identified yet. It might be water, a notoriously common source of *Cryptosporidium* spp.

Dr. Benadé wondered about the North Battleford water supply: was there a trail of evidence leading from all the sick people back to North Battleford faucets? The answer didn't come until April 25, when Scott Meekma, environmental protection officer for Saskatchewan Environment and Resource Management connected the dots: a contaminated watershed, no settling in the solids contact unit at the surface-water plant, and people with cryptosporidiosis indicated that tap water was contaminated with *Cryptosporidium* sp. and that North Battleford's public water supply had been unsafe for more than a month.

Two samples of finished water collected at the surface-water treatment plant late on April 24 were positive for oocysts of *Cryptosporidium* sp., as were samples of raw water collected on April 26 from the river intake. By April 28, a good settling rate had been achieved in the solids contact unit, after which no viable oocysts were detected in North Battleford's finished water.

Oocysts slipped into North Battleford's drinking water, and thousands of people got cryptosporidiosis. The government of Saskatchewan ordered an inquiry to determine how it came about, and several class action lawsuits were launched, causing more than $3.5 million (Canadian) to change hands. That was just the beginning of the spending.

Justice Robert D. Laing, commissioner for the inquiry, identified many factors that contributed to water contamination in North Battleford.

They included a watershed that had no protection; an outdated and underfunded treatment plant; a lack of educated, qualified staff with the necessary expertise; lack of appropriate monitoring of water treatment operations; a municipal government that did not place sufficient priority on drinking-water safety; and a provincial government that had passed responsibility for drinking-water safety down to municipal governments. Furthermore, similar factors were clearly affecting drinking-water safety in other municipalities.

Thus, North Battleford's experience with cryptosporidiosis set in motion many corrective activities. Laing's report, however, wasn't just the framework for a "to do list": it was a graphic illustration of how difficult it is to keep parasites out of tap water all the time and how challenging it can be to detect them when they're there. The prevalence of parasites in the environment will force water utilities to focus even more closely on these challenges in the future.

———

We've reached the point where all surface waters should be considered contaminated unless proven otherwise. In an unfortunate coincidence, we've also perfected the ability to deliver a disease-causing organism simultaneously to hundreds of thousands of people via water distribution systems. How have *G. lamblia, T. gondii,* and *Cryptosporidium* become so ubiquitous?

People found out about *G. lamblia* in 1681, when Antony van Leeuwenhoek, an inventor of early microscopes, famously saw the tear-shaped protozoan in a drop of his own feces. More than three hundred years later, we can't say when or where the parasite first infected humans, or whether beavers and other aquatic mammals had it first or caught it from us. We do know, however, that today *G. lamblia* is found all over the globe and that we don't need beavers to help us spread it to people and to surface waters everywhere. Nor do we need dogs, cats, sheep, cows, and other domestic animals, which can also carry it.[14]

Studies have found *G. lamblia* in the intestines of between 0.5 percent and 30 percent of people in various parts of the world. One gram of stool from an infected person can contain more than a million cysts of *G. lamblia.* As few as ten cysts can make you ill: imagine the potential of just one sick person in a watershed area.[15] Given the efficiency of this parasite in perpetuating itself, it's surprising that we don't all have it.

Toxoplasma gondii was discovered much later than *G. lamblia*. Appearing in the scientific literature in 1908, its life cycle wasn't fully understood until 1970. It had long since emerged, however, as a cause of disease and had already spread worldwide. Because humans—with the possible exception of cannibals—don't pass it from person to person, we haven't given it a boost in the same way we've spread *G. lamblia*, but we have aided this parasite in another way. We've spread it with the domestic cat, *Felis catus*.

Cats have been living with people for, perhaps, eight thousand years.[16] Most likely, the wild ancestor of today's domestic cat was *F. libyca*, a small feline of Africa and Asia with a relatively docile nature. Just how soon the animal began to travel isn't clear, but cats were sacred in Egypt, and they adapted well to life on ships—factors that would have favored their multiplication and spread.

Egyptians probably took cats to parts of what is now the Middle East (and *F. libyca* may have been domesticated there as well); the animals reached Greece by 500 B.C.; China by 200 B.C.; and the Romans subsequently brought them to northern Europe. The seafaring Vikings may have had a hand in spreading domestic cats as well. By 1000 A.D., domestic cats—and feral ones—were common in Europe and Asia, and despite persecution during the Middle Ages, they now live virtually everywhere on earth that humans do. So does *T. gondii*.

No one really knows how many cats there are, but estimates put the number of cats in the United States at about fifty million pets and forty million ferals.[17] A cat with an acute case of toxoplasmosis passes millions of oocysts in its feces, which are infective to humans and other animals within days. Studies have found that more than 45 percent of cats in colonies have antibodies to *T. gondii*.[18] We don't need to do the math to know that domestication of the cat was a very good thing for *T. gondii*.

Cryptosporidium has emerged from the background of human illness only in the past thirty-five years. Genetic studies have revealed that the parasite once known as *C. parvum* is actually two organisms, one that infects cattle and humans and one that infects only humans. The latter has multiplied in the same manner as *G. lamblia*—through human fecal contamination of surface waters. The other, like *T. gondii*, has doubtless benefited from domestication, and this time the animal is the cow.

Domesticated about nine thousand years ago from aurochs native to North Africa and Eurasia (now extinct), cattle have been successfully introduced to every continent except Antarctica. They didn't reach the

Americas until after European colonization, but now they are bred there in vast numbers. Earth is now home to more than one and a half billion of them. Many shed oocysts of *Cryptosporidium parvum*: studies have found that a majority of herds in the United States include infected animals passing oocysts in their feces.[19]

Laboratory testing indicates that both the Milwaukee cryptosporidiosis outbreak and the outbreak in North Battleford were caused by the type of *C. parvum* that infects only humans, likely from discharge of human sewage into surface waters. Many human cases, however, come from cattle. Ironically, water samples from the North Saskatchewan River in 1997 indicated that the majority of the oocysts in the river at that time came from agricultural lands: they were the type that infects both humans and cattle.

Put the spread of these parasites down to population pressure: more than six billion people now inhabit the earth. Living with various degrees of poverty, poor hygiene, inadequate sanitation, and simple ignorance, they continue to contaminate their surroundings. *Giardia lamblia* is the most commonly identified parasitic cause of diarrhea illness in the United States. *Cryptosporidium* is still emerging as a cause of illness: not only is it carried by land animals and transported by birds, but it turns up in oysters and other filter feeders in coastal regions where runoff enters the ocean. In recent years, scientists have linked numerous outbreaks of cryptosporidiosis to swimming pools and other recreational water, making the local swimming hole less than the idyllic place it used to be. *Toxoplasma gondii*, meanwhile, is apparently so ubiquitous that it is washing off land into the ocean in sufficient quantities to cause a serious decline in sea otters. It infects other sea mammals as well.

Now that we've aided and abetted these three invaders—and others— we find ourselves spending unlimited time and money trying to keep them out of our lives, still without success.[20] The next step in water treatment will use either ozone disinfection or disinfection via ultraviolet light to inactivate cysts and oocysts in drinking water. In the future, some water utilities may take yet another approach, the only one available to the people living on Cambodia's Stoeng Sangke: drinking water may have to be treated and delivered separately from water for other domestic uses.

These measures will do nothing to clean up the Stoeng Sangke, of course, and won't benefit the North Saskatchewan River or other contaminated surface waters. The changes required to bring back pristine surface waters will have to be far greater, if they are even possible. Meanwhile, *G. lamblia, T. gondii,* and *Cryptosporidium* spp. aren't the only parasites carried along with human migrations and activities. A number of other parasites have already spread, or are spreading, from their origins and are causing chaos.

FOUR

Illegal Aliens

The most "tropical" pathogens can break out from their motherland to the cool north and south as well as elsewhere; . . . our world has never been compartmentalized.

ROBERT S. DESOWITZ
Who Gave Pinta to the Santa Maria?

IMAGINE A DIAGRAM OF THE human body in which parasites represent the organs and other structures. The skin is mites, fly larvae, and micro-filariae.[1] Trails of malaria parasites, trypanosomes, worm larvae, and schistosomes show blood circulation. Muscles are made of *Trichinella* larvae and *Toxoplasma* cysts. Flukes and tapeworm scolices shape the liver. So many parasites crowd the intestines that it's difficult to find them all.

Now think of the body as a suitcase—luggage that can't be opened, x-rayed, or searched to reveal the parasites within. A packer and shipper of parasite relocation, your body takes along your parasites wherever it goes. The same is true for other parasite hosts, which means that innumerable parasites can travel unnoticed and spread to new environments around the world. This sort of travel is often a result of human actions—relocations aided by ignorance, stupidity, or covert activities, rarely by design.[2]

Put your finger down anywhere along the timeline of history, in any location where large numbers of people and domestic animals have passed through. You can be sure that many parasites passed through as well. Like the people and animals, some of the parasites didn't survive in their new homes. Others arrived in a friendly environment where they could complete their life cycle and flourish. North America is one landmass that has received a steady stream of people, domesticated species, and stowaway parasites.

—

The year is 1694; the place, Jamestown, Virginia, the oldest permanent English settlement in what is now the United States. The Atlantic slave trade has been booming on the west coast of Africa for two hundred years, and it will flourish for more than a hundred more. We can imagine a young man, typical of countless young men captured by slavers in western Africa, arriving in the New World after more than eight dreadful weeks at sea. Still alive after his ordeal, he is one of the lucky ones.

The ship berths at Jamestown on a fine morning in April, and the emaciated young man is dragged out into daylight, delivered to the colony, a slave for life. With his first bowel movement on Virginia soil, he—with countless others before and after—delivers something else from Africa: eggs of the hookworm *Necator americanus*. Each female hookworm that is attached to his intestine produces thousands of eggs every day, and on the plantations of South Carolina, where this African will spend the rest of his days, the parasite finds a home as well.

Hookworm eggs passed in feces need both warmth and moisture to survive. Deposited in a shady place where the soil is damp and contains abundant organic material, eggs hatch in a couple of days, releasing microscopic larvae. The larvae feed on bacteria and decaying organic material in the soil, growing to about two one-hundredths of an inch (about half a millimeter) long in under a week. Then the larvae can infect another human. They do so by penetrating exposed skin.

The conditions that allow hookworm larvae to find new human hosts were not hard to find in the American South during centuries of slavery. Slaves snatched from homes in Africa found themselves working barefoot in the fields, defecating directly on the ground, and returning repeatedly to the same outdoor latrines. Hookworm eggs deposited one week were infectious hookworm larvae the next, ready and waiting for the daily parade of bare feet.

Slaves were continually reinfected through exposure to contaminated soil. Anyone who arrived on the plantation without hookworm soon had it. But in a curious sort of serendipitous revenge, the arrival of the worm in North America was much harder on the white population than it was on slaves—hence the name *Necator americanus,* literally "American killer."

Caucasians are more susceptible to hookworm disease than blacks are, probably a result of natural immunity in people of African descent. This vulnerability was bad news for poor southern whites who also walked barefoot in the fields. Larvae, questing for a host in the soil beneath human feet, slipped under the outer layers of skin cells and burrowed through to blood vessels. Like *Ascaris lumbricoides* larvae, these wisps of life ride the bloodstream to the lungs before breaking out and crawling up the airways to the throat. Swallowed, they arrive in the stomach and then the intestine.

Now young adults, the parasites take a mouthful of intestinal lining as both an anchor and a source of nutrients. They grow to about a third of an inch (eight and a half millimeters) long—pale worms with the head end curved into a hook and a mouth that gapes as though the creature is yodeling. Four cutting plates, like circular saw blades arranged around the mouth, keep the worms attached.

For the next five to fifteen years, each worm will cost its host a little more than half a drop of blood each day by ingesting it or allowing it to leak into the bowel. Although this amount seems negligible, the main symptoms of chronic hookworm disease are those of anemia and protein deficiency, both results of intestinal blood loss. Hookworm infections can involve thousands of worms, and the bleeding is profoundly damaging over time, especially when the infected person's diet is poor.

The worms of the slaves turned on the masters, instigating a wave of anemia and undermining the health and economy of the South, taking a subtle, unintentional revenge. So many southerners fell victim to hookworm that the classic appearance of the chronic hookworm sufferer was the template for a stereotype of the poor southern white: so-called white trash, a gaunt, pale, and listless scarecrow, lazy and usually barefoot. In fact, these southerners were more sick than lazy, too anemic to get through a day's work.

When the matter of slavery came to a head in the American Civil War, hookworm was well entrenched, acting as a sort of environmental friendly fire in the South. According to historian Thomas D. Clark,

> By modern American military standards of physical, mental, and moral
> fitness . . . more than half of the Johnny Rebs [Confederate soldiers]
> who shelled the woods at Shiloh, Chancellorsville, and Gettysburg,
> or stood with Pemberton at Vicksburg, might have been kept at
> home. . . . No one can say just how much pellagra [niacin deficiency]
> and hookworm helped to sustain the Union.[3]

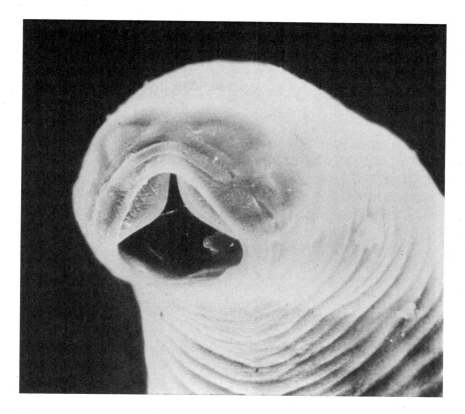

Figure 9. Cutting plates in the mouth of *Necator americanus* allow the worm to attach to tissue. From J. W. Smith, ed., 1976, *Diagnostic Medical Parasitology: Helminths,* photographic slide no. 40: hookworm: *N. americanus,* buccal capsule (scanning electron photomicrograph). Chicago: American Society of Clinical Pathologists. © 1976 American Society of Clinical Pathologists.

A Confederate army of undernourished, lethargic scarecrows fought comparatively healthy Union troops. Even in wartime, Confederate soldiers often went without footwear. They continued to spread hookworm wherever they went.

The worm, of course, picked no favorites; it had no political motives, no moral stance, and it treated all bare feet alike. In another grim example of unanticipated consequences, it visited its most horrendous violence on Union soldiers taken prisoner and interred in the Confederate military prison in Andersonville, Georgia. This notorious prison camp held, at times, more than thirty thousand Union troops. It became a shocking example of what hookworm can do.

The parasite may have been left in the Andersonville prison by southerners who built the enclosure, or possibly it arrived with prisoners who had already been in the South long enough to acquire the worms. Regardless of how it arrived, it could hardly have found better conditions for success: the prisoners had no immunity, sanitation, or shoes to protect them. Men defecated on the ground where they walked, ate, and slept. Before long, the ground teemed with hookworm larvae waiting to contact human skin. It was a rare and fortunate prisoner whose gut was not home to an army of hookworms.[4]

Vitamin deficiency brought on by poor nutrition and bloody diarrhea brought on at least in part by acute hookworm infection were so prevalent at Andersonville that in September 1864, the Confederate surgeon general sent Joseph Jones, an infectious-disease expert of the day, to investigate. Professor Jones was defeated before he began. Post mortems on soldiers revealed extensive damage to the intestinal lining, but, knowing nothing of the worm, Jones put the deaths down to "scorbutic dysentery" (bloody diarrhea caused by vitamin C deficiency): "There is no recognizable source of disease," he said, "in the waters or soil of Andersonville."[5]

In a sense, Jones was correct, but only because the existence of *N. americanus* was not recognized at the time and wouldn't be for almost forty years. Soon after the worm's discovery in about 1902, scientists realized that it was rampant in the southern United States. From that distant perspective, historians looked back and understood how it had arrived in the New World in the bowels of enslaved Africans, sapped the strength of the Confederate Army and the southern poor, and killed about a third of the prisoners at Andersonville.

Necator americanus wasn't the only dangerous parasite that came to the New World with the slaves. Both *Schistosoma hematobium,* which we learned about in chapter 1, and *S. mansoni,* a similar worm that lives in the blood vessels near the intestine, made the trip. Only *S. mansoni* found a suitable snail waiting for it, and the blood fluke still survives in northeastern South America and on a few Caribbean islands. *Onchocerca volvulus,* a parasite of Africa that causes river blindness, found the right conditions in parts of Central and South America and remains a problem to this day (see chapter 7). Mercifully, sleeping sickness stayed in Africa's tsetse belt, even though *Trypanosoma gambiense* was certainly introduced to North and South America by enslaved Africans:[6] the tsetse fly was absent from the New World, and African trypanosomes can't live without the fly.

Malaria came as well, but it was nothing new. Malaria was common in Massachusetts by 1640 and probably came to Virginia even earlier.[7] No one knows how the parasite first arrived, but it was well established in Europe, including Britain, and colonists came from malaria-infested areas. Historians speculate that the disease aided the British in pushing aside Native American populations.

All of these parasites became unwelcome aliens by chance, as accidental stowaways in a forced migration. No one involved in the slave trade was worried about introducing a few parasites to a new place and altering the course of history. That possibility was as invisible to the slavers as the parasites themselves, and humans weren't the only parasite hosts that were transported to North American soil.

Colonists came with a biological retinue from far away: pigs, cows, horses, grapevines, fruit trees, grains, and many other living things, all potential "suitcases" packed with other, unintended organisms. In 1622, hives of European honeybees, *Apis mellifera*, arrived in Jamestown at the head of a parade of bee parasites that continues into the twenty-first century.[8]

The honeybees settled in, spread to the wild, and made themselves indispensable. They didn't simply spend their time making honey and beeswax: the bees' busy foraging from flower to flower aided pollination in many plants. Wild animals benefited when honeybees pollinated wild fruit and nut crops, and farmers soon depended on the honeybee for peak crop production. Without honeybees, many of the crops introduced to North America—most of the fruits, vegetables, and flowers we still enjoy—would be in very short supply.

By the late twentieth century, honeybees in North America were worth hundreds of millions of dollars in honey production alone. Their pollinating activities were worth a hundred times that. Honeybees were pollinating apples, alfalfa, almonds, pumpkins, and many other crops. North American beekeepers, meanwhile, spent much of the twentieth century trying to prevent the arrival of bee parasites—mites they feared would wipe out their bee colonies almost overnight. The first such invader to get past them was *Acarapis woodi*, the tracheal bee mite.

Acarapis woodi lives in bees' tiny airways, where the female mite deposits her eggs. Hatching, they develop to adult mites; mated females then crawl out into the bee's external hairs to transfer to other bees, where the mites start the process over again. The infestation obstructs breathing and can shorten a bee's life: colonies that are stressed for other reasons don't thrive when infested with the tracheal mite. Healthy bees, however, suffer few symptoms.

Acarapis woodi was discovered in 1921 off the south coast of England on the Isle of Wight. At the time, most of the bees on the island suddenly died from the mysterious "Isle of Wight disease." When investigators subsequently found the mites, they thought they'd solved the mystery, but scientists now think that the bee losses were probably caused by a virus.[9] No one knows whether tracheal mites actually spread around the world from the island or whether they were simply noticed there first, but wherever they went, their undeserved infamy went with them, with far-reaching effects.

The fear that the tracheal mite might make its way to the honeybees of the United States prompted extreme measures: the Bee Importation Law of 1922 banned the importation of honeybees into the country. This approach worked for almost sixty years. Then, in the early 1980s, infected bees migrated on the wing from Mexico to the United States, a crossing no ban or border official could prevent.[10]

The mite became established in honeybee colonies in the United States and spread throughout the continent, but its success was not the catastrophe American beekeepers had feared. Dealing with the tracheal mite turned out to be merely a rehearsal for the challenge to come. *Varroa destructor*, a far worse parasite, was on its way, and it probably would have arrived in North America a lot sooner if not for the efforts to keep *Acarapis* out.

European honeybees introduced to eastern Asia in the late 1800s encountered the Asian honeybee, *Apis cerana*. They also encountered the Asian honeybee's tiny parasitic mite, *Varroa destructor*. *Varroa destructor* made its way from *A. cerana* to *A. mellifera* and found a suitable host. It invaded European hives and found that its life cycle is perfectly attuned to that of the bee. Both begin as eggs in the honeycomb.

An *A. mellifera* hive is a complex construction with honeycombs hanging side by side, each consisting of thousands of hexagonal beeswax cells set back to back. In the cells, bees store honey and pollen and raise young. Dropping from an adult bee in the hive, the female varroa mite invades a brood cell in the bottom where bee eggs incubate. The eggs hatch, and the mite lays her own eggs—typically four, thirty hours apart—in the brood cell. Meanwhile, bee larvae (brood) feed on royal jelly provided by

Figure 10. A varroa mite. Courtesy of Harvey L. Cromroy, University of Florida.

worker bees and grow. Tiny six-legged larvae soon emerge from mite eggs. Parasitic, they feed on young bee larvae and develop to mating adults in about a week. Male mites die in the brood cell, but females remain, attached to maturing worker and drone bees.

The female mite is less than a tenth of an inch (two millimeters) wide and only two-thirds as long: from the front, she looks like a tarantula hiding under an overturned dinner plate. She tucks herself neatly into a fold on the bee's abdomen, safe from any attempts by the bee to remove her and, making a hole in the bee's hard outer surface, sucks hemolymph, a fluid analogous to blood that bathes the bee's internal organs. Already settled and feeding on young bees when they emerge from brood cells, female mites usually remain in place until they're ready to drop off in the hive and begin the cycle again.

Well tolerated by *A. cerana*, *V. destructor* proved lethal to *A. mellifera:* heavily infested colonies typically die, sometimes within a few months.[11] The prudent course would have been to leave infested European hives in Asia to prevent the mite's spread, but humans followed familiar habits and brought European honeybees infested with varroa mites back to Europe from Asia. From there, infested bees went to South America (where imported honeybees had been thriving since the early 1500s), spreading the mites to a third continent. By the time *V. destructor* reached South America in the 1970s, the roads north were blocked by the Bee Importation Law. To get to the bees of North America, it looked like the mite needed a different route, but beekeepers ignored the law and once again brought the mites in.

Beekeepers often purchase queen bees, or even packages of honeybees, from other places to increase genetic diversity and improve the strain of their bees. The U.S. ban on imports put considerable limits on these activities, and after close to sixty years, some beekeepers were willing to disregard both law and risk. Bees were occasionally smuggled into the United States from outside. It was only a matter of time before an illegal shipment brought the mite as well.

In addition to selling queen bees and bee packages, beekeepers routinely move colonies of bees to places where crops need pollination, a mutually beneficial arrangement for beekeepers and farmers: the farmers' crops are pollinated and the beekeepers' honeybees are provided with plenty of pollen. However, selling bees and relocating hives spread bee diseases and parasites. In the fall of 1987, hives that had been moved from Florida to Wisconsin suddenly died off, and when beekeepers went looking for the cause, they found *V. destructor*. Frightened, other beekeepers checked their bees, only to find that hives in a dozen states were already infested. The mite was in the United States and spreading fast.

Even without human help, bees spread varroa mites: honeybees from different hives come in contact while visiting flowers, and sometimes individual bees drift from one hive to another. When a hive is in poor condition, bees from other hives tend to stage raids, coming away with *V. destructor* if it's infesting the sick colony. And when hives swarm—a queen bee is replaced each year, and the old queen departs the hive with a swarm to start a new colony elsewhere—their mites go with them.

By the end of 1987, states as far west as Nebraska and as far north as Maine had the mite, and wherever it turned up, honeybees crashed.[12] Two years later, *V. destructor* had a foothold all along the West Coast of the United States and most of the northern border with Canada. Canada passed legislation banning the importation of honeybees from the United

States, but this measure could only slow the mite's advance. The country had its own bee smugglers, and the political boundary did not affect the foraging and migration activities of honeybees.[13]

Varroa destructor crossed the Canadian border and infested bees in New Brunswick in 1989. It entered Alaska sometime in 1990 or 1991, and by 1995, every American state had the mite, with Wyoming the last to fall. The first report in Canada was on Vancouver Island, in March 1997. Virtually all wild honeybees died, and experts predicted that their absence would leave the area's wildlife with only half the normal supply of pollinated food sources. A third of managed hives were gone, and beekeepers were struggling to stay ahead of the mites with insecticides, a difficult task because the parasites become resistant to the chemicals and continue to spread and kill. Meanwhile, farmers with crops that needed honeybees searched for alternate pollinators.

If we humans had dropped canisters of the *V. destructor* on every country on earth, we could hardly have done a better job of dispersing them. Trade in European honeybees has now carried *V. destructor* to every bee-keeping area on earth except Australia, and Australia is unlikely to hold out indefinitely.[14] Ultimately, if *A. mellifera* can persevere, the bee is likely to develop natural resistance to the mite. Meanwhile, however, bee colonies in a number of countries are losing ground to a mysterious disease called colony collapse disorder, and we do not yet know what role tracheal mites, varroa mites, and other bee parasites may be playing in that decline. If we don't figure it out in time, four hundred years after Jamestown welcomed them, European honeybees may disappear from North America.

The histories of *V. destructor* and hookworm in the New World illustrate a curious and disturbing characteristic of many parasites: when they successfully infect a different species from the one they've evolved with, or even a population of the same species that hasn't been exposed to them, the disease they cause is unpredictable and often very much worse than it was in the original host. A parasite lurking in a healthy host is the proverbial wolf in sheep's clothing: it's dangerous and we can't see it coming.

Unlike the wolf, a parasite sometimes simmers for a long time before we recognize it, which allows it to get many more "sheep" before we wake up to the consequences of having moved something from one place to another. And sadly, we keep making this mistake and getting variations of the same result. To break this familiar pattern, we would have to conduct exhaustive examinations of every living thing that crossed our borders, right down to Santa's reindeer: reindeer have parasites too.

———

In December 1907, after twenty-one days at sea, the steamship *Anita* sailed into Cremaillere Harbor, near St. Anthony's in northern Newfoundland. On board were a group of Lapp reindeer herders and three hundred reindeer from Norway imported by Wilfred Grenfell, a physician and philanthropist who devoted his life to helping the fishers of Labrador and northern Newfoundland.[15]

Newfoundland is known as "the Rock," and for good reasons. The roughly triangular province blocking most of the mouth of the Gulf of St. Lawrence has steep and rocky edges everywhere except along its northeast shore. Encompassing 42,000 square miles (108,800 square kilometers) of windswept rock and dense forest, the island is rugged and beautiful. The Rock is still largely wilderness today, with most communities dotted along the shore and the human population concentrated in the south.

In northern Newfoundland, winters are long and cold, summers are short, and the thin, rocky soil does not lend itself to farming. Communities here are particularly isolated, and most people rely on the sea for their livelihood. In Grenfell's time, too, the sea was both the main source of food and the main route of transportation.

Reindeer had come to North America before: in 1892, herds had been shipped from Siberia to Alaska for food and as draft animals to haul sledges; their hides were used for clothing. Grenfell wanted reindeer in Newfoundland for the same reasons; during certain periods in deep winter, fishing was impossible, and native island caribou were elusive and hard to catch. People starved. Grenfell hoped that reindeer would provide food at such times and work as draft animals as well.

What Grenfell didn't know—and never found out—was that the reindeer came with a stowaway: a parasite that would later spread to the caribou herds on the island and inflict heavy casualties. The parasite was *Elaphostrongylus rangiferi,* a thin, threadlike roundworm that lives between the muscle layers of its host, often in the shoulders and haunches. Female worms poke through the walls of blood vessels and release their eggs directly into the blood. Blood carries eggs to the lungs, where they hatch, releasing microscopic larvae that migrate up the windpipe into the throat and are swallowed. Eventually, larvae pass out in the animal's droppings.

Like African captives brought to the American South centuries earlier, Grenfell's reindeer left droppings on the ground and spread their parasites to their new environment. Inevitably, some of the reindeer escaped captivity and joined native woodland caribou herds. Being the same species, they had no difficulty sharing both their genes and their worms.

The snails and slugs of Newfoundland fed on fecal pellets left by infected reindeer. Larvae in the droppings penetrated the mollusks' large fleshy feet and found them just as welcoming as the mollusks of Norway. The larvae developed into infective-stage larvae. Later, other caribou accidentally ate infected mollusks while grazing. Liberated by stomach acids, larvae promptly moved through the stomach wall into the peritoneal cavity, through the diaphragm and on to the spinal cord and brain. There, they grew into adult worms.

Young adult worms leave the nervous tissue and migrate along nerves to the muscles, where they mate, releasing more eggs into the blood. Adults live for years, if the animal survives the infection, and females continue to lay eggs throughout their lives.

Caribou with numerous *E. rangiferi* worms developing in the cranium and spinal canal appear stunned and confused, lose their fear of humans and predators, and often become separated from the main herd. They stagger about, walking in circles, and have difficulty standing upright because of weakness in the hind legs. Isolated and paralyzed, they are easily taken by poachers or predators, or they die of exposure and starvation. When a caribou herd is severely affected, nine out of ten newborn calves may be infected. Many die.

Grenfell's reindeer herd did well initially, numbering about one thousand animals at one time, but a century later, none remain on the island: they died, escaped into the island's caribou herds, or were killed for food. The parasite remains, however, and sporadically inflicts high casualties on the wild caribou herds of Newfoundland.

The disease is called cerebrospinal elaphostrongylosis, or CSE. It simmered undetected in Newfoundland caribou until the 1970s, when it caused an outbreak so widespread that it caught the attention of wildlife experts. More than sixty years after the worm's arrival, parasitologists identified it as *E. rangiferi,* marking the first time it had been found in North America. The parasite was well known in Scandinavia, however, and investigators soon figured out that the reindeer imported by Wilfred Grenfell were the source of the trouble.

Figure 11. A Newfoundland caribou infected with *Elaphostrongylus rangiferi*. Photo by Abra Whitney.

Initially, *E. rangiferi* did not appear to have spread over the entire island: the caribou herd on the Avalon Peninsula, the most southerly caribou herd in Canada, was not infected. Inevitably, however, the worm continued its slow march; it crossed into the peninsula, causing an epidemic outbreak in the southern herd in 1990. So far, *E. rangiferi* does not appear to have come to Alaska with the reindeer imported there, nor is it present in the Canadian arctic or subarctic regions, or Ontario, where reindeer may also have been introduced. At present, in Canada, it remains confined to Newfoundland. This worm, however, made Canada wary of a closely related worm, *Elaphostrongylus cervi*.

Elaphostrongylus cervi was first recognized in red deer in Scotland and was later found in deer in continental Europe. Game ranchers unwittingly introduced it to New Zealand when they imported red deer from the United Kingdom. And, in a familiar pattern, New Zealand game ranchers soon began exporting red deer to game ranches in other parts of the world.

In the red deer, *E. cervi* does very little damage, but it can have effects very similar to CSE in unfamiliar hosts. What if it were to escape game farms in North America and spread through native wild deer? In 1991, Agriculture Canada took a lesson from the Newfoundland experience and banned importation of red deer and fallow deer into Canada unless the exporter could guarantee that the animals were not infected with *E. cervi.* Unfortunately, no one could be sure that the parasite had not already arrived: more than ninety thousand deer had already left New Zealand, some of them bound for Canadian game farms.

Given the dreadful nature of the disease, we are fortunate that *Elaphostrongylus* spp. do not appear to pose any threat to human health. Animal parasites do infect humans, however, sometimes with similarly horrific results—a fact that creates a new level of concern when a parasite becomes established somewhere new. One such parasite is *Echinococcus multilocularis,* a tapeworm of foxes in North America and Europe that's spreading alarmingly.

—

If we were to visit an Alaskan village, we shouldn't be surprised to see someone skinning a red fox. Local people have trapped the foxes for their fur for centuries. The animals are common in the Alaskan wilderness and are bold in the villages, hunting voles and other small mammals and even venturing near dwellings. Unfortunately, red foxes in this part of the world often carry a tapeworm—the most dangerous tapeworm to parasitize humans—*Echinococcus multilocularis.*

A close relative of the diminutive *E. granulosus* that we met in chapter 2, *E. multilocularis* is even tinier: it grows to a maximum length of a little more than a tenth of an inch (three millimeters). In the natural life cycle, foxes, wolves, coyotes, dogs, and even cats host adult tapeworms in the intestine after eating infected wild rodents. In places where domestic dogs and cats share the hunting with infected foxes, the pets are likely to be infected as well.

People acquire the worm the same way rodents do: by accidentally swallowing tapeworm eggs passed in animal feces. An infected fox may have hundreds of tapeworms in its intestines and thousands of tapeworm eggs in its droppings, so even a tiny amount of feces can be infective. If you swallow some of these eggs, they pass through your stomach into your intestine and hatch. Larvae of *E. multilocularis* emerge.

Like *E. granulosus, E. multilocularis* begins its development in humans by migrating to the liver. The parasite is a single cystlike bud at first, but soon more buds form, attached to the first. If the mass were sliced through the middle, the inside would look like an irregular honeycomb of fluid-filled bubbles. The parasitic mass grows steadily larger.

In humans, the infection is a dead end for the parasite, and often for the host as well. It's a slow disease: an infected person may carry on for ten years or more before realizing anything is wrong. With more and more buds forming, spreading outward like expanding foam, the mass mimics a malignant tumor. And like a malignant liver tumor, the infection can spread. Buds break off and travel to other parts of the body, where they continue to grow, bud, and spread. They lodge in the heart and lungs and in the brain, obstructing ducts and vessels and interfering with organ function.

Once confined in North America to the Canadian North and Alaska, *E. multilocularis* had made its way to the American Midwest by the mid-1960s. In the 1990s, it was so common in some areas there that 50 percent of foxes were infected.[16] At the same time, these foxes spread quietly eastward, and the worm was highly likely to be traveling with them. Curiously, North American foxes are not expanding their range on their own—people are relocating them for sport—for foxhunting.

Many residents of the southeastern states enjoy foxhunting. The sport has weathered the changing landscape since colonial times but has had to adapt to land development and property rights of landowners. In many places, the hunt no longer goes across country; it takes place inside the boundaries of a private wild space surrounded by fencing designed to prevent foxes and other captive animals from escaping. These preserves, spanning hundreds of acres, are known as game enclosures or fox enclosures.

In most fox chases today, the fox is supposed to get away. A chase ends with the fox safely in hiding, but tall fences in every direction ensure that the fox is there to be chased again another day. This scheme makes for a hard life for the fox. Not only is the animal forced to run for its life repeatedly, but sometimes the worst happens: the fox isn't quick or crafty enough, and the hounds catch it and tear it to pieces. The numbers of foxes inside the enclosures are always in decline.

When an enclosure runs out of animals for the dogs to chase, operators must restock from outside. Imported foxes often come from out of state, and when they come from areas where *E. multilocularis* is already present, the worm is sure to come along for the ride. Infected foxes in enclosures leave eggs in their scat, and local voles and other wild rodents feed on the scat and become infected.

The infection spreads to dogs if they catch and eat infected rodents, and to humans who are exposed to dog or fox feces containing the eggs. People involved in the transport of captive wild foxes are at particular risk because they come in close contact with the animals. Smuggled foxes are often caged and transported under unsanitary conditions, so odds are good that people become contaminated with fox feces.

In 1989, the southeastern United States had about 150 fox enclosures—operations with a continuing demand for foxes. Some states forbade the import of foxes from out of state; others required a permit and a veterinary certificate. Many of the foxes coming into enclosures were illegally imported—smuggled.

In December 1989, the U.S. Fish and Wildlife Service staged a raid on a group of suspected smugglers in South Carolina. Cooperating with the South Carolina Wildlife and Marine Resources Department, the wildlife workers seized almost a hundred animals, among them fifty-seven live red foxes and eighteen gray foxes. They had the animals tested for diseases, including *E. multilocularis* infection.[17]

If you had swallowed those *E. multilocularis* eggs in the late 1970s, you'd probably have begun to feel the effects of your own *E. multilocularis* infection at about this time. It might begin with vague discomfort on your right side, just below your ribs, where a mass of parasitic tissue infests your liver. Your immune system has built a layer of fibrous tissue around the growth, but instead of killing the parasite, the barricade presses on blood vessels and liver ducts, causing the organ to enlarge and interfering with liver function. Bile doesn't drain from your liver as it should, and your skin takes on the yellowish cast of jaundice. At this stage, medical doctors often suspect liver cancer.

The parasite acts eerily like cancer. Occasionally, a bud breaks off and starts a new mass. Sometimes a bud is carried to another part of your body, where it continues to grow. If one moves down the common bile duct, it causes severe abdominal pain, mimicking a gallstone attack. If the parasitic growth continues unchecked, you will almost certainly die.

The only way to stop the growth and spread of *E. multilocularis* in 1989 was to remove it. Often, surgeons removed multiple alveolar hydatids from the liver only to see the disease return because of the worm's tendency to spread. Repeated operations to remove more parasitic masses prolonged lives but couldn't kill the parasite.

Progressively worsening headaches are an ominous sign that *E. multilocularis* may have moved to your brain. If so, scans will reveal brain lesions, and again only surgery can prevent the yellowish-green masses of parasitic tissue from continuing their relentless growth. Today, antiparasitic drugs combined with surgery give victims a chance at recovery, but there's no guarantee, and it might be a decade or more before you're sure the worm is gone.

There is no stopping the worm in the American Southeast, however. Three of the foxes seized in South Carolina had adult *E. multilocularis* in their intestines: the first one to test positive had more than three thousand of the worms. Worse, written records seized during the raid indicated that the smugglers had a network covering twenty-five states and some Canadian provinces and that more than three thousand animals, mostly foxes, had already been relocated to fox enclosures.[18]

If just 4 percent of relocated foxes were infected, this smuggling ring had already dispersed approximately 120 infected foxes throughout the American East and Southeast. And this number accounted for just one dealer. Another raid in 1994 netted 98 foxes illegally imported from Montana and Wyoming. The worm was found in 6 of the first 30 foxes tested—20 percent.[19]

More than ten years later, the hounds are still running. Fox-chasing enclosures still need to restock, and foxes are still being smuggled into the Southeast. We can be sure that *E. multilocularis* is still coming with them. If the parasite becomes established—and it probably will—no one will be able to get rid of it. Another parasite will have successfully expanded its range.

—

The New World hookworm, bee mites, and *Elaphostrongylus* spp. all came to North America from other parts of the world, but the Americas were not a clean slate before Europeans arrived. In a few cases, horrible parasites have gone the other way. One of them was *Cochliomyia hominivorax,* the nastiest fly on earth.

Let us now travel to Libya, Africa, in 1988. Early on a warm spring morning, a fly sheds her protective casing three-quarters of an inch (a couple of centimeters) down in the soft Libyan earth and works her way up to daylight. About twice the size of an average housefly, she is an adult female *C. hominivorax,* or New World screwworm fly. She is intimidating and inspires a sense of dread, with her shiny, slightly hairy blue green body marked by three black stripes and her shockingly large red eyes. *C. hominivorax* is perhaps the most unfriendly fly on earth, a real monster. In fact, the name *hominivorax* means "man eater."

This fly has one imperative—to find a mate and reproduce. Sexually mature in two or three days, the female can fly a long way, if necessary, in pursuit of a male. On the third day, she approaches a patch of trees and flowering shrubs where a male waits, feeding on flower nectar. He pursues and mates with her. In about four more days, she will lay eggs; her next task, therefore, is to find a place to deposit them, a place with a plentiful food supply for emerging maggots.

A hundred miles (170 kilometers) or more from where the fly emerged, a scratch on the flank of a domestic sheep catches her attention. She stops for about fifteen minutes, busily depositing more than two hundred eggs side by side in a single patch on the dry skin near the scratch. The wound oozes a little, and she pauses to feed before flying away. In a few more days, she leaves another egg mass near the unhealed umbilical cord on a newborn lamb. She leaves a third mass by a scalp wound on a man dozing in the afternoon heat.[20]

By the time the fly deposits her second batch of eggs, the first ones hatch and maggots invade the sheep's skin through the scratch. They feed on healthy tissue, creating a cavernous, putrid-smelling wound. A second female fly, attracted by the smell, deposits another egg mass beside the first, and before another day passes, two hundred newborn maggots join the others. Each buries itself head down near the center of the wound and feeds, breathing through its exposed posterior.

After about four days, the oldest maggots vacate, dropping to the ground and immediately burrowing down a few centimeters to pupate. The weather is warm, so they'll emerge as young adult flies in as little as seven days. The savaged sheep, meanwhile, succumbs to the infestation and secondary bacterial infection. By the time the first fly of the next generation pushes out of the ground on a warm spring morning, the sheep is dead.

The New World screwworm is, as the name implies, a parasite of the Americas. *Cochliomyia hominivorax* was formerly found only in the Western Hemisphere—throughout the southern third of the United States, Central America, and northern South America. Though the fly

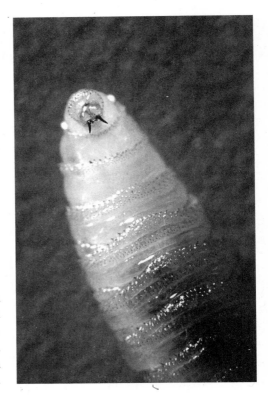

Figure 12. The head of a screwworm maggot: a mouth built for tearing at living tissue. Photo by John Kucharski, USDA Agricultural Research Service.

can't survive winters where the average temperature drops below 54°F (12°C) for an extended period, the roving habits of females during the warm months carry them far outside their winter range. Movement of infested animals can also transport flies, and in the past, screwworms have appeared as far north as the Canadian border.

The flies attack any warm-blooded animal, and as many as a fifth of infested animals die. A favorite site is the umbilical cord of newborns, and these attacks devastate the young of both wild and domestic animal populations. The fly is considered "probably the most economically important insect pest of mammalian livestock in the world."[21] Human infestations are frequent, and, untreated, they can be fatal. The human nasal sinus is a common site of infestation, where feeding maggots cause terrible destruction.

But the New World screwworm fly has a weak spot, and the life cycle of the female fly provides the crucial clue: she mates only once. If you rear huge numbers of the flies in captivity, sterilize them with radiation, and release them into infested areas, wild females mate with sterile males and produce infertile eggs. The numbers of wild flies drop off. After repeated releases of sterile flies, the insect dies out.

The first major eradication attempt was in the United States in southern Florida, where screwworm flies once survived the winter months and regularly spread north each summer into the southern parts of Georgia and Alabama. Beginning in late 1957, fourteen million sterile flies were released in southern Florida each week. As a result, the number of infestations immediately dropped off there and to the north.

In 1958, the program expanded, distributing more than fifty million flies per week in Florida, Georgia, and Alabama. The fly's end came fast: June 1959 saw the last case of screwworm infestation in Florida. Between that initial success and 1996, the "sterile fly technique" wiped out *C. hominivorax* in the United States, Mexico, and all the way south to the border between Panama and Columbia.[22]

The first case of Libyan screwworm myiasis (maggot infestation) was discovered on a sheep in March 1988: larvae were collected from the wound and identified at Al-Fateh University. Soon more cases turned up, all within a one-hundred-kilometer radius of Tripoli. What was *C. hominivorax* doing in Libya? Until then, the parasite had not been found outside of the Americas.

The flies hadn't drifted in on a wind from the west: a screwworm fly can travel a long way on the wing, but it cannot cross the Atlantic. Throughout the late 1980s, Libya imported well over a million farm animals each year, mostly sheep. The pest probably arrived on a ship or an airplane, possibly as maggots in the wound of an infested animal or as fly pupae in animal bedding. In 1988, about two million sheep came to Libya through regular channels, but none were good suspects in the search for the source of the fly.

Unconfirmed reports suggest that undocumented shipments of sheep arrived from Latin America and the Caribbean, and DNA evidence supports the theory that the fly originated in one of these two places: scientists studying the unique DNA patterns of screwworms from various countries have found that the Libyan flies differ from those of Central America and more closely resemble flies from further south and the Caribbean.

The arrival of screwworm in Libya was an immediate disaster for Libyan farmers—who knew nothing about this animal- and man-eating parasite—but it soon became an international emergency as well: the history of the parasite in the New World suggested what it might be capable of on another continent. Scientists feared that *C. hominivorax* would spread throughout most of the African continent as far south as the northern border of Namibia, using river valleys as routes of rapid spread. Wherever there was vegetation and a warm climate, it would probably thrive. It could also spread throughout the Arabian Peninsula and into all of the Middle Eastern and European countries bordering the Mediterranean. In all likelihood, it could survive the winter along the Mediterranean coast—Spain, Sardinia, Sicily, Greece, Lebanon, and Israel were directly threatened—and spread far into the territory to the north every summer, just as it had done in the United States.

As it spread, the screwworm fly would threaten livestock and stress wild animal populations. The fly's previous impact on white-tailed deer in North America suggested that damage to the large herds of antelopes in East Africa could be devastating—as many as 80 percent of newborns might be lost. Small populations of isolated or endangered species would likely be lost as well, and native people dependent on bush meat and other game would find their food supply threatened. The fly would curtail trade in live commercial animals and severely affect tourism motivated by wildlife.

Cochliomyia hominivorax would threaten humans as well; indigenous groups living far from sophisticated medical care would be particularly vulnerable, because an infestation can kill in just a few days. Small children and the elderly would be hardest hit. By all indications, the future predations of the New World screwworm fly in the Old World could be catastrophic.

The Libyan government moved quickly to ban all shipments of live animals from Latin America, a safeguard that came too late. The fly had arrived. It survived its first African winter, and 1989 brought 1,937 confirmed cases of screwworm infestation. In 1990, Libya had 12,068 cases. The infested area, not surprisingly, was largely agricultural, producing fruits, grains, nuts, vegetables, and livestock, mostly sheep. The nectar of native flowering acacia and mimosa trees provided the carbohydrates the adult flies required; the animals provided the protein.

In retrospect, considering the level of trade in live sheep from Latin America, it was only a matter of time before the dreaded fly spread, if not to Libya, then to some other location in the Old World. In one sense, the country was lucky that the fly arrived when it did: the sterile-insect technique had already been refined in the United States and Mexico, and with screwworm eradication still in progress in Central America, the expertise to deal with the emergency was at hand, as long as political barriers could be overcome.

An international collaborative effort was launched to eradicate the fly from Libya before it spread any farther.[23] Participants included eight countries immediately threatened by a screwworm infestation, four United Nations agencies, twenty-two donors, and several private businesses that supplied needed services. The plan was to combine a release of massive numbers of sterile insects in the infested area with surveillance and prompt treatment of any cases that emerged. The sterile flies came from the production plant in Mexico, which still produced flies for the screwworm eradication project in Central America.

The Libyan eradication project began on February 1, 1990. The endeavor was more complex than the American project because of the distance the flies had to travel: if the sterile flies arrived in Libya unable to compete with fertile males, the plan would not work. The flies had to be produced, packed for transport, shipped across the Atlantic, and released unharmed. Elaborate precautions and an unbroken chain of refrigerated trucks, planes, and trailers were deployed to ensure that the pupae were not exposed to the heat in the warm countries through which they traveled.

Screwworm pupae were packed in boxes and kept chilled so that they wouldn't emerge too early. During the first part of the eradication project, shipments went by refrigerated truck to Mexico City twice weekly, then on to Frankfurt, Germany, by air. In Frankfurt, they were transferred to another plane and flown to Tripoli. They made the entire trip at 50°F (10°C). By May 1991, a simpler route was devised: weekly shipment of pupae directly from the plant in Tuxtla Gutiérrez in Mexico to Tripoli, with a stop in Bermuda for refueling. Forty million flies made the trip each time, at a constant temperature of 68°F (20°C).

On the ground in Libya, pupae were stored in refrigerated trailers and warmed up gradually to control the emergence of adults. After a day or two at 79°F (26°C), the temperature at which adult flies emerge from the pupae, the boxes buzzed. A little pot of food in each box kept early arrivals happy until the rest had hatched, and when only 20 percent of the pupae remained, flies were ready for release.

On release days, Twin-Otter aircraft piloted by members of the Libyan Aeroclub flew 2.5 miles (4 kilometers) apart in the eradication zone, an area spanning 15,444 square miles (40,000 square kilometers) of land, stretching west of Tripoli into neighboring Tunisia and east beyond the Libyan town of Misratah. They dropped small cardboard boxes, each containing sixteen hundred screwworm flies, from an altitude of about 1,510 feet (460 meters). Individual planes dropped from three to ten boxes of flies each minute, aiming for a minimum distribution of eight hundred flies in each square kilometer on the ground below. If all went well, the boxes opened before landing, releasing the sterile flies, but if they did not open, a well-informed Libyan public popped the lids when the boxes hit the ground.

During the eradication, more than 1.2 billion sterile screwworm flies were released. On the ground in the eradication zone, inspection teams set up fly traps to determine how the flies were dispersing. They inspected animals, treated infections, and collected maggots for identification. Checkpoints on roads ensured that animals entering or leaving the area didn't carry screwworm.

The program worked quickly. The first sterile flies arrived in Tripoli in December 1990, and the last case of screwworm infestation was treated in April 1991. The dispersal of sterile flies continued for another six months to ensure that no fertile flies remained to reestablish the population. Eradication was declared a success in October 1991, and *C. hominivorax* has not been seen in Libya since. Ultimately, the eradication was a victory of international cooperation and diplomacy. It cost about $78 million.

Such experiences force legislators to race to stay ahead of the next alien species, the next wolf in sheep's clothing. Crossing international borders today means declaring any plant or animal material you're bringing with you to customs officials. Food, pets, even souvenirs made of natural materials are suspect. Still they come: parasites—as well as bacteria, viruses, and other life forms—continue to move. We seem to be slowly homogenizing life on earth, whether we mean to or not. Sometimes, parasites almost seem to have a master plan, like something out of a science fiction movie—as though they're scheming to stay ahead of *us*.

FIVE

Parasites in Control

In a surprising number of cases, parasitized animals are less likely to avoid predators. What causes such carelessness?

JANICE MOORE
Parasites and the Behavior of Animals

ACCORDING TO OLD TESTAMENT SCRIPTURES, after defeating the Canaanites, the "children of Israel" had a lot of trouble with fiery serpents. They

> journeyed from mount Hor by the way of the Red sea, to compass the land of Edom: and the soul of the people was much discouraged because of the way. And the people spake against God, and against Moses, Wherefore have ye brought us up out of Egypt to die in the wilderness? for there is no bread, neither is there any water; and our soul loatheth this light bread. And the LORD sent fiery serpents among the people, and they bit the people; and much people of Israel died. (Numbers 21:4–6)

In the millennia since, Arabian farmers have likely still thought less about the Lord than about the fiery serpent as they endured a typical attack of fever, nausea, and burning pain in an ankle or foot.[1] The extremity swells, and a red patch about two inches (five centimeters) wide develops. Worse, the lesion itches.

Invisible to the victim, the head of a female guinea worm, *Dracunculus medinensis* (the Latin genus name means "a small dragon or serpent"), lies in the flesh beneath the lesion. As long as a yardstick (about a meter), she has been moving through the tissues to this location, undetected, for about a month. Now ready to release her multitudinous young into the world, she needs the host's assistance, and she has a way to get it.

The red lesion gradually develops into a bulging fluid-filled blister over the course of about three days. Finally it bursts, and the suffering host feels better: the fever and nausea subside, but the blister remains intensely irritating. It itches and burns, and the host longs to plunge his or her leg into a pool of cold water for some relief. Now, too, the worm is visible.

With the rupture of the blister, about two inches (five centimeters) of spaghetti-like worm protrudes from a small hole near the center. About one-twelfth of an inch (under two millimeters) wide, she is delicate but easily visible. If we examine her microscopically, we might find that her uterus, teeming with tiny larvae, bulges out through her body wall or protrudes from her mouth.

Excruciating burning and itching persist—the discomfort has been compared to having a hot coal pressed to the skin—as the host limps to the nearest water hole. As soon as the excruciating lesion enters the water, the worm's uterus contracts and ruptures, and as many as half a million larvae swim free. Cool freshwater is just what they need. Little wormlike creatures drifting in the water, coiling and uncoiling, they are now in the only place where they have any hope of completing the next stage of their life cycle.

The lesion feels better temporarily, but most relieved victims miss the irony of the situation—the apparent contradiction of a worm that thrives in relatively dry regions of the world but must have standing water to reproduce. Plentiful water would actually lower the worm's chances of completing its life cycle: where watercourses dry up for at least part of the year, people gravitate toward pools and wells, which are frequently the only water sources in a dry season.[2] These water holes are used for everything—drinking, cooking, bathing, and soothing extremities when the guinea worm causes aggravating blisters. They bring the parasite and its hosts together.

Water is home to the cyclops, a tiny crustacean that eats other aquatic organisms, including *D. medinensis* larvae. The larvae survive being eaten and develop to their infective stage in the body of the cyclops. Then, when humans come to drink and accidentally swallow infested crustaceans, each larva finds its way through the human intestinal wall and begins a yearlong period of development that culminates with gravid female worms that literally lead suffering hosts to water.

The traditional home remedy for guinea worm is to wrap the free end of the worm around a twig and wait for more of the beast to emerge. For a few days, the worm has more larvae to release, and she does so each time the anguished host immerses her. It takes nearly a month for the entire worm to emerge from the lesion, wound around the twig inch by inch:

> And the LORD said unto Moses, Make thee a fiery serpent, and set it upon a pole: and it shall come to pass, that every one that is bitten, when he looketh upon it, shall live. And Moses made a serpent of brass, and put it upon a pole, and it came to pass, that if a serpent had bitten any man, when he beheld the serpent of brass, he lived. (Numbers 21:8–9)

The guinea worm has infected millions of people since early times, causing such infamous suffering that it may be the fiery serpent that plagued the children of Israel, as well as the serpent wound round the "rod of Asclepius," the familiar symbol of medicine. In the early 1990s, before the parasite started losing ground (see chapter 9), it emerged from more than three million blisters a year. When it appears, it is often accompanied by life-threatening secondary bacterial infection and debilitating pain. It keeps adults from work and children out of school for weeks or months and causes severe economic hardship.

Dracunculus medinensis leads a host to water like a head cold steers us to the tissue box; the difference is that the worm needs water even more than the host does. Although people often immerse extremities in water anyway, the worm's ability to incite a host to ease the lesion in the nearest pond is greatly to its advantage. This subtle type of host control is seen with many parasites, suggestive of a science fiction thriller in which an entity slips quietly into the mind or body of an unsuspecting character and slowly takes control of his every move. Parasites can't really do that, can they?

Unfortunately for luckless hosts, some can. One parasite whose controlling abilities have been studied is *Dicrocoelium dendriticum,* the lancet fluke. It's a small liver fluke of grazing herbivores, a leech-shaped worm about a third of an inch (eight millimeters) long that lives in the bile ducts and produces eggs that are flushed out of the liver into the intestine with bile. The infection is relatively rare in humans because it's almost always acquired by eating an ant—and it's in the ant, not the human, that the parasite becomes a deadly control freak.

If you are a fan of picnics—where ants occasionally invade the bean salad or drown in the lemonade—or a connoisseur of chocolate-covered ants, you might one day harbor a number of lancet flukes in your liver

Figure 13. Statue of Asclepius with a serpent wrapped around his staff. Exhibited in the Museum of Epidaurus Theatre, Greece. Photo by Michael F. Mehnert. http://creativecommons.org.

and pass their eggs in your stool.[3] If you are also okay with defecating behind the nearest tree while enjoying a picnic (or collecting ants), you might become one of the few humans to pass the parasite along.

A snail crawling and feeding under trees, or in meadows where infected herbivores graze, feeds on droppings and ingests *D. dendriticum* eggs. The eggs hatch, and the parasite multiplies inside the snail. After about three months, cercariae leave the snail, becoming encased in snail slime and left on the vegetation that the snail crawls over.[4] This material is reportedly attractive to foraging ants, which carry snail slime balls, each of which can contain hundreds of cercariae, back to the colony. Ants and ant larvae that feed on cercariae-infested slime balls become infected.

Now the parasite seems to be at a bit of a dead end: an herbivore gnawing on an anthill or cleaning up an ant trail with its tongue is not a regular occurrence. How does infective *D. dendriticum* pass from the ant to the next host? Essentially, the parasite forces the ant to offer itself up to be eaten.

One *D. dendriticum* metacercaria sacrifices itself for the rest: it moves to a location near the nerves that control the ant's mouth and takes control. Thereafter, in the cool of the evening, the infected ant crawls mindlessly to the top of a blade of grass and clings there with its mandibles until the morning sun's warmth releases it and it crawls down. Each evening, the ant returns to its high post, where it is much more likely than the average ant to be accidentally eaten by a grazing animal. During the day, of course, when the ant resumes its normal activities, it's available to careless picnickers and gourmet cooks.

The parasite's impact on people is not as direct as that of the guinea worm: it affects livestock in Europe, Asia, North America, and Australia, causing liver disease and requiring the destruction of many animal livers at slaughter. And we can only speculate whether it may, in the future, have a damaging effect on the efforts of those who think we should eat more insects.

Both the guinea worm and the lancet fluke affect the behavior of a host in a way that ensures the parasite has an easier time making the leap to the next host. The person with a guinea worm protruding from a foot is still the same person. The ant with *D. dendriticum* is like the legendary werewolf—normal during the day but seized by a strange compulsion at night. A real parasite horror story requires an entity that can take over completely, even change personality, making the body that it occupies a living ghost of its former self.

If ghosts haunt the empty waterfront of Kitsault, an abandoned town on the shores of Alice Arm, British Columbia, they may be ghosts of king crabs, *Lithodes aequispina,* one of the unfortunate hosts of a horrific parasitic barnacle.

Barnacles are not typically the substance of nightmares. The worst they usually do is cut your feet. But *Briarosaccus callosus* neither looks nor behaves like the barnacles we are used to seeing attached to rocks at the seacoast. This barnacle works its way through the body of a crab and then begins directing all the crab's activities for its own benefit.

Briarosaccus callosus is a tiny larva or nauplius—a mouthless, gutless creature with comblike legs—when it begins causing trouble for the crab. A female nauplius locates a crab and latches on near a thin area in the crab's hard shell. Abandoning legs and other structures, the parasite transforms into a sort of living hypodermic syringe and injects itself through the shell into the crab's soft insides. The crab is unaware that it has been invaded.

Once inside, the little mass of cells moves to a nerve cord in the underbelly of the crab and starts to grow. Tendrils wind around the nerve cord and grow into the surrounding tissues, round and about the organs like an expanding network of roots. At the same time, the main body of the parasite grows larger, pressing against the crab's shell with increasing force. Eventually it breaks through the shell between the crab's back legs and hangs there like a plump sausage. This part of the parasite is called the externa.

Now the barnacle is in control. The crab stops growing and molting and exists only to serve the parasite. An infected female crab can't produce eggs, but the externa is in the same place that a healthy female crab produces an egg mass after mating. The crab behaves as though the externa is her egg mass: she moves to deeper water, where she protects and grooms the externa as she would her own eggs. Curiously, the barnacle can even take over the bodies of male crabs: infected males are feminized and behave like female crabs with egg masses.

Male *B. callosus* living free in the water are attracted to the externa, mating occurs, and a new generation of nauplii develops within the sausage-shaped structure. When the nauplii are released, the hapless crab performs its final service to the parasite: puppetlike, it moves out of its hiding place and waves its abdomen back and forth, distributing nauplii into the surrounding water as it would its own offspring.

This scenario plays out in the waters off Kitsault more frequently than in most places because of the unusual geography of Alice Arm, one of the innermost arms of a network of fjords called the Portland Inlet System. The deep water in Alice Arm is renewed relatively slowly, so ocean currents don't carry away crab or parasite larvae: as a result, the water is home to a lot of king crabs, and many are infected with *B. callosus*.[5] Not surprisingly, the area supports a lucrative crab fishery.

The same quirk of oceanography linked Kitsault and its molybdenum mine with the fishers, the crab, and the parasite in the early 1980s. The parasite was nothing new in the fjord, but Kitsault was new, and it had the unreal air of a town lost in the wilderness. Like a movie set created on the spot, it was a complete community miles from anywhere. It had homes and apartment buildings, schools, shopping areas, medical facilities, entertainment, and all the amenities for miners and their families.

The mine opened in April 1981, and from the start, it enjoyed an unusual dispensation: it was the only mine in Canada allowed to discharge tailings directly into marine waters.[6] Scientists predicted that, like crab and barnacle larvae, tailings sediments and heavy metals would not be carried out of the fiord to pollute other waters. The Alice Arms Tailings Deposit Regulations saved the mining company lots of money, but the exemption also set the company at odds with environmentalists, local fishers, and the native people in the area. And, as though on cue, the king crab population in the waters of Alice Arm dropped off, and crab fishers came home with empty boats. They blamed the mine for killing off the crabs. In its own defense, the mine invoked overfishing and *B. callosus*, the castrating barnacle.

Imagine large numbers of crabs behaving as though they are producing offspring but actually producing none at all: because infected crabs don't reproduce, *B. callosus* can have a devastating effect on crab populations—and on crab fisheries. But was the parasite responsible for the loss of king crabs in Alice Arm, or were the mine tailings toxic to the crabs? Perhaps the two were interacting in some way. Was the crab parasite just a red herring, a scientific complication that happened to work in favor of the mine?

The guilt or innocence of the barnacle was never established, probably due to an unexpected, and unrelated, turn of events: the bottom fell out of the molybdenum market. At one time worth thirty dollars a pound, the mineral was earning less than two dollars a pound by 1982. Operating the mine was no longer feasible, and it was shut down.

A lot of people were happy to see the mine go, but its demise turned the storybook town of Kitsault into a modern northern ghost town. It was left vacant when more than a thousand people headed out to start new lives elsewhere. The houses and other buildings in the town sat empty for decades. In 2005 Kitsault was for sale for an asking price of $7 million (Canadian).

In the interim, one solitary couple lived in the isolated town, maintaining the buildings and properties. The pair must have felt a bit like Jack Torrance and his wife, Wendy, in Stephen King's *The Shining*, who became caretakers for an empty haunted Colorado hotel in the off-season. The job had its perks, however, and the caretakers enjoyed the wilderness and the seafood of Alice Arm—especially the salmon and the king crabs, which were still abundant in the fjord. *Lithodes aequispina* had survived, and doubtless its barnacle parasite along with it.

American millionaire Chandra Krishnan finally bought Kitsault for an undisclosed sum and reportedly intends to develop the town into a retreat for scientists and artists and a resort for ecotourism. He also hopes to produce films in the town, but not the sort that star a parasite that turns hosts into shells of their former selves with alien entities living inside.

Such a movie would be fiction: no parasite does to humans what *B. callosus* does to crabs. But some parasites can get into our heads, both literally and figuratively, and change us. One of them is that familiar parasite of cats, *Toxoplasma gondii* (the parasite that contaminated a water reservoir in chapter 3), and to understand what it does to people, let's look first at what it does to rodents.

—

The downtown core of any town or city is a likely place to find rats. We may not see them often, but they frequent the dim corners behind our favorite French pastry shop or pizzeria. They live in burrows, in buildings, and in the sewers, and they often emerge at dusk when they can go about their nightly foraging unnoticed. Ubiquitous, they are well adapted to life in human communities.

On a spring night in the evening shadows of a typical downtown alley, rats scrabble about searching for food. Delicious odors waft from the back entrance of a restaurant, where groups of friends, shop-talking colleagues, and couples dine, oblivious to the scavengers out in the street. Enticing smells come from the steaming dumpster too, and from the trash cans lined up along the wall. This scene presents a buffet of plenty, and it is a place of great activity; pigeons, crows, and seabirds visit during the day, along with flies, ants, cockroaches, and other insects. The occasional stray dog or feral cat pauses to investigate. Most of these creatures are not in evidence at night: the rats and mice appear to have the garbage and the darkness to themselves.

Like all rats, these are on the lookout for anything edible that humans have tossed out and for any crack that will allow them to break into food storage areas. Urban areas are lands of opportunity. As twilight deepens, more rats leave their nests and venture into the streets, foraging in the shadows, nosing through garbage, feeding in the sewers, and gnawing their way into buildings.

Something rats can't tolerate, however, is the scent of a cat. Countless generations of rats have learned, to their misfortune, that cats are dangerous. The need to avoid cats is so instinctive now that even though a rat may have never encountered or even smelled a cat before, it will still hastily remove itself from an area where it detects cat odor.

On this spring night, the smell of cat lingers in a dark passage by the pizzeria. Most rats that venture into the tempting space shy away quickly: "Cat!" their noses tell them, and they scuttle away from the scent, seeking the friendly smells of food and of home. But one lone rat in the alley is strangely unconcerned. It contentedly searches for food in the garbage scattered on the ground and investigates the cat smell with curiosity. It seeks out the damp source of the odor and wanders back to it repeatedly, loitering about, showing no fear.

Then, as though something has momentarily cut off the moonlight, the shadows in the alley deepen. Another presence stealthily blends in. Something approaches. The soft sound of a carelessly placed padded paw or the flick of a flexible tail in the debris signals to the rat that it is no longer alone. It looks up from its foraging and sees the cat. Yet it feels no fear. It doesn't run or try to hide but carries on with its activities, ignoring the predator's approach. The cat crouches, its eyes fixed on the rat, its muscles tense. This rat will not be going home.

Most of us would agree that something is amiss when a rat hangs about as though waiting to be eaten by a cat. If we knew that the rat was infected with *T. gondii,* we might ponder the coincidence that the cat is not only a typical predator of rats but also the definitive host of that parasite—the only host in which the parasite completes the sexually reproductive stage of its life cycle. Could there be a connection?

In fact, there is a connection. Research has shown that healthy rats consistently avoid the smell or presence of cats but that their innate fear is wiped out by a *T. gondii* infection (see chapter 3).[7] Infected rats don't avoid cats. They also show increased activity and decreased fear of

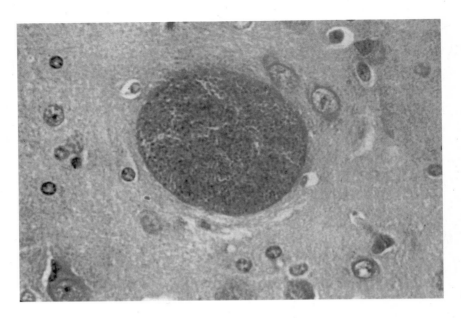

Figure 14. A cyst of *Toxoplasma gondii* in mouse brain tissue. From J. W. Smith, ed., 1976, *Diagnostic Medical Parasitology: Blood and Tissue Parasites,* photographic slide no. 87: *Toxoplasma gondii,* cyst in mouse brain (H&E stain). Chicago: American Society of Clinical Pathologists. © 1976 American Society of Clinical Pathologists.

unfamiliar things while behaving normally in most other ways: they still recognize the smells of food and of rat, and they mate and feed as usual. The parasite, living in the rat's brain and other tissues, is able to alter the animal's behavior in a specific way that makes the rat much more likely to be eaten by a cat, which is exactly where the parasite needs to go.

Studies with mice reveal changes in behavior as well. Infected mice move about more than healthy mice, are less likely to run away or hide, and tend to be more aggressive. Though some of these changes are different from the ones seen in rats, they still increase the likelihood that an infected mouse will be spotted by a prowling cat and promptly eaten.

After a satisfying meal of infected rodent, the cat's digestive processes break down the tissues surrounding the encysted bradyzoites and set them free in the intestine. What happens next is unique to cats. Bradyzoites plunge through cell walls in the cat's intestinal lining and begin to multiply inside the cells. The resulting crescent-shaped merozoites burst out, invade new cells, and multiply again, in a process that can repeat itself a number of times.

Eventually, the cycle culminates with the production of male and female cells instead of merozoites. Males fertilize females, and oocysts are produced—the stage of *T. gondii* that contaminated the Humpback Reservoir in Victoria, British Columbia, causing a waterborne outbreak of toxoplasmosis in humans. Each oval, thin-walled microscopic oocyst resembles a slightly flattened bubble with one or two glassy marbles inside.

When a cat has its first bout of toxoplasmosis, it expels millions of oocysts into the environment in its feces. There, the oocysts mature and wait to be eaten by a warm-blooded animal: almost any warm-blooded animal, including humans, will do. If conditions are right, an oocyst will still be infective after years in the soil. Virtually every region on earth is contaminated with these microscopic oocysts, especially areas with lots of cats and rodents—and wherever these animals thrive, one generally finds large populations of people.

The infection unfolds differently in humans and often goes unnoticed. Nonetheless, people all over the world—well over 50 percent of people in some areas—have antibodies to *T. gondii*, indicating that they have been exposed at some time in their lives. If the parasite can control the behavior of rats and mice, can it also affect the behavior of infected humans in some way?

The answer is almost certainly yes. Numerous studies have compared people who have chronic *T. gondii* infection with those who have never had it.[8] The results suggest some curious and alarming effects. One of the more curious observations is that the parasite appears to affect men and women in opposite ways. In 2007, Jaroslav Flegr, longtime researcher in this field, summarized the results of eleven years of personality studies: "[Infected] men were more likely to disregard rules and were more expedient, suspicious, jealous, and dogmatic. . . . [Results for women] suggested that they were more warm hearted, outgoing, conscientious, persistent, and moralistic. Both men and women had significantly higher apprehension . . . compared with the uninfected controls."[9]

Other studies suggest that chronically infected people have shorter attention spans and slower reaction times, which may increase their risk of accidents. The most disturbing association between *T. gondii* and behavior, however, is the suggestion that it may play a role in some cases of mental illness. Studies have found that a higher proportion of psychiatric patients have antibodies to *T. gondii* than does the general population. Moreover, infected rats treated with antipsychotic drugs don't undergo the behavioral changes that make them easy prey for cats.[10]

The difficulty with research on humans is that, of course, one cannot deliberately infect them and then objectively watch what happens. Information must be gathered from people who have had the disease, and a lot depends on their self-assessments of personality now and in the past. The possibility exists that men and women don't actually change in different ways from one another, but rather that their assessments of change, or their willingness to acknowledge personality changes differ in ways related to their gender. Alternatively, some personality traits might increase the risk of catching the parasite in the first place.

In the end, we still don't know for sure what effect *T. gondii* has on human behavior, though more people are asking the question than ever before. Tennis celebrity Martina Navratilova may well have asked it more than twenty-five years ago: she had a nasty case of toxoplasmosis in 1982 and subsequently found herself in court fighting an accusation of assault.

At one time, Navratilova had a great fondness for rare beef, and, according to one source, she had a particular weakness for steak tartare.[11] If you've never tried this delicacy, simply grind up fresh, raw sirloin steak, mix it with a beaten raw egg and a little onion, and roll it into little balls. No cooking required: tuck a caper into the center of each ball and garnish with some freshly ground black pepper and a little chopped parsley or chives. Delicious, but beware. Steak tartare is much riskier than chocolate-covered ants. A brief indulgence in the summer of 1982 probably led to what Navratilova called "the million dollar illness," and to what parasite specialist B. H. Kean later called "the steak tartare defense."[12]

Top-seeded Navratilova was looking forward to the U.S. Open in September 1982. The event was the only major tournament she had not yet won, and she was determined that this would be her year. But she was not feeling well. For weeks she had been tired and weak; her muscles felt strained, she was having muscle spasms in her arms and legs, and she was unusually emotional. Most frightening of all, the lymph nodes in her neck, armpits, and chest were enlarged, making her doctor wonder whether she had cancer. She needed to be at her peak of physical fitness, but she just wanted to sleep. On the eve of the U.S. Open, her condition was identified: toxoplasmosis. Navratilova was one of the few unlucky healthy adults to suffer serious symptoms.

Navratilova and Gary Wadler, the tournament doctor, wondered where she picked up the parasite. Cats, perhaps? At first they suspected the pet cats of Rita Mae Brown, a former partner of Navratilova's. Navratilova had visited Brown recently and remembered noticing that the house cats had their paws in the munchies. Cats with toxoplasmosis can easily have many infective oocysts on their paws, and Brown's cats might have deposited some oocysts on the snack food. The cats, however, tested negative. Steak tartare was next on the list of suspects. It was impossible to prove that the meat was the source of the parasite, but it seemed a good bet: Navratilova had enjoyed uncooked beef shortly before visiting Brown.

The infection couldn't have come at a worse time, and the long-awaited tournament turned into a different kind of struggle for Navratilova. Wadler advised her to withdraw from the tournament and rest, telling her that she would not have enough energy to play a long match, but Navratilova had a strong desire to win and a deep sense of responsibility to the other players. She forged ahead without saying anything publicly about her illness. Only a handful of people knew she was ill.

As Navratilova prepared for the quarterfinal match against Pam Shriver, she promised herself that she would win in two sets, before her strength deserted her. Her energy, however, didn't last even that long. She won the first set 6–1 but felt the draining effects of the parasite in the second set: she was slowing down and she knew it. Shriver won the second set in a tiebreaker. Now Navratilova knew she was in trouble; she didn't have the strength to play a third set. In fact, she could hardly get out of the chair. Competing on rubbery legs that refused to move, she lost to Shriver 6–2.

The loss was a difficult moment for Navratilova. She had been so determined to win the tournament, she was feeling wretched, and she knew that a crowd of sports reporters and photographers were poised to get comments and pictures. Wobbling on weak legs, in tears, and with a towel over her head, she tried to avoid them and make her way to the relative safety of the locker room. But escape was impossible.

Reporters and photographers were waiting for her under the stands. Navratilova moved through the crowd as quickly as she could. Photographers snapped pictures. She asked them to stop. One photographer was so determined to get pictures of the miserable tennis player that he continued to photograph her, pursuing her paparazzi style and snapping pictures so aggressively that he was later described as "stalk[ing] her like a hunter."[13]

Navratilova felt attacked. She wasn't ready to face the public, and she didn't want anyone taking pictures of her in her weakened state. She lost her temper. Accounts relate that when the reporter stopped to reload one of his cameras, Navratilova walked over and seized another that was slung over his shoulder. She wrestled it from him and, walking away, opened the camera to expose the film, destroying his pictures.[14]

Despite this encounter, Navratilova, who was known for her willingness to talk to the press, gathered herself together in the locker room and appeared at a press conference after the match where she finally admitted to her debilitating illness. The day was a huge disappointment for her, and she said as much.[15]

If Navratilova was devastated by the way the day had turned out, the aggressive sports photographer was incensed. He launched a $2 million lawsuit claiming that Navratilova had assaulted him. He maintained that she had injured his shoulder, arm, and hand. His lawyer later claimed that she had "twisted [the] sports photographer's arm like a pretzel."[16]

Leading up to the court date, doctors Kean and Wadler pondered what part *T. gondii* had played in the unfortunate events of that September day. Undoubtedly the parasite had ruined Navratilova's tennis game. Surely it had made her weak and fatigued. Navratilova weighed fifty pounds less than her accuser, was four inches shorter, and had just played a long tennis match, after which her legs barely held her up. She could not have been much of a physical threat to anyone. But had the parasite influenced her behavior in any other way?

The doctors considered the possibility that the parasite was in Navratilova's brain, causing acute inflammation, which could affect her behavior. They knew that *T. gondii* can run amok in people with weakened immune systems and cause psychotic symptoms. This effect is not seen in otherwise healthy people, but some do suffer from hallucinations, delusions, anxiety, and depression. Still, this medical argument had no proof.

It remains without proof today. We know that the parasite is found predominantly in the muscles and nervous system and that it affects chemicals involved in brain function even after the acute disease passes. We know that it appears to cause subtle behavioral changes over time, but no one knows when these apparent chronic effects kick in or why.

In the end, Martina Navratilova never claimed "the parasite made me do it," although it may, in fact, have influenced her actions. Rather, "the steak tartare defense" maintained that she had probably contracted toxoplasmosis from eating raw beef and that the debilitating physical effects of the infection were the cause of her loss on the tennis court. The same debilitating effects made her much too weak to have been a physical threat to a photographer after the match. The argument worked.

All the evidence suggesting that *T. gondii* affects the behavior of individuals who harbor it in their muscles and brains raises a chilling question. In countries where a high proportion of people have the parasite, could it affect behavior at a cultural level? Could it influence a national attitude, mold an apprehensive nation of moralistic women and suspicious men? Could it lead to conflict?

Social scientists have studied and theorized about how culture shapes personality and worldview, but there is also reason to wonder how a shared personality trait, or aggregate personality, might shape culture. If *T. gondii* plays such a role, then the aggregate personality in nations where a majority of the population has the latent infection should be different from that where the infection is rare. Prevalence of chronic toxoplasmosis—the percentage of the population infected—does vary widely from country to country, from more than 50 percent in Argentina, Brazil, Jamaica, and Yugoslavia to less than 10 percent in Norway, South Korea, and the United Kingdom.[17]

Preliminary research suggests that "nations with high *T. gondii* prevalence [have] a higher aggregate neuroticism score."[18] In this work, researcher Kevin Lafferty uses "neuroticism" to define a standardized measure of guilt proneness. The study also suggests that high *T. gondii* prevalence might result in stronger gender roles and a shared desire to avoid uncertainty. Some nations, however, do not fit the pattern, and Lafferty does not reach definite conclusions.

We shouldn't hold our breaths for an answer to how *T. gondii* is affecting world history. Many forces act together to shape culture and national attitudes; scientists will never be able to isolate toxoplasmosis completely from other influences and measure its effects exactly. Tantalizing results like this one raise more questions than they answer. Does a tendency toward "neuroticism" make people more likely to catch the parasite rather than the other way around? Might another factor—such as genetic predisposition or environment—lead to both neuroticism and high risk of toxoplasmosis? How might increasing multiculturalism in many nations change the dynamics? Could *T. gondii* affect different cultures in different ways? If any of these elements are influencing the picture, then we really don't know anything.

Parasitic infections typically come with a handful of common symptoms that help us recognize them, but *T. gondii* isn't the only one to affect people in different ways. Another parasite that tends to end up in the human brain is the larval stage of *Taenia solium,* the pork tapeworm, and it sometimes causes bizarre behavioral changes that are much less subtle than those attributed to toxoplasmosis. Typical symptoms include seizures, headaches, depression, and cognitive decline (the loss of intellectual brain function), but psychiatric diseases, including psychosis, are also seen fairly often.

One such case was reported in the medical journal the *Lancet* in 2004: "A thirty-five-year-old Indian farmer ... [suffered from] restlessness, insomnia, auditory hallucinations, wandering, social withdrawal, poor self care, blunted affect, delusions of persecution, and violent outbursts."[19] In a similar case, also in India, a twenty-five-year-old was irritable and restless, suffered bouts of anger, saw snakes and fires that didn't exist, and heard "divine voices."[20]

—

Few animals share their diseases with humans as famously as pigs do: trichinosis is a familiar pig-related disease, and so is swine flu. Another they share generously and often is *Taenia solium,* the pork tapeworm. Actually, we should say that we share the tapeworm with pigs, because the adult worm resides in the human intestine.

A person who harbors a pork tapeworm often has an intestinal companion more than three meters long, a prolific egg factory that releases microscopic eggs into the feces for years if left undisturbed. Conveniently for the worm, pigs are partial to human feces as a food source, and when egg-laden feces are deposited or spread as fertilizer on ground where pigs forage, the feces are ingested and with them, tapeworm eggs.

Inside the pig, the parasite's life is similar to that of *T. saginata* in a cow. Eggs hatch, releasing tiny spherical larvae (onchospheres) that move through the intestinal wall and hitch a ride in the animal's bloodstream. They climb out into muscles and organs, where each one builds itself a glossy cysticercus, a little cyst like a hollow pearl, with the larva clinging to the inside wall. Now the developing larva is called a scolex and looks a bit like a toadstool with a thin neck and a large, fat, rounded head. The scolex has some features that toadstools lack, however—two rings of barbed hooks at the tip and four circular suckers around the circumference.

The tapeworm is ready for its next host if the pig is slaughtered and the pork is eaten raw, or rare. Now in the gut of a human, the pearl turns itself inside out, exposing the scolex, which promptly attaches itself to the wall of the intestine with its armature of hooks and suckers. It grows from its free end, adding proglottids and getting steadily longer. The oldest proglottid moves farther away from the head on the end of a long strip as new pieces are added. In just three months, the creature looks like a frilly ten-foot (three-meter) noodle stretched out in the intestinal current. Mature proglottids, strung end to end, start producing eggs and the cycle starts again.

All too often, the storyline goes wrong. If you are passing thousands of tapeworm eggs in your feces every day and are not scrupulous about washing your hands, or if you live in a place where the sewage and sanitation systems hail from the Dark Ages, the eggs may not end up in the sewage treatment plant or even in the mouths of pigs. Humans who harbor tapeworms often transfer eggs from dirty hands to their mouths and to the mouths of other people via the objects and food that they handle. Untreated feces in the environment contaminate food and water with eggs. Then, people unwittingly take the place of pigs in the worm's life cycle.

The results can be devastating. Onchospheres make themselves at home in the muscles, as they do in pigs, but they also tend to migrate to the brain, and there they can cause chronic problems, both physical and psychiatric. This was the fate of the two psychotic young men in India: both were diagnosed with neurocysticercosis; both had many cysticerci under the skin and in the brain.

The same species of worm was accused of playing a leading role in the death of Kevin Keogh, the chief financial officer of the city of Phoenix, Arizona, in 2004. His final moments were tragic and sensational. According to media reports, on the afternoon of December 8, drivers on Camelback Road in Scottsdale, Arizona, noticed a Mercedes-Benz traveling at about thirty-five miles an hour.[21] As they watched in disbelief, the driver climbed out of the car through the driver's window. Casually dressed in loafers, a sweatshirt, and blue jeans, he climbed onto the roof of the car,

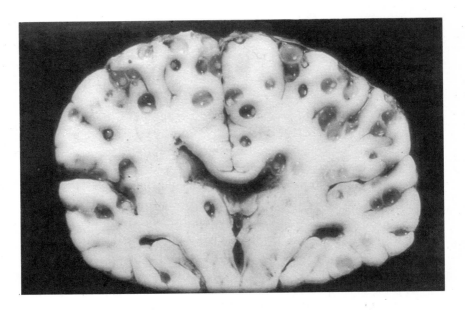

Figure 15. A cross-section of human brain with numerous cysticerci of *Taenia solium*. Photo by Ana Flisser.

stood up, and spread his arms as the car continued to speed, driverless, down the street.

To all outward appearances, this startling behavior was a case of car surfing, a terrifyingly dangerous game usually indulged in by young people who challenge each other to see who can stay on the car the longest and who can land upright when they are finally thrown from the vehicle. Not surprisingly, car surfers are often seriously injured or killed. Not waiting to be thrown, Keogh jumped to his death. He rolled and hit an orange tree, his lifeless body coming to rest beneath its branches. His car, meanwhile, continued down the street until it collided with a vehicle waiting at a stoplight. By a great stroke of luck, no one else was injured.

Phoenix was stunned. The man who did this was not the Kevin Keogh they knew. Keogh was a well-respected businessman not given to flamboyant or risky behavior. Usually well dressed and quiet, he was good at his job and had settled in comfortably at city hall. Everyone who knew him was shocked at his death—and even more shocked by the manner in which he died.

Soon the story got even stranger. "Official's Bizarre Death Has Equally Odd Explanation" claimed the *Arizona Republic* on December 9, and the

Arizona Daily Star wrote "Worm in Brain a Rare and Horrifying Affliction."[22] Health writers warned of the dangers of travel to exotic places and pointed to Keogh's death as an example of what could happen. The city manager of Phoenix was quoted as saying that the Keogh family believed the death was a result of central nervous system damage by a parasite. Reports quoted Keogh's wife, Karlene, as stating that her husband had a parasite in his brain, which he had picked up in Mexico in 2001.

If his wife was right, Keogh must have swallowed the eggs of a pork tapeworm at some point during his trip to Mexico. The eggs, passed in human feces, were probably in contaminated food or water. Onchospheres had entered Keogh's bloodstream, and some of them had traveled to his brain and settled there as pearly cysticerci. In Central America, this sequence of events is shockingly common.

After he returned home, Keogh had continuing health problems, and after consultation with several doctors and a short hospital stay in February 2002, he learned that he might have neurocysticercosis, *T. solium* tapeworm larvae in the brain. He suffered from seizures and mental confusion, typical symptoms of neurocysticercosis, but the diagnosis was still uncertain. Medical test results were suggestive of cysticercosis but not definitive.[23]

Keogh and his wife kept quiet about his health troubles and carried on with life. He received albendazole, a drug that kills the tapeworm larvae, but if the cysts were there, they would remain in Keogh's brain and muscles. Depending on their location, they could continue to cause trouble. Still, the couple had no inkling of the tragedy to come. Nor did they suspect that Keogh might be a danger to other people.

After Keogh's death, officials, family, and physicians speculated that neurocysticercosis had affected Keogh's judgment. He did things he would not ordinarily have done, made poor decisions, and lost sight of what was socially appropriate. Backing up the theory, medical specialists agreed that *T. solium* cysticerci in the brain could cause bizarre behavior and affect decision making. The case appeared to be solved.

Then, almost a year later, Kevin Keogh's death reappeared in the news. Rebecca Hsu, assistant medical examiner for Maricopa County, ruled the death a suicide. Though she could not rule out neurocysticercosis as a contributing factor in his bizarre behavior and fatal leap, the autopsy she had conducted had failed to turn up any encysted *T. solium* larvae, dead or alive, in his brain.

The new reports questioned the financial dealings at Phoenix city hall at the time of Keogh's death, and now said that Karlene Keogh had acknowledged that her husband had been depressed and dealing with a lot of stress at the time of his death. A new theory about the cause of Keogh's death emerged: he had apparently committed suicide as a result of extreme pressures and possible irregularities at work. Independent audits of Keogh's financial activities on behalf of Phoenix, however, found nothing wrong.

Yet another year went by, and the mystery still nagged at Karlene Keogh, at Kevin Keogh's friends at city hall, and at the people of Phoenix. Karlene Keogh, far from satisfied with the suicide ruling, had not been idle: she had hired an attorney. Experts who reviewed Kevin Keogh's medical records, including forensic psychiatrist Steven Pitt, forensic pathologist Michael Baden, and psychology professor Kiran Amin, all agreed that the known facts were not consistent with suicide. None of them ruled out neurocysticercosis. Following the submission of their professional opinions by Keogh's attorney, Philip Keen, chief medical examiner for Maricopa County, amended the cause of death on Kevin Keogh's death certificate to "undetermined."

Kevin Keogh had medical symptoms consistent with neurocysticercosis and a travel history consistent with that diagnosis. His medical and neurological problems dated back to the illness he experienced after his trip to Mexico. One medical test provided an equivocal result—it was neither negative nor positive—a suspicious finding. However, other tests and an autopsy found no evidence of *T. solium*.

Though doctors were unable to confirm neurocysticercosis, Keogh's symptoms and test results were suspicious enough for his doctor to decide to treat him with albendazole. Keogh believed he had the worm larvae in his brain, and Karlene also apparently believed the larvae were there. But we have no proof. We will never know for certain what caused Kevin Keogh's dangerous and self-destructive behavior on that December afternoon, but *T. solium,* a common worm that can be difficult to recognize, may have been responsible.

SIX

In the House of Mirrors

As I was going up the stair
I met a man who wasn't there;
He wasn't there again today.
I wish that man would go away.

HUGHES MEARNS
"Antigonish"

WESTERN MEDICINE, textbook definitions, and the court of public opinion in developed countries agree: parasites are bad. Similarly, modern parasitology textbooks give the impression that we understand what parasites do and how they do it. But when we drag a parasite out into the light and examine it from every angle—medical, cultural, historical, environmental, and emotional—we find that it has as many faces as a clown in a house of mirrors. It means different things to different people. The significance of a parasite is in the eye of the beholder. To test this statement, simply present a freshly passed *Ascaris lumbricoides* worm to a modern general practitioner of Western medicine, a practicing allergy specialist, and a Chinese physician from the fifteenth or sixteenth century. The GP will send it to the laboratory for identification and prescribe an antiparasitic drug; the allergy specialist may point out that, while the worm is detrimental in many ways, evidence suggests that it protects against allergies and autoimmune diseases; the Chinese physician may bake it and reduce it to powder for use as an aphrodisiac.[1] Clearly, parasites can have roles and uses that don't immediately occur to the average host: they are, and have long been, widely misunderstood.

Tapeworms, for example, can hear. Or so we are told by various medical authorities of the eighteenth and nineteenth centuries.[2] Western tapeworms of the time were apparently greatly aroused by music, particularly church organ music, forcing their hosts to seek a quiet place for a little relief. In Chinese medicine, practitioners did not discuss plans to eradicate an intestinal tapeworm aloud, lest the target learn of the plot.

Chinese doctors also once believed that intestinal worms could turn their heads downward and that treatment was effective only if the head was up.[3] Worms naturally turned their heads down, patients were told, during the second half of the lunar month and could be tricked into turning upward again by passing roasted liver or another equally delectable treat under the host's nose. Perhaps this practice is the origin of the belief, still in circulation today, that one can lure a tapeworm out by placing milk or meat by the host's mouth, like an offering to evil spirits.

All of these ideas may sound outlandish, but they would not have surprised Dimitri Tsafendas, the man who assassinated Henrik Verwoerd, prime minister of South Africa, in 1966. Tsafendas had a long and adversarial relationship with his intestinal tapeworm that went far beyond the usual parasite-host relationship and ultimately played a part in his crime. He claimed that the tapeworm made him do it.[4]

In 1935, thirty years before Tsafendas knifed Verwoerd in the South African House of Assembly, a physician in Mozambique treated him for a suspected tapeworm infection. Should a worm appear, Tsafendas was instructed to submit it for examination. After taking the medication, the teenager indeed passed a long strip of tapeworm segments—which his stepmother, Marika, immediately flushed down the toilet, banishing the worm from sight but not from mind. The worm's species was never established, and, worse, no proof existed that the whole worm had gone into the sewer.

Sixty years later, Tsafendas remained convinced that his tapeworm lived on, both in his body and in the sewer beneath the house where he had lived in 1935. For Tsafendas, the worm was all powerful: it spoke to him at night and gave commands, it struggled inside him, it held him prisoner. He longed to be rid of that worm and to have it exposed to public view so that people would, at last, understand.

Tsafendas really did have a tapeworm, at least until he was treated in 1935. The worm inhabited his intestine for a time, absorbing nutrients from his bowel contents and contributing proglottids and eggs to his feces. It may have been there for some years. The infection probably didn't affect Tsafendas's health much: intestinal tapeworms generally cause few symptoms, if any. And we can only speculate about whether Tsafendas had neurocysticercosis (see chapter 5): *Taenia solium* was present in Africa, though *T. saginata* was more common. Other tapeworm species were less likely to be the culprit.

Tsafendas had valid reason to worry: if the head of the parasite was not attached to the strip of proglottids in the toilet, it might still be attached to his intestine. If so, it could regenerate, and the lad knew it. Tsafendas had a fear of harboring a worm in his guts—a fear that most of us can sympathize with—and no one could convince him that his worm was dead. When Marika Tsafandakis flushed the tapeworm instead of collecting it, she not only ended any hope of identifying its species, she gave it immortality.

For thirty years after the tapeworm incident, Tsafendas wandered the globe, touching down in South Africa, Mozambique, Canada, the United States, Greece, Portugal, and numerous other European countries. But wherever he went, he couldn't get away from the worm. He was in and out of hospital in various places, treated for abdominal problems, parasites, and psychiatric illness. If the beast was still with him at the end of these travels, as he believed, it was an extraordinarily old worm.

Nonetheless, Tsafendas believed the worm was invincible and claimed that it was responsible for his actions on the day that he walked into the House of Assembly in South Africa with two knives concealed under his jacket. In front of hundreds of people, he stabbed Henrik Verwoerd four times, killing him. Overpowered by the crowd, Tsafendas made no attempt to get away.

Predictably, Tsafendas was found mentally incompetent and spent the remainder of his days in a psychiatric institution. The idea that an intestinal worm could dictate a political assassination might have been credible to some in the 1800s, but it doesn't measure up in today's scientific world. Yet, to write the tapeworm off as a figment in the imagination of a madman is to miss an opportunity to examine the roles this immortal parasite has played in the history of South Africa.

Why did Tsafendas want to kill Henrik Verwoerd? What did he, or his tapeworm, have against the prime minister of South Africa? Verwoerd, often referred to as "the architect of apartheid," engineered a political system that drew a line of prejudice and hatred between white and black South Africans. Tsafendas, the illegitimate son of a Greek father and a black Mozambican mother, had one foot on each side of that line but could not live comfortably on either side.

Tsafendas spent his adult life prior to the assassination dreaming of living near his family in South Africa, a country that tried hard to keep him out. He repeatedly applied for visas, but despite the fact that his father lived in the country, he was repeatedly denied.[5] He could not win this battle any more than he could win his battle with the immortal tapeworm: if Verwoerd was a symbol of apartheid, Tsafendas's tapeworm was a symbol of the insoluble dilemma faced by a man in limbo under the apartheid system.

Henk Van Woerden, who researched Tsafendas's life, sees the tapeworm in another light: he describes it as a social distraction, a way that South Africans and the world at large could come to terms with a political assassination without delving into the significant underlying social issues. Tsafendas emerged neither as a hero for the antiapartheid camp nor as a political opponent of the ruling party. He was simply a madman who was convinced that an intestinal worm was controlling him; his claims about the worm combined with his history were damning evidence of his insanity. No other explanation was required.

In the event, what mattered to Tsafendas was that he believed the worm existed and that it was a malevolent dictator, commanding him to act. Unfortunately, proving the presence of something is much easier than conclusively proving its absence. This poses a problem when treating imaginary parasites, which are much more common than you might expect.

—

Blair Higgins (a pseudonym), a British car salesman, was twenty-eight when he first noticed the bugs crawling and jumping about in his hair.[6] They bit him and caused annoying itching that would not go away. As he studied them over more than a decade, he came to believe that they were laying eggs in his scalp. The eggs hatched, he thought, to produce the minute bugs that he observed. The bugs were able to fly as well, and after laying their eggs, they flew away. They were unlike anything known to medicine.

Drifting from doctor to doctor, Higgins tried to find a cure for his infestation. No one helped him. No one else could see the bugs. He applied antiseptics and insecticides repeatedly. The bugs were immune to everything. He even shaved his head. They persisted. They hatched and crawled. They jumped and bit, laid eggs, and flew away. More eggs hatched.

Higgins was frightened that the creatures would spread and infect other people. As though to validate his fear, the bugs were at their most active when he was around lots of people. Crowded places like buses, pubs, and planes were torture chambers for Higgins. Eventually, he was asked not to come back to his favorite bar. His friends deserted him, or he, them.

Resolving to live alone with his parasites, Higgins left his wife and quit his job, changing employment many times. He found sanctuary of a sort at sea with the merchant navy. There, his contact with other people was limited, and if he couldn't sleep at night, he could knock himself out with liquor.

When Higgins was forty, a doctor finally referred him to a dermatology clinic, where he told his story. He drew pictures for the doctors there, illustrating the bugs' life cycle, and he wrote a description of the parasites, his experiences, and his thoughts about a cure (figure 16).

The doctors at the dermatology clinic looked him over carefully and made a serious effort to find the creatures he described. They noted that his skin was normal—no bites, no rashes, no parasites that could be seen with the naked eye. They did a skin biopsy of his scalp and found that the tissue looked entirely normal under the microscope as well. They admitted him to hospital, giving him a bed in the dermatology ward, but they treated him with pimozide, a sedative and tranquilizer. Later, he was moved to a psychiatric ward and given other tranquilizers.

Though Higgins's list of solutions hints that his sense of humor was still intact despite his trials, he was not joking. He had endured as much as he could take. After his psychiatric assessment and subsequent unsuc-cessful treatment with tranquilizers, Higgins went to a service station, where he bought gasoline, poured it over his head, and ignited himself. Surprisingly, he survived the fire without serious injury—and so did his parasites. Not long afterward, however, he tried another of the options on his list: he made a noose and hung himself. This time he was success-ful. To him, his parasites were a problem worth dying to solve: to the rest of us, they were an inexplicable delusion.

Of all of the varied perceptions of, and interactions with, parasites, the hardest to accept are the ones of parasites that apparently don't exist. "These people are crazy," we say, "deluded. They need help." Certainly. But try walking into a room crowded with people (friends are okay, but strangers are better) and announcing loudly that you have just been to the doctor and received a diagnosis of scabies. Watch as the group quickly provides you with lots of personal space.

Nonchalantly scratch at exposed areas of skin, and notice how many others are doing the same. Note that the very mention of scabies has made

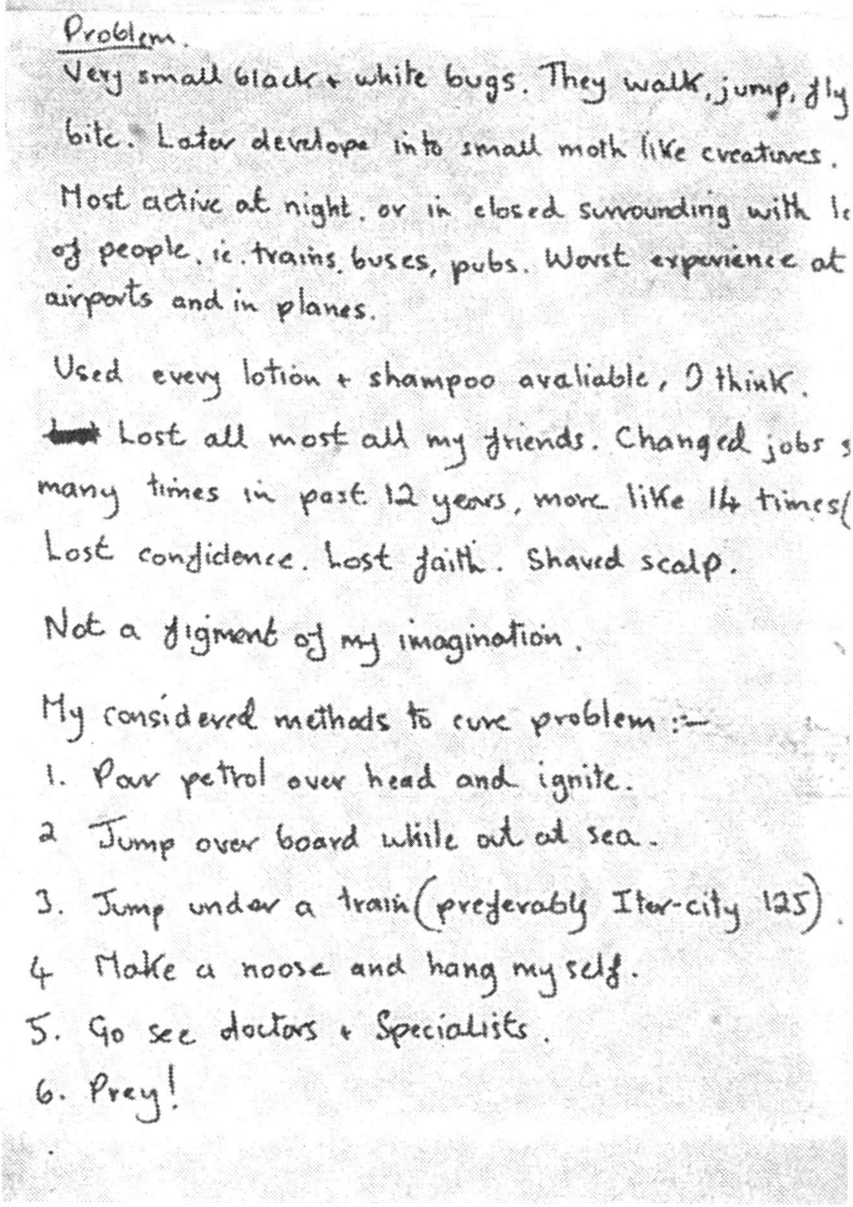

Problem.

Very small black + white bugs. They walk, jump, fly bite. Later develope into small moth like creatures.

Most active at night, or in closed surrounding with lc of people, ie. trains, buses, pubs. Worst experience at airports and in planes.

Used every lotion + shampoo avaliable, I think.

~~Lost~~ Lost all most all my friends. Changed jobs s many times in past 12 years, more like 14 times(

Lost confidence. Lost faith. Shaved scalp.

Not a figment of my imagination.

My considered methods to cure problem :—

1. Pour petrol over head and ignite.

2 Jump over board while out at sea.

3. Jump under a train (preferably Inter-city 125).

4 Make a noose and hang myself.

5. Go see doctors + Specialists.

6. Prey!

Figure 16. "Blair Higgins's" note to dermatologists. From B. E. Monk and Y. J. Rao, 1994, "Delusions of Parasitosis with Fatal Outcome," *Clinical and Experimental Dermatology* 19 (4): 342. © 1994 *Clinical and Experimental Dermatology.* Reproduced with permission of Blackwell Publishing Ltd.

you more aware of skin sensations—little tickles, clothes brushing against you, breezes ruffling the fine hairs on your arms. Each time you feel something—or imagine that you feel something—you want to look to make sure nothing is there.

Chuckle and say, "Ha, gotcha!" and see how many in your audience are genuinely amused. Our revulsion at the thought of something living on, or in, us is strong. If you don't remove yourself from the twitching crowd—and even if you do, everyone will continue to twitch for some time—or convince them of the truth, things are likely to get ugly. You are wise not to mention that some of the people in the crowd probably already have a few of their own external parasites. By the time we reach middle age, two out of three of us, even in the West, have a healthy population of rather peculiar mites living on our faces.

Demodex folliculorum is a long, thin creature that looks as if someone cut a plump earthworm in half and stuck a knobbly head with eight stumpy legs on the severed end. The mite drags a long tubular body behind it wherever it goes. It doesn't go very far, but spends its time plugged into a hair follicle, feeding on dead skin cells and secretions. Its tail may protrude above the skin, next to the hair, like a microscopic finger pointing at the host's friends and colleagues. If we could see the mites there, the effect would be quite intimidating, but follicle mites are less than two-hundredths of an inch (half a millimeter) long and virtually invisible to us, even close up.

Fortunately, we're blissfully unaware of our face mites, and the crawly itchiness of a louse scare does fade. We forget it. Imagine, though, if the crawly sensations were to continue. What if they never went away? What if they were accompanied by the sound of something crawling on your body, and by the sensation of something biting, stinging, the almost imperceptible movements of something. As though you were spending a night in a haunted house, you dread each moment: what is that noise? What is chewing on the skin just below my elbow? What is that *thing* moving through the hair above my ear?

For most of us, the disorder known as delusions of parasitosis, or delusional parasitosis, seems incredible. However, it is not as rare as we might think, and it is becoming more common. Typically, victims believe that bugs, mites, or insects are living on or in their skin, and they cannot be convinced otherwise. When they are able to describe their parasites, the creatures usually don't match any known medical pest.

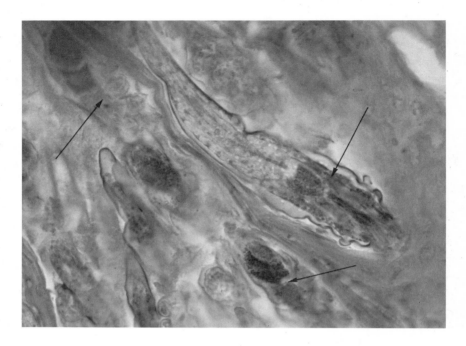

Figure 17. A cluster of face mites, *Demodex folliculorum,* in hair follicles. Arrows point to three individuals. Photo by the author.

The habit of collecting many small specimens in matchboxes or other tiny containers—bits of dirt or lint, skin scrapings, hair, or harmless insects found by sufferers on their bodies or in their homes—is so typical of delusional parasitosis that it has a name: the "matchbox sign." But the samples look like pocket fluff to everyone else. "There is nothing there," others say. "This is bits of skin; that is shreds of facial tissue."

Another feature typical of the delusion is the determination to be rid of the parasites by any means necessary. Frantic sufferers dig and scrape at their skin, producing rashes and wounds. Some apply insecticides to their bodies, often in dangerously toxic amounts, burn their furniture, euthanize their pets, or abandon their homes and families.

Because individuals with delusional parasitosis cannot prove to others that their infestation is real, they often go from doctor to doctor and consult a variety of specialists—who, in turn, cannot prove that the infestation is *not* real. Often, patients become hostile toward health professionals, especially when told that they are mistaken or crazy.[7] About a quarter succeed in convincing someone other than a physician that the horrors are real. Then, the delusion becomes *folie à deux,* the madness of two.[8] The documented case of Marie Duval (a pseudonym) and her husband illustrates how destructive *folie à deux* can be.[9]

—

On an otherwise unremarkable day in 1967, Marie Duval (a pseudonym) went out in the small French village where she lived in search of her family doctor. She was not looking to consult him about a medical problem or to settle a bill—those days were over. Today she had a loaded hunting gun, and she intended to use it. Fortunately for the physician, the bullet went wide. Failure did not deter Duval, however: again, she took aim at the terrified man and fired. For the second time, she missed.

Duval hadn't slept for a week. She was tortured unbearably, day and night, by parasites that infested her skin and hair. No one would help her. No one believed her except her husband, Gilles. In fact, the couple believed that the doctor was scheming against her and turning others against her as well, making it impossible to get help. Moreover, they thought he was the perpetrator of the dreadful infestation. He refused to listen, refused to treat the parasites, refused to give her sleeping pills. His indifference was impossible to bear. She couldn't stand it any longer: she believed she had to kill him.

The nightmare had started years before, when Duval began noticing a crawling sensation in her skin and scalp. Hordes of tiny creatures seemed to be moving about on her, crawling and creeping invisibly under the surface and scurrying around the roots of her hair. She thought she could hear them moving when other noises didn't drown them out. She watched for them, studying herself in the mirror and scrutinizing her skin. Duval discovered that she *could* see them when she combed her hair—tiny insects that made a crawling noise. She eventually captured a few. She carefully imprisoned them in a matchbox and took them to her family doctor.

The doctor studied the contents of the matchbox and saw nothing but debris—perhaps a strand of hair and some bits of skin. He looked at her skin and at her scalp and hair and found nothing wrong, except a few small lesions where she had scraped at herself in an effort to catch the tiny invaders. Seeing nothing out of the ordinary, he told Duval there was nothing wrong with her.

Duval soon had more problems. She concluded that part of her discomfort came from a scabies mite infection that she had picked up from her pet cat.[10] Furthermore, she deduced that the scabies infection was part of a town epidemic; she believed that her neighbors and other townspeople had scabies infections and that the parasite was sure to keep spreading. Nobody listened to her.

Duval doubled her efforts to catch the tiny monsters so that she could prove to her doctor that they existed. She brought numerous small specimens in containers to his office for examination, but each time, he failed to find any parasites there. He did not believe that she had insects in her skin, and he didn't believe that she had scabies mites either.

Duval knew that she wasn't crazy: she could see the devils! They were crawling all over her! They were eating her alive. Surely the doctor should be able to see them too. Gilles knew they were there. Why wouldn't the doctor admit they were? Desperately, Duval turned elsewhere for help. She took her story to the police and to the mayor, but they also treated her as if she were crazy. For more than two years, Duval sought help. No one but her husband believed her.

When she ultimately tracked down her doctor and her shots went wide, Duval gave in to total frustration, rushing at the doctor with a stick and hitting him on the head until she was finally subdued. In short order, she was committed to a mental institution. The parasites went with her. Neither scabies mites nor any other parasite known to science, her attackers were tiny terrors that only she could see. Duval and her parasites would remain locked away for more than twenty-five years.

The typical delusional parasitosis sufferer is an older woman or a younger man. Often, the victim has a history of drug abuse, particularly cocaine use, or intense emotional stress. Marie Duval, for instance, had not had an easy life prior to the onset of her delusions and her subsequent attempt to kill her doctor.

Duval came from a poor French family and was barely literate. Her father had committed suicide by hanging himself when he was in his fifties, and her alcoholic mother had lived only to sixty-eight before dying of an undiagnosed form of dementia. Duval's husband was also an alcoholic and had been imprisoned in a German prisoner-of-war camp for five years during World War II. The couple had two daughters, who apparently caused their mother considerable trouble while they were growing up.

Duval's torment, then, came at the end of a long string of hardships. Many people have suffered delusional parasitosis after enduring much less:

the delusions can arise following retirement, loss of a spouse, leaving home, surviving a flood, or some other disturbing event. And the affliction has been plaguing people for a very long time: it was first described in medical literature in the late 1800s.[11]

In *folie à deux,* the victim of the phantom parasites usually has a strong, dominating personality, whereas the person who shares the delusion is emotionally weaker and may be highly sympathetic to others. When these empathetic sufferers are removed from the dominating person's influence, they generally recover.

Gilles Duval believed his wife when nobody else did, and he continued to threaten the doctor, even after she'd been hospitalized. Eventually, however, he realized that his wife had no parasites. There were no creeping, crawling insects. There was no plot. There was nothing in the matchboxes but bits of fluff and dead skin cells. The parasites were a delusion. For him, this realization put an end to the confusion.

⎯

If any real parasite could have caused Higgins's and Duval's suffering it would be the scabies mite, *Sarcoptes scabiei.* The name is legend, though the mite is relatively uncommon in the West. Anyone who has been imprisoned in a developing country, however, particularly in an overcrowded prison with scant medical attention and little opportunity for good hygiene, has probably met the beast. Even prisons in the developed world are subject to frequent outbreaks of this torturous mite. To understand why, you have to understand its lifestyle.

The adult female scabies mite, measuring slightly more than a tenth of an inch (about a third of a millimeter), looks like a pale gooseberry with eight tiny stubby legs, except that scabies mites are not striped as most gooseberries are. The mite is nearly circular when viewed from above, and her legs seem to poke straight out of the plump body, as though stuck on as an afterthought. Two pairs of legs are positioned close beside the small protruding head. The other two pairs are harder to spot because they poke out farther back from beneath the rounded body.

The female mite is a miner of skin. Jacking up her hind end with long bristles attached to the posterior pairs of legs, she chews her way headfirst through the skin and disappears in two or three minutes. She burrows and builds a long winding cave just beneath the surface; the tissue she tunnels through is her sustenance as well.

Once the mite goes down, she never comes back up, instead continuing to tunnel for up to two months. As she slowly proceeds, she leaves a trail of fecal pellets and eggs in the tunnel. Hatching in about a week, *Sarcoptes scabiei* larvae migrate to the surface, feeding on dead skin cells and oils as they go. The fecal pellets and the activities of the parasites cause an intense, unrelenting, notorious itch. Because the numerous larvae inevitably grow up and mate, producing more females to tunnel and produce eggs, a scabies infection doesn't clear up on its own, which explains why the infestation has been called the "seven-year itch." And because all the immature mites crawling about on the surface of the skin are easily brushed off onto other people, scabies is highly contagious in close quarters.

Scabies roars like a brushfire through prisons, crowded slums, extended-care institutions, armies, and even hospital wards. The very mention of scabies brings a wince to the faces of health care workers, social workers, and police officers, to name just a few. The mite's bad reputation bears some responsibility for the tragic death of Victoria Climbié in England, in 2000.[12]

Victoria Climbié was born in 1991 in the Republic of the Ivory Coast, a small coastal country in the western bulge of the African continent. At the age of seven, the little girl left the Ivory Coast with her great-aunt, Marie-Therese Kouao, who had convinced Climbié's parents that she could offer their daughter a better life in Europe. Sadly, they trusted the wrong person: instead of getting better, Victoria Climbié's life was about to get a lot worse.

Kouao got Climbié into Europe with a fake passport and changed the girl's name to Anna. The two started their life together in Paris, with Kouao using the child to claim welfare benefits from the French government. The scam didn't last long: soon, the French authorities began checking into Kouao and demanding money back. It was time to go. The woman and the little girl moved on, arriving in England in the spring of 1999.

In England, Kouao and Climbié moved into a hostel and, again, Kouao applied for benefits, which sustained the two until Kouao found employment as a cleaner. In June, the woman struck up a relationship with Carl Manning, a reclusive bus driver from the West Indies. She won him over quickly. The two became a couple, and by July, Kouao and Climbié had moved out of the hostel into Manning's small flat in North London. The arrangement proved disastrous for all three: Manning and Kouao began a campaign of escalating child abuse.

In mid-July 1999, Climbié's babysitter asked her daughter to take the child to Central Middlesex Hospital because of marks and abrasions on her skin and because Climbié was losing control of her bladder. The babysitter suspected that someone was abusing the girl, and her concerns were passed along to hospital staff. The two women did not inform Kouao of their intentions, and Climbié was in hospital hours before Kouao was told she was there.

When Kouao arrived, however, she explained away the suspicions of abuse: the girl had scabies, Kouao claimed, and she had been scratching and digging at herself; her skin wounds resulted from the mite infestation and the terrible discomfort it was causing. Climbié left the hospital with Kouao the following day with a diagnosis of scabies and instructions for treatment of the parasite. No one, apparently, took a sample to confirm the diagnosis.

Just nine days later, Climbié was back in hospital, this time North Middlesex Hospital, with scald injuries to her head and face. Again, Kouao claimed that the injury was self-inflicted: Climbié had poured hot water over her own head, Kouao said, to relieve the terrible itching of her scabies infection. Kouao's story was a bit far-fetched, and staff at the second hospital didn't accept it: the little girl was not only injured but malnourished and unkempt. Climbié was admitted to hospital.

Climbié remained in hospital almost two weeks, during which time nurses noticed that she ate as though she were starving and became incontinent whenever Kouao visited. Suspicion mounted. In the meantime, they received confirmation that scabies had indeed been diagnosed at her previous hospital visit, so again, the scabies infestation was accepted without laboratory confirmation. Then, somehow Victoria Climbié fell through the cracks again: despite the hospital staff's deep suspicions of abuse, the child was sent back home to Kouao and Manning.

Distressingly, though Climbié's case was reported to various authorities, no one made a serious or effective effort to intervene. A social worker and a policewoman who went to the house to check on the little girl received no answer at the door and later claimed that they were reluctant to return because they were afraid of catching scabies from her, or from the environment in the flat.

From August 1999 to February 2000, Victoria Climbié endured horrific abuse at the hands of Kouao and Manning. The girl was forced to sleep in the bathtub in an unheated bathroom, clad in nothing but a plastic bag because she was wetting the bed. Her hands and feet were bound with masking tape. Her toes were struck with a hammer, and she was beaten with belts, bicycle chains, and wire coat hangers. She was burned with cigarettes. She was not fed.

On February 24, 2000, the driver of a cab in which Climbié, Kouao, and Manning were passengers noticed that Climbié was unwell. He brought them to North Middlesex Hospital again. Climbié was starving and suffering from hypothermia: her body temperature was about 80.6°F (27°C). Her legs were tucked up in a permanently bent position, and her muscles were wasted, suggesting that she hadn't moved for many days. She was barely conscious. She was quickly transferred to a pediatric intensive care unit, but all efforts to help her failed. Victoria Climbié died the next afternoon. An autopsy report documented 128 separate external injuries to her body.

Climbié's death provoked a storm of outrage in England. Kouao and Manning both went to prison, social workers lost their jobs, and doctors were investigated for malpractice. People pointed fingers at the medical system, the child protection system, and the police. Critics of the system cited lack of government funding and racial prejudice as contributing factors in the little girl's death.

A statutory inquiry ordered by the U.K. secretaries of state for Health and the Home Department found no fewer than twelve instances in which Climbié might have been rescued and was not: in at least three of them, the tiny, nasty scabies mite was a scapegoat for the lack of action by those who could have helped. And the bitter truth is that she may never have had mites at all: no mite was ever properly identified. None were ever collected from her skin. It was not the mite itself but the reputation of the mite—its emotional impact—that held incredible power.

The murderous duo of Kouao and Manning prompts an uncomfortable return to the disorder known as *folie à deux*. At the time, what her guardians did to Climbié was given far more attention than why they did it. But the question is obvious. Why did they torture and starve an eight-year-old girl to death? What were they thinking?

Some features of the Climbié case are eerily reminiscent of *folie à deux*—not in the child but in the adults. Could Climbié have been the victim of delusional parasitosis, or *folie à deux* by proxy?[13] Kouao explained away the lesions and wounds on the girl's body by claiming they were caused by scabies. She claimed that Climbié poured scalding hot water over her head to rid herself of the mites. Though medical professionals accepted the scabies story, and Climbié was treated for scabies, there is considerable doubt that she ever had the parasites. Did Kouao believe in the mites? Did Manning?

Furthermore, Kouao and Manning both apparently believed that Climbié was possessed: their physical abuse of her reportedly was an effort to drive out the devil. Her problems with urinary incontinence and, later, fecal incontinence as well were evidence to them that she was controlled by evil spirits. Climbié made remarks to various adults suggesting that she was being controlled by witches or the devil—and at least one of those adults suspected that she had been coached to say these things.

Kouao and Manning asked for help at various churches, seeking a sort of exorcism in at least one fundamentalist church. In fact, they were apparently en route to another exorcism the day before Climbié died when the taxi driver redirected them to a medical facility.

Kouao was a bold and dominating person. She approached Climbié's parents and convinced them to send one of their children to France with her. She smuggled a child who was not her own across international borders using a fake passport and then applied for welfare benefits under false pretenses. And she insinuated herself into the life of the reclusive bus driver, Carl Manning, eventually moving herself and Climbié into his home.

After Climbié's death, Manning was like a man emerging from a trance. Once he was removed from the situation, and the overwhelming control of Kouao, he looked back on the events with horror. Unable to understand how he could have allowed the abuse to go on, he couldn't account for his thought processes during that time. In testimony at his trial for Climbié's murder, and at the public inquiry that followed, he said that he had been in a different frame of mind at the time—a frame of mind incomprehensible to him later. He revealed all the terrible details of Climbié's last months. He pleaded guilty and publicly apologized for his actions.

In contrast, Kouao denied everything, loudly and repeatedly, accusing Manning of lying and insisting that she had loved the little girl. Even when confronted with overwhelming evidence to support Manning's testimony, Kouao admitted no guilt and expressed no remorse. It wasn't her fault that Climbié had been controlled by the evil spirits, she said. The wounds weren't real. She had done everything she could: the child was healthy; the doctors at the hospital had killed her.

Whether or not we are willing to categorize demons and evil spirits as parasites (and they do fit the definition, though they cannot be collected and pickled in a jar), scabies certainly are parasites, and Marie-Therese Kouao and Carl Manning resemble Marie Duval and her husband, Gilles, closely enough that we might well ask whether the murderous pair had a deadly case of *folie à deux* and whether Victoria Climbié was a victim of delusional parasitosis by proxy.

———

Nasty as they are, scabies mites do not deserve such a damning reputation that we would go to any lengths to avoid them, even neglecting a child or abusing a fellow human being. Other creatures, such as lice and fleas, that creep and crawl around on our outsides are similarly maligned: they evoke such a feeling of revulsion that we tend to react out of all proportion to the threat. This reaction is probably because, in the West at least, we know we can get rid of them. In the twenty-first century, it's almost illegal to have them: they are evidence of neglect, or self-neglect, if they go untreated.

If we could transport a handful of people from medieval England into a crowd that has just heard the words *scabies* and *lice*, the new arrivals would wonder what all the fuss is about. In their day, everyone had lice. Lice were a good thing: in the eighteenth century, lice were thought to protect children against diseases, and as late as 1950, some people in England believed that a child who could support a hefty population of head lice must be quite healthy.[14]

Head lice are small but visible to the naked eye. The females grow to a little less than a tenth of an inch (about two millimeters) in length. Long and thin with six legs attached to the thorax and an extended abdomen, head lice look somewhat like tiny, pale amber wasps at first glance. Each hairpin leg ends with a wicked-looking sickle-shaped claw that can wrap around a hair and defeat the most rigorous attempts to shake the beast off. Wrapping left and right claws around a hair on each side, a louse can hang suspended like a high-wire gymnast preparing to do a somersault in midair.

Lice suck blood. They have teeth to chew through the outer protective layer of skin and then anchor themselves in place. Next, tiny stylets probe for a blood vessel, and the parasite pumps out a blood meal. Being fed upon by lice can have consequences for the host: the bites itch and the host scratches, leading to more irritation and sometimes infection. Lice are well known for transmitting nasty diseases too, although the body louse is the main culprit; head lice are not particularly famous as vectors of disease.[15]

Female head lice lay eggs like little cocoons with a trapdoor at one end. Each one is glued securely onto a hair, where it remains as an empty shell long after the newly hatched youngster departs through the opened trapdoor. The eggs, or nits, are visible to the naked eye, but they are tiny and hard to see clearly. They resemble specks of skin or other debris, but they can't be washed away. Secure on our heads, they have been with us since prehistoric times, and for most of that time, they haven't inspired much concern.

The colorful account of the death of Thomas Becket, archbishop of Canterbury, illustrates how acceptable it was to have multitudes of lice in medieval England. Born in 1118, Becket was the son of a successful English merchant, who became friends with King Henry II. King Henry wanted more control over the church, and he installed Becket as archbishop in 1162 with that objective in mind, but his plan didn't work. The two had a falling out.

In late December 1170, four knights, bent on doing King Henry a favor and probably hoping to advance their own social standing, confronted Becket in Canterbury Cathedral. Aided by a fifth assassin, they attempted to drag Becket out of the building, but he couldn't be budged. They brutally murdered him on the steps of the altar, spreading his blood and brains across the cathedral floor. He apparently offered no resistance, merely forbidding them to hurt any of the horrified onlookers. The assassins walked away in bloodied boots, leaving the archbishop's remains sprawled on the cold stone.[16]

Becket's remains lay in the cathedral until the following morning, when a group gathered to clean him up and prepare him for burial, and this is when Becket's lice stole the show. The body had cooled, sounding the eviction alarm for a multitude of the tiny parasites living in his numerous layers of clothing. A record of the exodus describes body lice "boil[ing] over like water in a simmering cauldron."[17]

Body lice are fussy about the temperature of their living quarters. They don't live on the host as head lice do, but remain in the clothing close to the body, laying their eggs on the fabric and visiting the skin only to feed. When the host dies, they soon get cold and go looking for warmer accommodations, a habit that, in Becket's day, made looting a body or preparing it for burial a good way to acquire a few more of them. This phenomenon inspired a verse by Gordon Bottomley a century ago:

Figure 18. A body louse,
Pediculus humanus corporis.
Photo by the author.

A louse crept out of my lady's shift—
Ahumm, Ahumm, Ahee—
Crying "Oi! Oi! We are turned adrift;
The lady's bosom is cold and stiffed,
And her arm-pit's cold for me."

"The lady's linen's no longer neat;"—
Ahumm, Ahumm, Ahee—
"Her savour is neither warm nor sweet;
It's close for two in a winding sheet,
And lice are too good for worms to eat;
So here's no place for me."

The louse made off unhappy and wet;—
Ahumm, Ahumm, Ahee—
He's looking for us, the little pet;
So haste, for her chin's to tie up yet,
And let us be gone with what we can get—
Her ring for thee, her gown for Bet,
Her pocket turned out for me.[18]

Bet may not have been one of those attending the lady's body, or pilfering her possessions, but she was undoubtedly the beneficiary of a good many body lice if she wore that gown!

Body lice are rare today, at least in the West, both because we wash our clothes frequently and because we wear fewer of them. In 1170, people wore their clothes for many days without removing them, much less washing them, and in winter they wore many layers to keep warm. Becket reportedly wore eight layers of clothing, including three woolen coats. It would have taken a while for his body heat to dissipate and his body lice to exit that textile labyrinth. The onlookers laughed and cried at the sight, but they did not think any less of their archbishop.

The four knights suffered disgrace, and King Henry II endured a flogging by eighty monks armed with branches as he walked through Canterbury dressed in sackcloth. In contrast, despite multiple layers of unwashed clothing and a notable population of body lice, Archbishop Becket was soon sainted. The endless stream of pilgrims traveling to his shrine at Canterbury was immortalized by Geoffrey Chaucer in *The Canterbury Tales* more than two centuries later.

Looking back through history before and after Becket's death, we find that humanity has consistently been kinder to lice than we are today.[19] Early Chinese physicians used a paste made from hundreds of lice to treat headache, and they had other lousy cures for fever, corns, and even ingrown eyelashes. Western physicians used lice to treat epilepsy, malaria, and toothaches. To cure jaundice, they recommended a dozen lice crushed in wine, and a particularly inventive treatment for urinary trouble involved introducing live lice into the urethra.

In sixteenth-century Mexico, the poor, who had nothing else to give, presented little bags of lice to their king as a tribute. Northern Siberian maidens threw lice at the men they desired. Not surprisingly, given all these varied uses for lice, indigenous folk of many parts of the world have also been known to eat them, some even going to the trouble of cooking them first.

Even today, a louse has its uses. Research has shown that the DNA of a person who has been fed upon by lice can be identified in the parasites many hours after the bite. When lice feed on two people successively, DNA analysis of the remains of the blood meal will show a mixture of the two individuals' DNA profiles. This technology might help confirm close contact between two individuals, such as a rapist and victim or kidnapper and prisoner.

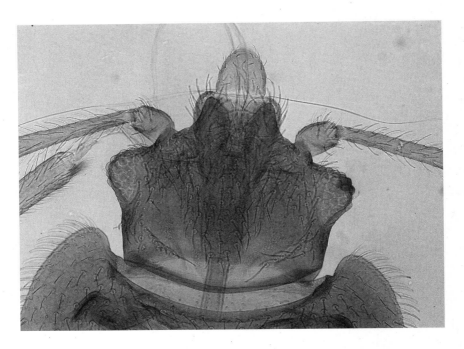

Figure 19. The head of a bedbug, *Cimex lectularius*. Photo by the author.

Similar investigations have focused on other blood-sucking parasites, particularly the bedbug. The adult bedbug is only about a fifth of an inch (five millimeters) long. If you met one under your pillow, it would look a bit like a drab, flat ladybug the color of dried blood. Magnified to many times its actual size, it would display a body covered with bristles, six hairy legs sticking out to the sides, a round head with bulging raspberry-shaped eyes, and a snout like Andy Capp's.

The bulbous snout houses a feeding tube that probes in the skin until it pierces a blood vessel. Another tube injects saliva loaded with anticoagulants to prevent the blood from clotting, and the bug takes its meal. It feeds more slowly than the mosquito, taking about eight minutes to finish the job. The irritation caused by its bite, however, can last much longer. To bedbugs' credit, they don't appear to transmit diseases.

Robert Buckman calls bedbugs "the cat burglars of the parasite world."[20] They come in the night, often just before dawn, feed, and disappear without being detected. They go back to their hiding places—creases in the bedding and mattress, crevices in the bed frame and night table, spaces under the edges of carpets. If the bedbug you meet under your pillow is a female and she gets away (the bugs can run quite quickly), she will produce hundreds of eggs in her lifetime, and the young nymphs will all feed on you if you are the only one sleeping in the bed.

If you sleep away from home in a bug-infested room, your blood and with it your DNA will remain when you leave, and if, for any reason, you don't want anyone to know where you slept, that reminder of your presence could be a bad thing. Like lice, bedbugs have the DNA of the people they have bitten in their stomach contents, and scientists have been able to identify the DNA of individuals from that source.

Like lice, bedbugs acquired their bad reputation rather recently. At one time, having a healthy population of bedbugs available was the equivalent of a well-stocked medicine cabinet. Two millennia ago, the insects were highly valued in Western medicine as a treatment for malaria: the afflicted took seven of them with beans before a malarial paroxysm struck. The same medicine minus the beans was used to treat the victim of a viper bite, and mixed with tortoise blood, bedbugs were believed to eradicate warts. Ironically, a mixture of crushed bedbugs and egg, presumably raw, was used to treat nausea. In China, a slightly less nauseating mixture—ten bedbugs soaked in good white wine—was used to alleviate choking.

Today, if a Western physician were to treat malaria or snakebite with bedbugs, a malpractice suit would probably soon follow, but if the many historical uses of bedbugs seem like bad medicine, they pale beside an ancient use for flies and maggots: the people of ancient Persia (present-day Iran) needed maggots for "the punishment of the boats."

The punishment of the boats was a form of capital punishment in which the perpetrator of an offense was essentially eaten alive. The particulars in one example, a fatal case of sibling rivalry, were recorded by the classical philosopher and writer Plutarch.[21] This drama began with the death of the Persian king Darius II in 404 B.C.

Darius had two sons. The elder, Artaxerxes, assumed the throne after his father's death, becoming Artaxerxes II. As often happens, Artaxerxes' younger brother, Cyrus, frequently referred to as Cyrus the Younger, wasn't happy with the arrangement. He too wanted to rule, and he plotted to murder his brother and seize the throne.

Cyrus had their mother, Parysatis, on his side, and when his plot failed, Parysatis interceded with Artaxerxes on his behalf. Cyrus escaped punishment and promptly made himself scarce, relocating to Sardis (in present-day Turkey), where he began plotting anew.

In the spring of 401 B.C., Cyrus set out from Sardis with an army to depose Artaxerxes. He had kept his intentions so secret that even his soldiers didn't know where they were going or why. It's hard to miss an approaching army, however, and Artaxerxes met his brother at Cunaxa, a town near the Euphrates River. A battle ensued. Ultimately, Cyrus broke through the bodyguard of Artaxerxes and was set to win, but at the crucial moment Cyrus was fatally wounded by a young Persian defender named Mithridates.

Artaxerxes took credit for Cyrus's death, bribing and bullying Mithridates into silence, but one evening when Mithridates had celebrated too long and consumed too much wine, the truth came out: he was the one who had killed Cyrus, he announced, not the king. His drunken boast was a big mistake. Artaxerxes was infuriated, and he condemned Mithridates to the punishment of the boats.

"The boats" were designed to fit together like a clamshell, forming an enclosed prison with openings for the hands, feet, and head. The condemned Mithridates was laid on his back in the lower boat, and the second boat was lowered over him. As he lay unable to move, day after day, he was always positioned so that the sun shone directly on his face.

Mithridates was fed every day, and a drink made of milk and honey was forcefully poured down his throat. If he refused to eat or drink, his tormentors tortured him by pricking his eyes until he cooperated. They did not make him drink all of the milk and honey, however: some of it was saved and smeared over his face. The sticky mixture, along with sweat, feces, and urine building up in the boat, attracted a great many flies in the hot Middle Eastern sun. The flies fed, and having found a good food supply for their young, laid eggs in the boat and on Mithridates' skin. Days passed, and multitudes of flies visited the prisoner in the boats, leaving masses of eggs.

The maggots fed as soon as they hatched. Inside the boat, they swarmed over Mithridates, consuming all the food they could find. Where his skin broke open in the heat and filth, they fed not only on the milk and honey and excrement but on his flesh as well. Mithridates' daily ration of food and drink and the sweet mixture regularly applied to his face ensured a steady food supply for flies and maggots. His suffering would only get worse.

Mithridates survived the hellish torture for seventeen days, and in the end he must have welcomed death. Afterward, Artaxerxes had the upper boat lifted to reveal the remains. The friend who had delivered him from the murderous Cyrus had been half consumed; his corpse boiled with maggots.

The Persians were not the only people to use flies and maggots to deliver torture and punishment: history records similar examples in other parts of the Middle East, and even among the Spaniards in the West Indies. However, given the multiple personalities of other parasites such as tapeworms, lice, and bedbugs, we should not be surprised to learn that maggots have another side—a silver intestinal lining.

Physicians through the centuries have noticed that when some wounds become infested with maggots, they heal faster and the patient is less likely to succumb to infection. Ambroise Paré, a barber-surgeon who treated the wounded after the 1557 battle of Saint-Quentin in France, took note of the amazing recovery of a patient whose wound was both serious and maggot ridden.[22] Dominique-Jean Larrey, a surgeon in Napoleon's army in Egypt, noted similar apparently miraculous recoveries.

Larrey identified the relationship between maggots and recovery but left the arrival of the diminutive healers to chance and even removed them for aesthetic reasons when they did appear, a frequent occurrence in Egypt. John Forney Zacharias, a physician in the Confederate army in the American Civil War, took the next intuitive step and deliberately introduced maggots into dirty, festering battle wounds. The maggots consumed all the dead tissue before dropping out to pupate, leaving clean healthy tissue to heal.

Most fly maggots that infest wounds consume dead tissue and tissue that is breaking down, as in the case of the tortured Mithridates. Many do not invade healthy tissue, which is why they are so useful in cleaning up infected wounds and ulcers. They eat only the tissue that needs to be removed, and they appear to produce secretions that fight off infection in the wound. Before the days of antibiotics, they were a boon to medicine.

It took another war to bring maggot therapy into its own: World War I produced another wave of dirty, infected, untended wounds, and another group of intuitive physicians who noticed what maggots could do for a wound. From then until antibiotics came on the scene, medicinal maggots were commonly used. Today, with the increasing problem of bacterial resistance to antibiotics, the use of medicinal maggots is once again on the rise, and maggots are available commercially in the United States and other countries for treatment of stubborn unhealing wounds and ulcers.

Even the much-reviled parasitic worm is regaining some respect, if not popularity. Apparently, playing host to the occasional worm can actually protect us from other diseases, particularly those that cause our immune systems to turn against us and make us ill: allergies and autoimmune diseases.

Evidence for the proposed benefits of worm infestation comes from two directions. First, allergies and autoimmune diseases are much more common in developed, industrialized countries, and within these populations they tend to be more common in people who don't have high exposure to things like dirt and farm animals—people who are less likely to be exposed to parasites. Second, research with animals shows that helminth infection does alter the immune response, and numerous accounts now exist of people who have successfully treated disease with worms. Hookworms have found use in treating hay fever and asthma. *Trichuris suis,* the whipworm of pigs, has helped patients with inflammatory bowel disease achieve remission. People with multiple sclerosis tend to have milder disease if they also have worms.[23]

Perhaps the easiest way to ease oneself toward acceptance of this idea is to take our parasites back into the house of mirrors and try to see them in an entirely new way. Some of our parasites, the ones whose ancestors lived in our prehuman ancestors, the ones that evolved right along with us, have *always* been with us, though infestations in hunter-gatherers were likely to be light. With the advent of good sanitation and antiparasitic drugs in the West, we've been forced to live without them for the first time in history, and we're just beginning to realize how much we miss them.

The current theory on why being worm free could be a bad thing examines the way that human immune systems respond to organisms in the environment. We encounter some organisms consistently: things that live on our skin and in our mouths, intestines, and genital tracts; and bacteria and fungi common in the air and soil or found in foods and in water. Because these things are very common, our immune systems have evolved to ignore them. Before sanitation and food inspection, parasitic worms were common as well.

Worm infestations are also long-term host-parasite relationships. A powerful immune reaction would be necessary to evict an adult worm—a reaction so strong that it would do considerable damage to host tissues at the same time. Indeed, some of the worst effects of parasitic infestations are due to the body's attempts to get rid of the invaders. Our immune systems, fortunately, have evolved to refrain from launching self-damaging attacks on our "old friends," the worms that evolved with us.[24] Immunologically, we've learned to tolerate them.

Research has shown that when the human immune system is exposed to parasitic "old friends," an unexpected thing happens. Immune cells are activated whose function is to suppress, or dampen, the activities of other immune cells. Among those suppressed are the cells that would react strongly to the parasite, as well as others involved with allergies and autoimmune diseases—conditions in which the immune system goes into action when it shouldn't. In allergy, the body reacts to things in the environment that are harmless. In autoimmune disease, it attacks and destroys its own tissues.

The theory is that when we are not exposed to worms, our immune systems don't receive the training they need to act appropriately, and they overreact. An extension of this theory suggests that allergies and autoimmune diseases are the result of defects in our immune systems—defects that have been hidden by parasites all this time but are now free to make our lives miserable. The diseases that may be eased by exposure to parasitic worms include allergies, Crohn's disease, inflammatory bowel disease, multiple sclerosis, atherosclerosis, Alzheimer's disease, Parkinson's disease, certain cancers, and even some psychiatric disorders.

The medieval people who counted on head lice to protect them from disease might justifiably nod to each other: "We told you so." They'd be further gratified to learn that recent research with wild mice and their lice suggests that lice have the same benefits: they somehow regulate the immune system so that it doesn't attack when it shouldn't.

In light of these revelations, we can imagine allergy and autoimmune disease sufferers of today, as well as those who favor preventive medicine, deliberately setting out to become infested with parasites. In fact, such services are already offered: "helminthic [parasitic worm] therapy" is available in some places for those who can afford it, and researchers in this field have no trouble finding volunteer subjects. One day we may all take a supplement along with our vitamins—a pill to make our immune systems think we have worms.

SEVEN

The Parasite Felonies

Some circumstantial evidence is very strong, as when you find a
trout in the milk.

HENRY DAVID THOREAU
Journal

FORENSIC PARASITOLOGY IS A DISCIPLINE that doesn't exist in any
formal sense. Unlike the insects of interest in forensic entomology, which
are virtually certain to arrive in a more or less predictable fashion whenever there is an exposed corpse—and thus provide important information
about a crime—parasites become involved in crime in wildly unpredictable ways.[1] They may be red herrings, as in the case of Victoria Climbié,
instruments of torture and capital punishment in the hands of ancient
Persian kings, or imaginary masterminds of political assassinations—but
such opportunities are rare.

Occasionally a crime investigator stumbles on a parasite and grasps its
significance. Likewise, the occasional individual or group may attempt to
use a parasite to do harm. The difficulty—and the beauty—of these
human insights lies in the particularity of parasites. Lacking the right host,
the right environment, or the right opportunities, the parasite falls flat.
Thus, a parasite can provide specific information and insert a fascinating
twist into an already unusual situation.

On an August day in 1982, all was quiet in Ventura County, California.[2]
An abandoned car in a roadside meadow baked in the sun, while all

around it wild oats bowed in a gentle breeze. At the edge of the field stood a tall eucalyptus tree casting a wide circle of shade beneath its spreading branches. Around the roots of the tree and beyond, the ground began to rise and the oats gave way to a thick ground cover of brushy native plants.

Eventually, the deserted car attracted attention. A search-and-rescue team was called in to conduct a ground search of the area. The team began its search late in the day on August 5, combing the tall wild oats in the field and searching in the brush on the slope and around the tree. In such situations, searchers hope to find someone in need of assistance, or perhaps even no one at all, but they are always prepared for the worst.

The team did not have to search long. The remains of a young woman lay in the shade of the eucalyptus tree, poorly concealed under a heap of brush and grass. She had been dead for several days. When the search-and-rescue team found her, the sun was already setting, and homicide experts had yet to arrive on the scene. As a result, the corpse remained under the tree for one more night.

Police removed the body the following day and requested a complete autopsy. Meanwhile, detectives combed the site for evidence. The detective in charge of the case searched for anything that might help identify a murder suspect, sifting through the brush where the murderer had gathered plant material. As he disturbed the growth at the margin of the field, the detective unknowingly picked up a crucial clue. In fact, he didn't know he possessed information—evidence that would lead to a conviction—until twenty-four hours after he left the murder scene.

The autopsy revealed the imprint of fabric on the victim's neck, evidence of blows to the head, and sperm cells in the vagina. She had been beaten, raped, and strangled. The evidence also told investigators that her final moments had played out in the field under the eucalyptus tree. She was soon identified as a young woman who had last been seen on the evening of August 3, two days before her body was discovered.

On August 6, a suspect was brought in for questioning. He was a man with a history of sexual assault, and he admitted that he had been with the victim on the evening of August 3. He denied any knowledge of her death, however, and denied having been to the field where her remains were found. Police suspected that he was lying but couldn't be sure: they had no evidence linking him to the murder scene. The detective who questioned the suspect also examined him physically and noticed that he had a number of lesions that appeared to be insect bites on his buttocks and lower torso. The bites were clearly very itchy: the suspect had scratched them raw.

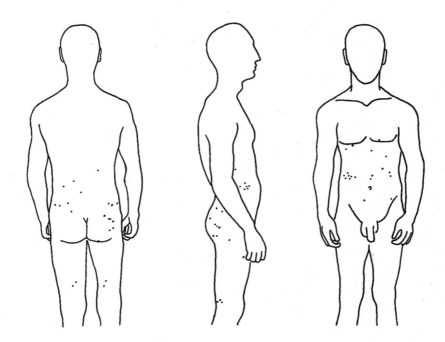

Figure 20. The pattern of bites found on the murder suspect. From J. G. Prichard, P. D. Kossoris, R. A. Leibovitch, L. D. Robertson, and F. W. Lovell, 1986, "Implications of Trombiculid Mite Bites: Report of a Case and Submission of Evidence in a Murder Trial," *Journal of Forensic Sciences* 31 (1): 304, figure 3. © 1986 ASTM Int'l. Reproduced with permission of Blackwell Publishing Ltd.

The next day, the detective in charge of the investigation woke up to find that he had been bitten by something. A large number of raised, irritated red bites had appeared overnight. They were clustered on both hips, one bunch under the place where his gun holster normally pressed against him and another bunch on the other hip well below the waist, under his uniform. He also found bites on his legs just below the point where the tops of his boots would be. Curiously, he had no bites where his skin was usually exposed. The bites were maddeningly itchy; he could not resist the urge to scratch.

The experience wasn't new to this detective. He had suffered the bites of chigger mites in another state, and he wondered if the same creature, or at least a close relative of it, had bitten him this time.

Chigger mites are the larval form of trombiculid mites—mites that prey on invertebrates such as snails and earthworms and do not trouble people. Only the larvae are parasitic on humans, and then only by accident. In the normal course of events, chiggers hang about in low vegetation in tight little patches and climb onto passing reptiles, amphibians, rodents, or birds. They climb onto human skin when the human is unfortunate enough to go wading through brush, bramble, or damp marshy growth where they lurk.

A chigger is too small to be seen without a good magnifying glass, but if you could see it, you would probably mistake it for a minute tick. It is mostly body, a broad oval body that appears far too large and heavy to be dragged around by the six slender, segmented legs provided for its transportation. Adult trombiculids are more attractive, with eight legs and a velvety red or yellow coat. At about four-hundredths of an inch (a millimeter) in length, adults are visible to the naked eye.

Unlike ticks, chiggers do not suck blood, nor do they burrow into the skin like scabies mites. Using their mouthparts, they scrape through the outer layers of skin and inject enzyme-rich saliva into the tissue beneath. The enzymes break down the tissue, producing liquid food. The human immune system's first response is to partition off the bite site, which results in a hard tube through which the larva can continue to draw food. Subsequent immune response by the body causes the intense itching that makes chiggers so unpopular. Undisturbed, they'll remain feeding for several days, but human hosts, driven to distraction by the itching, usually scratch them off.

The pattern of bites on the murder suspect, and on the detective who searched the murder scene, was typical of chiggers. The tiny larvae prefer to wedge themselves into tight spaces so that they have something to brace themselves against while they gnaw through skin. Thus, bites tend to occur where clothing presses against skin: at waistbands, the tops of socks or boots, around the hips, under a gun holster, or anywhere else where clothing is tight.

The bites on the two men matched as well. They were between one- and two-tenths of an inch (about four millimeters) across, red, and raised. Bites that had not been scratched had a vesicle in the center, like a tiny fluid-filled blister. Bites that had been scratched were crusted over and had turned purplish, like little bruises. They were typical chigger bites. The lesions on the murder suspect appeared to be about two days older than those on the detective.

The investigators had only one problem: chiggers were not present in Ventura County, or so local entomologists believed. No one had ever reported a case of chiggers attacking a human there. To prove the bites were the work of chiggers, police needed the chiggers themselves. Entomologists were recruited to go back to the field and search for trombiculid larvae beneath the eucalyptus tree and in the surrounding brush.

The search was a success. Scientists collected chigger larvae from the local lizards, mice, and wood rats, and, after moving about in the brush, they found chigger larvae on their own bodies, preparing to feed. This isolated, heavily infested patch of chigger mites was in a place the pests had never been seen before. The entomologists identified the mites as *Eutrombicula belkini,* a species that was known to attack humans in other parts of California and that had been identified just once before in Ventura County—from a reptile in 1950.

If the mites had been more common in Southern California, the trial of the suspect might have turned out differently, but, as effectively as footage from a hidden camera, the chiggers placed the suspect at the scene, a place he had denied ever being. The fact that *E. belkini* was so rare in Ventura County made it highly unlikely that he had been bitten anywhere else. Moreover, the apparent age of the bites when he was examined placed him at the scene at the correct time to have been the killer. The verdict was "guilty."

The way that *E. belkini* larvae insinuated themselves into this crime was stunningly bad luck for the murderer and pure serendipity for law enforcement. Neither side could have predicted the sequence of events. This case wasn't the first time, however, that a parasite linked a murderer to his victim, and to a crime scene. A much earlier case involved none other than Joseph Jones, the same man who investigated the deadly diarrhea epidemic at the Confederate prison camp at Andersonville but missed the hookworm (see chapter 4). In 1876, the professor missed another opportunity to discover an important parasite, but he recognized its calling card and identified the perpetrator with it nonetheless.[3]

In 1876, Donaldsonville, Louisiana, was a small community on the banks of the Mississippi River. At the edge of town sat the little one-story house and general store of Narcisse Arrieux. The building faced the river, protected from the unpredictable whims of the waterway by the riverside road and a wide levee. Not far away, behind the dwelling, lay extensive mosquito-ridden wetlands. The store took up the front part of the house, and Arrieux lived in the back in two smaller rooms.

On the evening of December 27, 1876, sometime after 9 P.M., four burly men came into the store, where Arrieux minded the counter alone. They asked for liquor, but when Arrieux turned away to fill the order, one of the men picked up a heavy iron weight that lay on the countertop and struck the storekeeper on the head. As Arrieux staggered from the blow, the other three men joined in the attack. They beat him with iron weights and with a short hickory branch with a lead knob on the end that one of the men produced from inside his clothing.

With Arrieux incapable of further resistance, the assailants robbed the man and left. Their victim lay on the floor near the counter in an expanding pool of blood. He had multiple head wounds, and blood was pooling inside his skull, pressing on his brain. His skull was so severely fractured that pieces of bone protruded through his scalp. Lead weights lay about, matted with blood and hair. One, hurled at the dying man, had gone wide and smashed through the back window into the yard outside.

Though mortally injured, Arrieux was still alive. As blood flowed freely from his head wounds, the pressure in his brain was relieved and he regained consciousness. He managed to stand up and get to the door and lock it. Then he stumbled and staggered around the store and his two private rooms, holding onto the furniture and walls for support, leaving a heavy trail of blood everywhere he went.

The blood of Narcisse Arrieux—splattered and drying on the floor, the bed, the desks, and running down the front door, the door posts, and the walls—was the usual mix of red and white blood cells and plasma, but it contained something else as well. Within many of the red cells, a more unusual cell was hiding. Tiny organisms, wisps of nebulous cytoplasm, spread out and grew, feeding on the hemoglobin in Arrieux's red blood cells and dumping their waste products inside the cell; malaria parasites were at home in his red blood cells. Though invisible, they too were splattered around the inside of the store, dying as the blood clotted and dried through the night.

Arrieux checked the condition of the store and rooms and looked in his desk to see if money had been stolen. He spread newspapers on the floor and had a bowel movement. He even tried to start a fire. Then he simply sat down in a chair near the stove and died. As his body stiffened, his unbalanced weight tipped the chair, and his body was discovered the following morning, lying crookedly on top of it.

The police of Donaldsonville were quick to make an arrest: on December 28, they apprehended four suspects in the murder. One of them, Wilson Childers, had suspicious red patches on his wool coat and his shirt. Were they bloodstains? Childers claimed the spots were red paint from a freshly painted whiskey barrel, but the police had doubts. Pieces of fabric were cut from the left breast of the shirt and the left sleeve of the coat so that the stains could be analyzed and identified.

Neither an expert microscopist nor an adequate microscope was available in Donaldsonville, so the police sent five pieces of fabric to New Orleans for analysis. The samples were taken to Joseph Jones, then professor of chemistry and clinical medicine at the University of Louisiana in New Orleans. Jones was an acknowledged expert on blood, particularly the blood of malaria patients.

In the southern United States of the 1800s, warm evenings and early mornings regularly brought the steady whine of hungry mosquitoes from low-lying swamps and wetlands into human communities. The insects entered homes through open doors and windows, hid in cool corners and cupboards, and when an unsuspecting human wandered near, the bloodsuckers struck. People knew, of course, that mosquitoes were an irritating nuisance, but they did not know that the insects spread malaria and other diseases, including yellow fever. Scientists had not yet figured out how these diseases spread from one person to another.

Jones had seen lots of blood from malaria victims. He had probably seen the tiny parasites themselves, living inside red blood cells, without realizing what they were.[4] Also unidentified was malaria pigment, the waste products of *Plasmodium* spp. that are visible in the blood once the organisms have passed their earliest stages. Jones didn't know what malaria pigment was, but he could see it, and he knew it was unique to the blood of malaria sufferers.

Jones examined the fabric samples and conducted some tests, quickly confirming that the stains were blood and that the blood was human. He was also able to tell the police that the stains came from an individual who was suffering from malaria, or had suffered from it very recently. He could say this with absolute certainty because he saw the typical black specks of pigment in the blood on Childers's clothing.

Later, investigators asked Jones to analyze two pieces of wood, one of mahogany and one of cedar, that had been cut out of two bloodstained

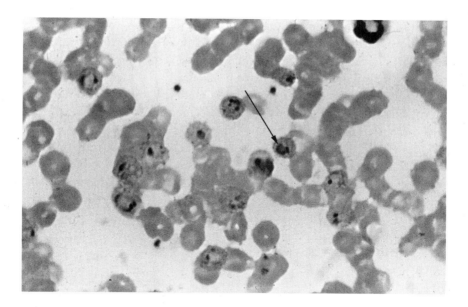

Figure 21. *Plasmodium vivax* in human blood. The arrow points to a clump of malarial pigment. Photo by the author.

desks at the store. He also visited the grisly murder scene at the little store by the river and examined other bloodstains. In each case, he found the same thing: blood from a person with malaria.

In late May 1878, Jones testified at the trial of Wilson Childers and the three other accused men. He recounted in detail how he had determined that the stains on Childers's clothing were blood rather than paint and explained how he could tell that the blood was human. A witness for the prosecution, he described "abnormal substances observed in connection with the colored and colorless or white blood corpuscles; black pigment or melanemic particles . . . in masses of various sizes. . . . Many of the particles . . . were spherical, others irregular and angular, some entirely free, others incased in a hyaline mass," which told him that the blood came from someone with malaria.[5] He produced the pieces of wood from the two desks in the shop and demonstrated that they fit precisely into the holes left in the desks, which had been brought to the courthouse for that purpose.

The police in Donaldsonville had not been aware of Arrieux's illness until Jones recognized the telltale specks in the blood on Childers's clothing and made the diagnosis. In independent testimony, two other physicians confirmed that Narcisse Arrieux had indeed been ill with malaria and that he had been battling it for some weeks prior to his death. The testimony of Jones and the other two physicians established a link between the accused and the victim, and, combined with other damning testimony, helped ensure that the four accused men were convicted. All four were sentenced to death by hanging.

Jones wrote about his experiences in detail, an indication of how unusual the case was.[6] The parasite's role was, in fact, so subtle that it might easily have been missed. If we were to predict how malaria might expose a criminal, we'd probably imagine it causing incapacitating illness, preventing escape, or forcing its victim to seek medical attention. In 1999, malaria apparently did provide such a clue, and if the theory is true, the parasite may have saved a lot of lives.

———

Sometime between April and December of 1998, a mosquito took a blood meal from a young man in eastern Afghanistan, injecting him with the sporozoites of a malaria parasite.[7] Not from Afghanistan, the man's background was murky: he carried a Canadian passport and spoke with an Algerian accent. The name on his passport was Benni Antoine Noris.

Noris had entered Afghanistan from Pakistan in April through the Khyber Pass, a centuries-old trade route that rises to 3,500 feet (1,067 meters) above sea level through the rugged and dusty Safed Koh Mountains. The steep-sided pass is the shortest route from Peshawar in Pakistan to Kabul in Afghanistan. It has long been a route for both smugglers and the military, and those who cannot get through in vehicles go through the hills with donkey trains.

During his stay in Afghanistan, Noris spent time in al-Qaida terrorist training camps, learning the essentials of hand-to-hand combat, self-defense, and hand weapons. He also reportedly studied bomb building, sabotage, assassination, and the means to destroy infrastructure such as airports, military bases, and utilities. In January 1999, he emerged from Afghanistan a trained terrorist, one of five Algerians instructed to form a cell in Montreal and to launch a terrorist attack on the United States. The group hoped to have the attack coincide with the millennium—January 1, 2000.

Noris and the other members of the team traveled separately, intending to enter Canada by different routes. They planned to meet again in Montreal and begin to put their plot together. That meeting never happened: Noris was the only one of the five to get into Canada without being detained. Unknown to him, however, he did not travel alone. He brought the instrument of his own failure with him: a quiescent case of malaria that would flare up at just the right time to prevent him from committing a heinous crime.

After returning to Canada, Noris carried on alone. He cobbled together a new team recruited from untrained associates and planned to build a bomb, take it across the border into the United States, and detonate it in Los Angeles International Airport on the eve of the millennium. His new team helped with assembling the bomb components and provided him with money; an accomplice in the United States would help him plant the device. The task of transporting the bomb across the border was his alone.

As the millennium approached, Noris still did not know he had malaria. The disease often hides for six months before causing the first malarial paroxysm, and in rare cases, it waits a year or even longer. Thus, not until Noris left Montreal in November 1999 did he begin feeling ill with flulike symptoms.

Noris and an accomplice, Abdelmajid Dahoumane, met in Vancouver and assembled the bomb in the back bedroom of a motel bungalow. The chemical brews they were working with created noxious toxic fumes that caused headaches and sore throats; though the December air was chilly, they had to leave the windows open to avoid breathing too much of the poisonous air inside. Noris may have believed that all of his symptoms were caused by the chemical exposure. He struggled on, using painkillers and antiseptic throat spray. Meanwhile, *Plasmodium* sp. was multiplying in his blood and destroying red blood cells.

On December 14, preparations were complete. The men packed the bomb components into the spare-tire compartment of a rented Chrysler 300M sedan and caught a ferry to Vancouver Island. They parted there, and Noris boarded a second ferry from Victoria to the American port of Port Angeles, Washington. The U.S. immigration inspector at the ferry terminal on the Canadian side was suspicious of Noris, but he found no specific reason to detain him. The ferry left Canada less than ten minutes later.

When the ferry docked less than two hours later, U.S. customs officials were waiting. Noris's rented Chrysler was the last car off the boat. When he pulled up at the customs checkpoint, the inspector, Diana Dean, saw a slim, uneasy-looking driver: on this chilly December evening, the man couldn't seem to sit still. He was sweating and fidgety. Dean suspected he was nervous and described him as acting "hinky." She asked him to get out of the car.

Moments later, Noris made the customs staff even more suspicious when he handed a Costco shoppers card to inspector Mark Johnson instead of a valid piece of identification. At least four inspectors surrounded him now, and they proceeded to search his pockets, the items in the trunk of the car, and the contents of the spare-tire compartment. They soon discovered the bomb materials, though they did not immediately realize what they had found. Noris ran.

The frantic terrorist did not get far. Hoping to evade his pursuers, he rolled under a parked truck but was discovered. After crawling out from under the truck, he fled again, running into the street. He must have known his energy was flagging, and he had no hope of outrunning the customs officials: he tried to commandeer a passing car, but the driver accelerated and threw him off. His pursuers jumped on him. He did not escape again.

U.S. officials learned that Noris's real name was Ahmed Ressam and that he was an Algerian immigrant to Canada who had initially entered the country in 1994, using false French documents, under the name Tahar Medjadi. When customs officials discovered the fraud, he concocted a tale of imprisonment and torture in Algeria and played the Canadian immigration system. He was allowed to stay in Canada and to request status as a political refugee. Medjadi/Ressam collected social assistance for a time and then supported himself by shoplifting, stealing from tourists, and peddling stolen passports, credit cards, and other documents. He was caught several times, but each time, Canadian judges released him.

By 1998, Ressam was deeply involved with other Algerians in the Montreal area who were connected to terrorist groups, including Osama bin Laden's al-Qaida. He heard about the al-Qaida training camps in Afghanistan and wanted to go there, but he was a known criminal, and he was being sought by Canadian authorities for immigration violations. He needed a new identity.

Ressam broke into a Montreal church, stole a baptismal certificate, forged the necessary signatures on it, and gave himself a new past. He used the fake document to obtain a valid Canadian passport and officially became Benni Antoine Noris. Though Canadian authorities were looking for Ressam, they lost track of him from that moment until he showed up in Port Angeles with fake identification and a case of malaria.

What made him so fidgety and sweaty that night? Surely Ressam, a seasoned criminal and trained terrorist who had used false documents many times, would not have lost his composure at this last critical road-block. He had been living as an illegal immigrant, sneaking across inter-national borders, committing petty crimes, telling lies, and participating in terrorist activity for years. He should have been calm and steady. He handled the customs inspector at the ferry boarding without difficulty, but Port Angeles was a different matter.

A credible theory suggests that *Plasmodium* sp., which had been hiding in Ressam's liver finally started multiplying to vast numbers in his blood. Myriad red blood cells burst, releasing merozoites and setting off a malar-ial paroxysm as he arrived in Port Angeles. As he drove off the ferry in Port Angeles, with enough explosives stuffed in his trunk to blow a huge hole in Los Angeles International Airport and in the millennium celebra-tions of millions, he must have been feeling wretched: he would have been exhausted, confused, and dripping with sweat. For Ressam, the timing was deadly. After all his plotting and secrecy, the parasites simply handed him over to the authorities.[8]

While Ressam awaited trial, he earned yet another name: "the millen-nium bomber." Soon, he began cooperating with U.S. intelligence, pro-viding investigators with information about other terrorists and groups he had been involved with. In April 2001, a U.S. federal court convicted Ressam of plotting to commit an act of terrorism. He faced a possible sentence of 130 years. Sentencing was delayed, however, in the hope that he would provide even more information, and by the time he was sen-tenced in July 2005, he had apologized for his actions and renounced terrorism. Recognizing his good conduct and cooperation, Judge John Coughenour sentenced him to a reduced prison term of 22 years.

What would have happened if Ressam hadn't been apprehended in Port Angeles? Would he have been able to plant his bomb successfully? We'll never know, but his arrest and the information on terrorist cells that he has provided have likely had a significant ripple effect in the twenty-first century. Though we can't thank malaria for much that's good, perhaps we can thank the parasite for delivering Ressam into authorities' hands.

Still, malaria fingered Ressam by chance rather than by design: literally, the parasite was in the right place at the right time. Engineering such an event would be difficult, which is why parasites are so rarely used as weapons—but they have been used.

——

On October 4, 1940, a Japanese plane flew low over Chekiang Province south of Shanghai, China, and very soon rats in the town of Chuhsien discovered an increase in their food supply: it was raining rice and wheat.[9] The rats, eager to exploit an opportunity, came out to feed, and when they did, they encountered a parasite that troubles rats everywhere—the rat flea. The fleas, of course, were the real payload, with the grain thrown in to bring the rats. And even the fleas were more than they appeared to be. They were parasites carrying deadly bacteria: *Yersinia pestis,* the agent of the black death, or plague.

Although humans have their own fleas, *Y. pestis* is most often transmitted to humans by the Oriental rat flea, *Xenopsylla cheopis,* parasite of the black rat, *Rattus rattus.* When an infected flea bites a human, it transmits the *Y. pestis* bacteria. The bacteria settle into lymph nodes in the armpit, groin, or neck, causing swellings called buboes. This is bubonic plague. From there, the bacteria may move into the bloodstream or into the lungs, changing to a disease that is passed directly from person to person without the need of a flea's assistance—pneumonic plague.

Victims of the black death suffer fever and chills, headache, weakness, and extreme tenderness at sites with buboes. *Yersinia pestis* can multiply to vast numbers in the blood until every drop contains thousands of organisms. Hemorrhage and blood clots cause limbs to turn black and gangrenous. Death comes quickly. Untreated, bubonic plague kills up to 60 percent of its victims.[10] When the plague struck London in 1665, seven thousand people died each week.

Given the potential of *Y. pestis* to kill a lot of people fast, it is not surprising that the Japanese tried using it as a biological weapon. The United States thought about using it too: Leon A. Fox of the U.S. Army Medical Corps suggested in 1933 that the military could spread the plague by dropping infected rats from planes.[11] The idea conjures up a crazy image of feverish rats dragging tiny parachutes up the street. If the Japanese borrowed this idea, they made an intelligent modification.

As the rats munched their way up and down the streets of Chuhsien, the fleas jumped on board and started feeding, passing on *Y. pestis*. Rats carried the fleas into human houses and other buildings, where the insects turned to biting people when the rats died. Before long, Chuhsien, a town with no history of plague, had a small plague epidemic on its hands. The scenario was repeated in another Chinese town about three weeks later, with similar results. Altogether, about 121 people died of plague—a significant death toll in which a manipulated parasite played a part.

More recently, *Schistosoma hematobium*, the proposed nemesis of Bronze Age Jericho (see chapter 1), was a candidate for parasitological warfare—an odd choice because schistosomiasis takes much longer to develop than do diseases like the black plague. The example of Jericho does show, however, that *Schistosoma* spp. can work as a biological weapon, if you can wait years for results. Most causes won't wait that long, but Tamil militants in Sri Lanka banked on another, more easily used feature of the disease: its power to scare people who don't understand the parasite. Parasites' horrible reputation can far exceed their true destructive ability. Like the fear that monsters hide under the bed, the notion that a parasite lurks in the shadows can be powerful—possibly a better weapon than the parasite itself.

The militants, mostly angry young Tamils, were the product of decades of conflict between Buddhist Sinhalese and Hindu Tamils in Sri Lanka. Since 1948, when the British agreed to political independence for the island, the Sinhalese—accounting for three-quarters of the population—had gradually marginalized the Tamils and denied the unique Tamil cultural identity. The Tamils fought back, but they made little political progress. A spiral of conflict and violence ensued, reaching a crescendo in July 1983, when Sinhalese mobs responded to the deaths of thirteen Sinhalese soldiers by massacring about three thousand Tamils.

When the violence was over, 150,000 Tamils were homeless. Many fled to India or to the West. The remaining young Tamils had limited access to higher education and employment. Restless and frustrated, many turned to violence and terrorism, joining the Liberation Tigers of Tamil Eelam or other Tamil guerrilla groups. One of these groups sent a disturbing and threatening letter to the Sri Lankan government:

> The Ceylon Government has announced that it will get the help of the devil to fight the terrorists—that is to subjugate the Tamil race. It is now quite apparent to the whole world that the Government is doing exactly that by its diabolical acts against innocent Tamils. Hence it is quite fit and proper for the Tamils to counter the Government in a similar manner, and with this object in view, we have formed an operation squad to wage total war against the Government in all parts of

Ceylon. One strategy is to wage a biological war which we believe will cripple Ceylon in a few years. Doctors and scientists have got over their scruples and [are] now working on methods to implement the following:

1) Sending qualified volunteers to bring infected material, cultures and infected water snails to spread Bilbariasis [sic] (River Blindness) in the canals and reservoirs of the Mahaweli at several points. It may take some time before infected people come to the hospitals, but by that time the damage will have been achieved.[12]

The letter then threatened the introduction of yellow fever, leaf curl (a disease of rubber trees), and diseases of tea bushes.

"Bilharziasis," after Theodor Bilharz, who first observed the eggs, is an older name for the disease caused by *S. hematobium.* In the letter, the Tamil group was threatening to introduce the same type of parasite that may well have been the scourge of Jericho. However, their inspiration was more likely to have come from the spectacular misfortunes of Egypt after the completion of the Aswan High Dam on the Nile, when the incidence of bilharziasis exploded along the Nile and above the dam.

Before the Nile River was dammed, the river valley flooded every year, transforming the dry, cracked land into a fertile floodplain with water and silt from deep within the African continent. When the water receded, Egyptian farmers planted food crops in its wake. But the annual flood was fickle. In drought years, it was brief and small, flooding only part of the plain; then the crops failed and Egypt went hungry. In other years, it was an angry inundation, spilling over dikes and sweeping away villages.

Egypt built the Aswan High Dam to produce hydroelectric power and to control the flooding in the Nile River Valley. In turn, the dam created the enormous body of water that is now Lake Nasser. Downstream, seasonal flooding ended, and irrigation made agriculture possible throughout the year. Unfortunately, the gentle flow and stable water levels also created perfect conditions for the snail host of *S. hematobium.* The snail proliferated in the lake and along the edges of the river and irrigation canals, setting the stage for schistosomiasis.

Before the dam, about 5 percent of people living in the river valley between the dam site and Cairo had schistosomiasis. After construction was completed in 1971, human cases increased sevenfold in just four years. And above the dam the situation was even worse: those who came into contact with the water were at serious risk of catching the disease. Soon, three-quarters of fishers on the lake had the worms.

Sri Lanka faced a similar possibility. On the eastern side of Sri Lanka, the Mahaweli Ganga River runs for about two hundred miles (more than three hundred kilometers), tumbling down from the central highlands and meandering across the plains on a crooked course to the Bay of Bengal. The plain, slowly rising from sea level, is in the dry zone—the southeast, east, and north of the island—and receives little rain from February to September.

The plain was contested territory in the long-standing Sri Lankan ethnic conflict, and the area was specifically targeted by the Tamil threat. Historically, the dry zone had been Tamil territory, sparsely populated and supporting only about a quarter of the island's agriculture, mostly rice. Other crops, mainly rubber, tea, and coconut, were grown in the wet zone, where the majority of the island's population lived.

By the late 1970s, a major irrigation project was under way on the Mahaweli Ganga. The government poured money into the project in an effort to bring large areas of land under cultivation, and people—mostly Sinhalese—were migrating into the area. The increased production of rice and other crops, as well as electricity from hydroelectric dams, significantly reduced Sri Lanka's need to import these products. The Mahaweli Ganga Program became a gem of the Sri Lankan economy.

The Tamil plan to introduce infected snails could work if the environment were right. If the snails could establish a breeding population, the parasite would also become successfully established. And the prevalence of rice farming in the Mahaweli Ganga irrigation project would guarantee human exposure to the water. In 1952, *Schistosoma* sp. was discovered in India about one hundred twenty-five miles (two hundred kilometers) south of Bombay. Thus, the snails would likely prosper in Sri Lanka. Fortunately, history does not recount any concrete attempts to carry out the threat, nor has the island experienced an epidemic of schistosomiasis.

But perhaps schistosomiasis was not really the plan. A curious error in the text of the terrorist letter casts doubt about the group's true intent. The letter mentions river blindness and bilharziasis: bilharziasis is a common name for schistosomiasis, but river blindness is not. "Infected water snails, . . . canals and reservoirs" add up to schistosomiasis, but river blindness refers to a parasitic disease caused by a roundworm, *Onchocerca volvulus,* that is transmitted by black flies. Sometimes a crab serves as a host for *O. volvulus,* but a snail won't do. And *O. volvulus* does not prosper in slow-moving, flood-controlled irrigation projects. It requires fast-flowing water. Sri Lankan conditions favor the black flies, not in the plain where the water moves slowly and people are plentiful but close below the dams and in the highlands where the river is wild and fast.

To introduce river blindness (onchocerciasis), the Tamils would have needed infected black flies (species of *Simulium*) and fast-running streams. The flies deposit egg masses on rocks or water plants near the surface. Larvae, hatching from the eggs, attach themselves with sticky glue and hooks to submerged rocks. They battle the constant drag of the current with an anchoring thread and reel themselves in with this thread if they are dislodged. With stalked plumes (cephalic fans), they sieve microscopic food from the river as it rushes past. After a few weeks, they pupate, become adult flies, and ascend to the surface inside air bubbles.

If black flies infected with *O. volvulus* were released in Sri Lanka, the females, naturally, would be hungry. They would torment any Sri Lankan unlucky enough to be wandering by the stream, slashing through skin with their bladelike mouthparts and feeding on blood. Meanwhile, they would deposit the microscopic larvae of the worm in the wound.

Over the next year, the larvae would mature into adult worms residing either in the skin or deeper in the body of their unfortunate host, often gathered together in tumorlike nodules. They would mate and begin producing young—microfilariae—which migrate in the skin and might be sucked up by a biting black fly, assuming that the insects survived in their new locale and the host again strolled by the stream.

The microfilariae left behind to die in the human host cause most of the dreaded symptoms of onchocerciasis. Dying in the skin, the microfilariae can cause a maddeningly itchy allergic skin rash. Over time, the skin thickens and darkens, cracks, wrinkles, and sags, making the victim look prematurely old. When the microfilariae die in the eye, they cause the blindness that gives the disease its name. The adult worms carry on producing microfilariae for up to fifteen years.

Unfortunately for terrorists waiting for a rush of seriously ill people to show up at the hospitals, neither the adult worms nor the migrating microfilariae tend to cause significant immediate health problems. More serious developments, such as blindness, generally take many years to develop and don't strike everyone who has the worms. As well, the infection is now relatively easy to control and treat with the drug ivermectin; in fact, health officials could probably easily eradicate a new focus of infection in a geographically isolated area such as Sri Lanka.

If the Tamils had really used *O. volvulus* as a biological weapon, they would likely have been disappointed with the results. They probably

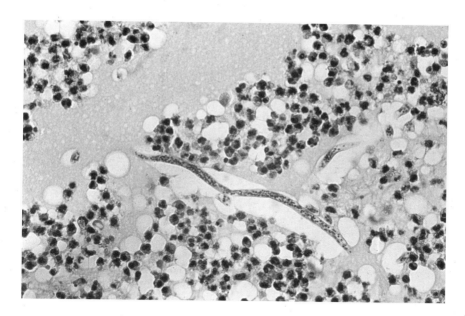

Figure 22. Microfilariae of *Onchocerca volvulus* migrating through skin. Photo by the author.

meant *S. hematobium* in any case, and the reference to river blindness was likely either a red herring designed to confuse or an unfortunate error. Perhaps the real intent was not to introduce a parasite at all but to create fear that they would do so. Terrorism, after all, is about creating terror.

Practical jokes, in contrast, are about getting a laugh, and sometimes a measure of revenge.

The pig roundworm, *Ascaris suum,* was both weapon and evidence in a dangerous piece of mischief in Canada in the early 1970s. This parasite, previously thought to be harmless to humans, might have killed a quartet of university students, had they not had easy access to good medical care.[13] The drama began in mid-February, when the four were suddenly stricken with a bizarre illness.

Twenty-five-year-old Dan Matthews (all the names in this account have been changed) was the first to arrive in the hospital emergency department. After feeling rotten for about three days, he had no appetite and was running a fever. More alarming, he had a bad cough, his heartbeat was rapid, and he was wheezing like an asthmatic. In fact, by the time he arrived in the emergency room, his skin had a distinct blue cast from lack of oxygen. He was in respiratory failure.

X-rays showed opacification in Matthews's lungs, meaning that something was taking up space where air should be. Blood tests showed a high white blood cell count, suggesting an infection, and Matthews's blood had an unusually high number of eosinophils, the white cells that respond to allergies and parasitic infections. Doctors also found that Matthews's liver was enlarged. He was admitted to hospital with a diagnosis of pneumonia and given antibiotics. The drugs didn't help. Twenty-four hours later, his condition remained the same except that a rash had appeared all over his body.

On day two, the mystery deepened when twenty-three-year-old Michael White arrived in the hospital emergency department, wheezing, blue, and in respiratory failure. His lung X-rays looked similar to Matthews's; his white blood cell count was high, with a higher than normal number of eosinophils, and his liver was enlarged. The two men appeared to have the same infection. When doctors looked for a connection between the two, they discovered that, indeed, the students lived in the same rented house.

Doctors still did not know what was making the students ill, but the unusually high eosinophil counts suggested that a parasite might be involved. Eosinophils are white blood cells that contain enzymes useful for destroying foreign substances that invade the human body. When an invader appears, eosinophils proliferate and travel to the site of invasion. When they are close enough, they burst, releasing potent enzymes in an attempt to destroy the enemy. Eosinophils increase in rather specific circumstances, including certain parasitic infections. The doctors promptly sent samples of the students' sputum and stomach contents to be tested for parasites.

Nevertheless, no parasite was immediately evident. Matthews remained in an oxygen tent, struggling for breath, and antibiotics didn't appear to be having any effect. Without a diagnosis, physicians could only watch and wait. Day three came without an answer to the riddle, and roommate number three, twenty-one-year-old Scott MacDonald, arrived in the emergency room in respiratory distress.

MacDonald had the blue look now so familiar, but he was not as ill as the first two men. His lung X-ray looked similar, though not quite as alarming, and his white blood cell count was high. His liver was not enlarged, and his eosinophil count was normal (but it would rise substantially later). He joined his roommates in hospital.

The three became four the next day, when yet another roommate, twenty-three-year-old Andrew Langille, turned up in the emergency department. He was the healthiest of the four, suffering from a dry cough and some wheezing, but only when he exerted himself. His white blood cell count was normal, and X-rays of his lungs showed little damage. Nevertheless, doctors kept him in hospital, where they could keep an eye on his condition.

Two other men, also students, had been sharing the same rented house. One of them was not ill and seemed to have escaped the disease. The last man, Allan Robson, a twenty-three-year-old student from the United States, had recently moved out. He had not been paying his share of the rent, and they had asked him to vacate his room a few weeks before the trouble began.

At about the same time that Langille went into hospital, the results of testing on Matthews's sputum and stomach washings came back. The parasite had been found, and it was no ordinary human parasite. Both specimens contained many tiny, wriggling wormlike creatures, between one- and two-tenths of an inch (four millimeters) long and coiled at the tail end. They were identified by a specialist in parasitology as the larvae of *A. suum*, the pig roundworm. This finding was a first: the medical literature contained no reports of anyone treating a human case of infection with *A. suum*.

Ascaris suum is not supposed to infect people. Though it probably shares a common ancestor with *A. lumbricoides*, the large intestinal roundworm of humans, the two worms are considered separate species. Today, scientists still debate whether *A. suum* can develop to an adult worm in a human host. Its life cycle, however, is virtually identical to that of *A. lumbricoides*, the worm that Vice-Admiral Sir James Watt suggested may have plagued Captain James Cook. From the lungs, larvae travel up the windpipe, down to the stomach, and thence to the intestine.

When the microscopic larvae of *A. suum* hatch and leave the intestine, they may go first to the liver and wait there for a couple of days, like an army waiting to set off on a campaign. This progression is not known in human infections involving *A. lumbricoides* but has been studied in *A. suum* in pigs. It may explain why the first two men had enlarged livers: their bodies' attempts to get rid of the parasites in the liver would have inflamed the organ. From the liver, larvae move to the lungs, where they break out of tiny blood capillaries into the air spaces.

Each emerging larva causes a tiny bit of blood to leak out of the capillary into the lungs. When large numbers of larvae arrive in the lungs at once, the bleeding and swelling can be serious. White blood cells, including eosinophils, flock to the lungs to help in the fight, and dead and dying cells and larvae begin to pile up. An X-ray at this point shows material filling up the air spaces in the lungs, and explains a pneumonia-like illness exactly like the symptoms the four young students had when they arrived in the emergency room. If enough pus, dead cells, and dead larvae build up in the lungs, the infection can be fatal.

The lack of experience with pneumonia due to *A. suum* in humans left doctors with scant available advice on how to treat the victims. To begin, they treated the symptoms. As soon as they knew what they were dealing with, doctors treated Matthews, White, and MacDonald with prednisone, a drug used to control inflammation. With the battle in their lungs turned down a notch, they soon began to improve. Langille, who had not been as sick as the other three, was not treated with the drug, and he recovered without treatment. Prednisone, however, is not an antiparasitic drug: it would not kill the larvae.

Any larvae that had survived the lungs and the stomach would have continued on into the intestine. No one knew what would happen then. The larvae might die because they were in the wrong host, or they might mature. Maturation takes time, so stool tests for worms would have to wait. In the interim, attention turned to figuring out how the pig parasite had gotten into four humans in the first place.

The worm itself gave them an obvious answer: Allan Robson, the evicted roommate, was a student in parasitology. He would have had access to eggs of *A. suum*, a parasite that is most unlikely to infect four young men by chance in the middle of a Canadian winter. And, upset at being turned out of the house, Robson had a reason to do his roommates an ill turn.

Thinking back, the sick men remembered a weekend meal they had shared about two weeks before being admitted to hospital. The unaffected roommate had gone curling for the evening. Robson had, presumably, just vacated his room, or at least, he was not socializing with the people who had turned him out. The four sat down to a supper prepared from the contents of their shared refrigerator. That evening, the four friends ate something—probably milk or cold meat, something raw—that was contaminated with vast numbers of infective eggs of *A. suum*. The eggs were invisible in the food, but they were ready to hatch as soon as they hit a warm intestine.

The four men swallowed all of the eggs, apparently, at that meal. All of the eggs then hatched at once, and the larvae left the intestine together, migrating through the lungs in a swarm, which explains the seriousness of the pneumonia experienced by Matthews and White and the short period of time in which all four men were hospitalized. Although the unaffected roommate was carefully watched for signs of infection, and other students who had visited the house around that time were tested as well, no one else became sick.

Local Canadian newspapers closely followed the tale of the "parasite killer," but more than three weeks passed before anyone saw or heard from Robson again. He had precipitously departed for the United States at about the time his former roommates began getting seriously ill. A warrant was issued for his arrest, with four charges of attempted murder to back it up. At Robson's family home in the northeastern United States, his parents stated that they had not seen him for some years. Police could not find him. He had simply disappeared.

Andrew Langille had the easiest time of the four men in his initial sickness, but in early March, he could boast of being the one with the most intestinal parasites. His stool samples contained a massive number of immature but healthy worms of *A. suum*. MacDonald also had a great many worms, while Matthews and White, the two who had endured the worst of the illness, turned up no worms, immature or otherwise. All four were treated with antiparasitic piperazine, a drug to kill the parasites, to be sure the last worm was gone.

The young men's dramatic illness provided a wealth of information about the activity of *A. suum* in a human host and challenged the belief that this parasite neither causes disease in humans nor matures to adult worms in the human intestine. Though the parasites were wiped out with medication before they had time to reach maturity, the abundant immature worms found in two of the men suggested that the parasite could indeed mature. No such compelling evidence had turned up before, nor has any appeared since.

All four victims recovered from their ordeal, although lung and liver damage took time to heal. After about three weeks, they were all discharged from hospital together, just in time to see Robson show up with a lawyer in tow and surrender to police.

Robson was arrested and held without bail for nine days, until his first appearance in court. At his preliminary hearing, the judge decided he was unlikely to disappear again and set him free on bail. Robson requested and received a publicity ban on the evidence against him; thus, a sensational news story fell silent in the local newspapers. The trial of the "parasite killer" commenced promptly.

If the worm served as Robson's weapon and then betrayed him, it also likely got him off the hook. Robson wasn't convicted. Indeed, how could he have intended to murder anyone with a weapon that he, and everyone else, believed was not capable of causing disease in humans?[14] If he did seed the food in the house with *A. suum* eggs, his malicious prank was reminiscent of the chocolate cake of urban myth that was reportedly frosted with laxative icing—not nice at all but not meant to kill.

Robson probably believed that his roommates would merely be mildly ill for a couple of days—allowing him to take a little revenge for their perceived harsh treatment of him. Initially, he might have snickered to himself, enjoying the knowledge that they had unwittingly swallowed pig parasites and that he was the only one who would ever know. His was an eviction, and a revenge, that delivered more than anyone could have predicted—a story that has endured in the history of North American parasitology.

EIGHT

Emerging Parasites

The fear that new plagues are in the making is not unjustified. In most parts of the world we are unprepared for any new pestilence. We have not enough water, not enough food, not enough shelter, and no peace.

I. J. LOEFLER

"Microbes, Chemotherapy, Evolution, and Folly"

WE WOULD BE MISTAKEN TO think that we have already met and catalogued all of the life forms that can parasitize humans or that no new human parasites will evolve in the future. As we change, and as we change things in our environment, our parasites change as well. The body louse of humans is a fairly recent example of parasite evolution.

In twelfth-century England, Archbishop Thomas Becket was a suitable host for body lice because he wore many layers of fabric that were seldom washed (see chapter 6). Anthropologists remind us, however, that people didn't always wear clothes. Our remote ancestors had body hair that is thought to have gradually disappeared from humans between 1.7 million and 3 million years ago. Thereafter, humans went naked until they started wearing clothing, perhaps a hundred thousand years ago. Humans must have lived a long stretch of time without suffering infestations of lice on their bodies. Where did body lice come from then?

The current theory is that body lice evolved from head lice after humans started wearing tailored clothing that kept the insects close enough to the skin to be comfortable.[1] Lice didn't have to move far from the head to the trunk and had only to learn to cling to fabric rather than hair: the switch may have happened more than once. One might argue that humans were directly responsible for the appearance of a new species of louse: the body louse emerged because we created a home for it. It then proceeded to indirectly kill millions of humans by transmitting epidemic typhus and other diseases.[2]

The original tailor could justifiably invoke the law of unintended consequences: no one anticipated the emergence of body lice or epidemic typhus when people started wearing clothes, nor did anyone understand the threat posed by body lice until long after the parasite had emerged and become commonplace.[3] People knew only that clothing provided warmth and protection. The emergence of the body louse was a classic case of an advantageous change having an additional, unfortunate, and unexpected result.

The simplest definition of an emerging parasite today is any parasite that suddenly grabs our attention. The parasite might be genuinely new—like body lice were when they first appeared—a novel organism evolving to occupy a new niche. This path is relatively rare, but parasites can emerge in other ways.

Parasites sometimes spread from animals to humans and cause disease that then spreads in humans; like secondhand goods, these parasites are new to us but not really new. Intrusions into wild space can allow parasites to make this transition, as well as domestication of wild animals, but changes in diet are also suspect: today people are eager to try new and different foods, or use different methods of food preparation, increasing the chances of ingesting live organisms they haven't been in contact with previously.

For various reasons, a known parasite sometimes emerges dramatically in a new place; the screwworm emergency in Libya that I describe in chapter 4 is one example. In more subtle ways, parasites once associated with the tropics increasingly emerge in the West as throngs of world travelers return home after eating, drinking, swimming, walking barefoot, and feeding blood-sucking insects in exotic travel destinations. Doctors in the West are facing their first cases of malaria, trypanosomiasis, or schistosomiasis. Emergence happens as well when a once-rare parasite meets up with conditions that enable it to infect large numbers of people, like *Cryptosporidium* spp. in waterborne outbreaks. Increased environmental contamination paired with a growing tendency to cook food lightly also contributes.

Some emergent parasites aren't really any more common than they were before: rather they suddenly become visible to us. For example, we might finally discover what causes a familiar set of symptoms: hookworm emerged in the early 1900s when scientists in the United States finally recognized it as the health problem behind the "white trash" stereotype (see chapter 4). Or new diagnostic methods might enable scientists to identify a population that's already infected.

Today, the emergence of a parasite almost invariably follows human actions, or a whole string of human activities that change conditions— leading to an unintended consequence.

Naturalist Charles Darwin wondered about the evolution of lice, though no evidence exists that he connected body lice with the invention of clothing. While on his famous voyage aboard H. M. S. *Beagle,* Darwin collected various species of lice, which he later donated to naturalist Henry Denny's studies of the parasites. Darwin is better remembered, however, for his close contact with another blood-sucking insect that was transformed into a serious health menace for humans by human innovation.

In March 1839, a species of triatomid bug (kissing bug), or benchuca, fed on Darwin while he was traveling in the province of Mendoza, Argentina. In his diary, he wrote, "It is most disgusting to feel soft wingless insects, about an inch long, crawling over one's body. Before sucking they are quite thin, but afterwards they become round and bloated with blood."[4] This was probably not the only time Darwin was bitten: in the same diary entry, he describes catching a benchuca in Chile and releasing it on a tabletop:

> If a finger was presented, the bold insect would immediately protrude its sucker, make a charge, and if allowed, draw blood. No pain was caused by the wound. It was curious to watch its body during the act of sucking, as in less than ten minutes it changed from being as flat as a wafer to a globular form. This one feast, for which the benchuca was indebted to one of the officers, kept it fat during four whole months; but, after the first fortnight, it was quite ready to have another suck.[5]

Fascinated by nature, Darwin probably knew the benchuca as well as anyone at the time, but he didn't know that he was toying with the insect vector of *Trypanosoma cruzi,* a parasite that would infect millions in later decades and by the year 2000, kill forty-five thousand to fifty thousand people each year. He didn't know because American trypanosomiasis, or Chagas' disease, had not yet emerged: no one knew that the parasite existed, that it multiplied in the hindgut of triatomid bugs, or that it infected humans and other vertebrates.

Attracted by body heat, the bug typically feeds when its victim is sleeping. It prefers to bite through the thin skin in the corner of the eye or near the margin of the lip—hence the name "kissing bug." And like a kiss, the bite is typically painless. Unlike the tsetse fly and the mosquito, however, the kissing bug doesn't pass the parasite to the next host with its bite. Infectious trypomastigotes are in the bug's feces.

Animals often acquire trypanosomes by eating food or water contaminated with bug feces or by eating the bugs themselves. Humans are less likely to ingest bugs and bug feces, but a curious coincidence of events enables the parasite to infect humans: feeding causes the bug to defecate, leaving a tarry pool of feces teeming with trypomastigotes of *T. cruzi* near the bite site. When the bitten human scratches or rubs a bite, smearing bug feces into the tiny wound, or into the eyes or mouth, the parasite gains entrance. Transmission of *T. cruzi* to people, then, depends on the bugs' defecating on human skin before leaving the scene.

If triatomid bugs didn't defecate on their victims, people would have served as a food supply but seldom acquired the parasite. But the bugs do, and Chagas' disease emerged in human populations. By the end of the twentieth century, some sixteen million to eighteen million people in South and Central America had trypomastigotes of *T. cruzi* circulating in their bloodstreams.

The trypomastigotes are so tiny that one of them could curl up inside a human red blood cell. They look like long transparent sea serpents, with one end rounded and the other tapered, and a diaphanous ruffled fin runs down their length, thinning to a long whiplike tail. The fin is an undulating membrane, and a flagellum runs along its outer edge from end to end, trailing beyond the tapered end to form the tail. But here the comparison fails: this serpent swims backward; its tail precedes it through the deep waters, or in this case, through the fecal drop of the kissing bug and the blood of humans.

For the unwitting bite victim, especially one who doesn't notice the bug, the first sign of trouble is a swollen red chagoma at the site of infection—an immune response intended to mop up the invaders and destroy them. However, the immune cells are co-opted instead. Engulfed by these cells, the trypomastigotes round up into small forms called amastigotes and multiply. Eventually host cells are destroyed and emerging trypomastigotes spread. They are carried to the lymph nodes and then disperse

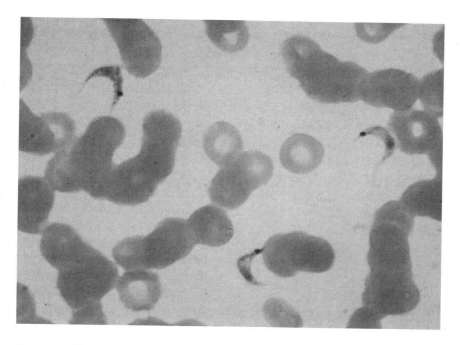

Figure 23. Trypomastigotes of *Trypanosoma cruzi* in blood. Photo by the author.

through the blood, invading cells everywhere they go. They change to amastigotes and multiply, bursting out as trypomastigotes, destroying the host cell, and dispersing through the blood. Muscle and nerve cells are particularly hard hit.

At this stage, Chagas' disease can kill in just a few weeks. For some, though, the initial symptoms are mild, the infection goes unnoticed, and the parasite persists for decades. As time passes, cell destruction takes its toll: muscle cells of the heart often become so damaged that the victim finally dies of heart failure. In other cases, nerve function in the esophagus or intestine is gradually destroyed so that the organs become enlarged and flabby and no longer work as they should.

For the duration of the disease, trypomastigotes circulate in the blood and hide in cells. The number of trypomastigotes in the blood may be so small that they are undetectable with routine laboratory tests, but infected people can still pass the disease along if they are bitten by another kissing bug, or if they donate blood or solid organs, and pregnant women can pass it on to unborn babies.

Kissing bugs live in palm trees, woodpiles, cracks and crevices in homes, and thatched roofs. They hide by day and venture out at night to feed. One species, *Triatoma infestans,* is responsible for the bulk of human infections because it lives almost exclusively in human dwellings. Dilapidated or crude housing and thatched roofing create ideal conditions for the bugs, and people sleeping in these dwellings at night provide a ready food supply.

How did one species of triatomid become an almost exclusive inhabitant of human dwellings? Scientists think that the bug originated in the Cochabamba Valley of Bolivia and that it began to feed on humans in a significant way as long as five thousand years ago. It probably moved into human dwellings when humans in that area domesticated the guinea pig (otherwise known as the cavi, or cuy). Guinea pigs, one of the few wild animals domesticated in South America, were not household pets then: they were food.

When wild guinea pigs came indoors, or were kept in pens, they presumably brought their trypanosomes along, and *T. infestans,* which fed on the rodents and transmitted the parasite, came too. Guinea pigs were traded and dispersed throughout the continent from their original place of domestication, and the bugs were dispersed as well. Hiding in cracks and crevices in homes and pens, they discovered a new and highly reliable food source. They multiplied and spread on their own, flying during the hours of darkness to other dwellings.

Human dwellings were such a comfortable environment that *T. infestans* became domesticated as well; almost everywhere but Cochabamba, they forsook the wild and stayed indoors. Though almost all species of triatomid bugs are potential vectors of *T. cruzi, T. infestans* became the principle vector of the parasite in human infections throughout most of South America. To humans, this event appeared to be the first emergence of the parasite.

Four-thousand-year-old human mummies from South America's Atacama Desert with *T. cruzi* DNA in their tissues prove that humans have suffered from Chagas' disease for a very long time, and they support the theory that kissing bugs became domesticated at about the same time as guinea pigs.[6] Presumably, however, the parasite was already present in animal species on the continent when the first people arrived, and sporadic infections most likely occurred even before *T. infestans* invaded homes.

In 1909, *T. cruzi* emerged in a different sense: Carlos Chagas discovered the parasite in triatomid bugs, and subsequent research at the Oswaldo

Cruz Institute in Rio de Janeiro proved that triatomid bugs transmitted the parasites to animals. In 1916, Chagas linked trypanosomes to a common illness of children in South America. He also perceptively noted what Chagas' disease had become: a disease of the poor and marginalized. In a 1920 publication, he wrote,

> The great foci of the insect are formed by the houses of primitive construction whose walls and roof furnish propitious shelter for the [blood-sucking insect]. It is the small cottages and huts of the country, roofed with grass and with imperfect walls, that are the most heavily infested. In the rural cities the well-constructed houses are sheltered from contamination; but the [blood-sucking insect] is always found in abundance in the poor houses that are always situated on the outskirts of these cities.[7]

With the advent of blood transfusion, the parasite invaded the cities as well, arriving in the blood of migrants and contaminating the blood supply. By the 1970s, some 25 percent of blood donors were infected in some regions, and literally thousands of people were acquiring Chagas' disease through blood and blood products every year. Routine screening of donors for trypanosomiasis did not get under way until the 1990s.

Other events in the 1970s set the stage for a third emergence of Chagas' disease. This decade witnessed the beginning of a massive wave of northward human migration: the immigration of Latin American people into the United States. Today, a million or more infected people may be living in the United States.[8] Many will suffer the long-term effects of the parasite later in life, but if these people donate blood or organs in the interim, they could pass on their parasites to others. Transmission by donor organs has already been documented.

In April 2001, a thirty-seven-year-old American woman came to the hospital feeling unwell. She had received a donor kidney and pancreas almost a month earlier, and now she had an unexplained fever. The fever persisted, and four days later a smear of her blood showed trypomastigotes, the typical crescent-shaped blood forms of *T. cruzi*. The woman had Chagas' disease, and she almost certainly had not caught it from a kissing bug.[9]

Kissing bugs do occur in the United States, and animal testing has confirmed the presence of the parasite, but human cases acquired from bugs inside the United States are very rare. People in the United States are not exposed to the bugs as much as those in Latin America—they don't tend to get bitten. In addition, the U.S.-based parasite may be a less virulent strain.

The transplant patient's organ donor, however, was an immigrant from Central America who had acquired the parasite before coming to the United States: the transplanted organs contained the parasites. Though the woman was treated for the next four months with nifurtimox, a drug specially obtained from the Centers for Disease Control, she died of Chagas' disease in October 2001, with the dubious distinction of being the first American organ recipient to die as a result of *T. cruzi* acquired from a transplant. Two other people who received organs from the same donor also contracted Chagas' disease, but neither died as a result. Thus, *T. cruzi* has not emerged in the United States and other Western countries by spreading out in the environment; it has emerged in the blood supply and in organ transplant programs. Although screening tests are now available, they are still not universally used.

Charles Darwin died in 1882, long before the discovery of *T. cruzi*, so he never knew about the dangers of offering a finger to a hungry kissing bug. We can't be sure that the bugs that bit Darwin in Argentina were *T. infestans,* or that they carried *T. cruzi*; however, he wrote in his journal that he was attacked at night, while sleeping in the village of Luxan, which suggests a house-dwelling species, and in Argentina, *T. infestans* is the usual culprit. The naturalist suffered from chronic health problems, and scientists debate whether he had Chagas' disease. If so, he weathered it for more than forty years. Living in England before the days of blood transfusions and organ transplant, he did not pass it on.

—

If body lice found a future in fashion and *T. cruzi* found one in medical advances, a common but little-known amoeba called *Acanthamoeba* has successfully exploited both human inventions at once, moving from soil and water into human eyes. The advent of widespread contact lens wear coincided with the unexpected emergence of this parasite.

Acanthamoeba spp. live in the environment all over the world, in freshwater and saltwater, soil, mud, sewage, and other decaying organic material. They appear in swimming holes, water reservoirs, and water distribution systems. In these locations, they are not parasitic; they feed on bacteria in water and organic debris.

Under the right circumstances, *Acanthamoeba* spp. can also feed on living tissues of animals. Human infections were once exceedingly rare, involving the occasional invasion of the brain, eye infections stemming from an injury contaminated with soil or plant material, and infections in people with compromised immune systems.

The first case of acanthamoeba keratitis (infection of the cornea of the eye) was reported in 1973. In the 1980s, more cases appeared. At first, no one paid much attention, but eventually doctors noticed that the people experiencing destructive acanthamoeba infections of the cornea virtually all belonged to a select group: wearers of soft contact lenses. The infection mimics a viral infection and is often mistaken for one: the eye feels irritated and scratchy at first, becoming red and sensitive to light. Patients often experience severe pain out of proportion to the degree of inflammation, and vision becomes blurry. Antibacterial and antiviral drugs are not effective. When the first cases appeared, no treatment worked, and early patients suffered permanent vision loss or even lost the eye.[10]

Some victims had had direct exposure to places where *Acanthamoeba* spp. are known to lurk: they had swum or showered while wearing lenses, lounged in hot tubs with their lenses in, or used well water. However, as more information became available, homemade lens solutions that included tap water came under scrutiny. The amoebae seemed to be coming out of the tap.

Inside household plumbing pipes, water distribution systems, water cisterns, and even contact lens cases, communities of microorganisms called biofilms form when living organisms adhere to surfaces. (Even properly treated water is not completely sterile.) They secrete a biological glue to hold them in place and to protect them from toxins in the water. This film snags more organisms floating by so that a patch of biofilm grows, containing a variety of aquatic organisms. Over time, the biofilm becomes extensive, particularly in places where water flows slowly and in locations distant from sites of chemical disinfection.

Thus, even in treated water systems, the inside of a plumbing pipe presents a strange underwater panorama: a bizarre variety of life forms that have either slipped in through the water treatment plant, leaked in through cracks and tiny passages in the pipes, or been introduced by humans working on the mains. The biofilm ecosystem is a mixture of

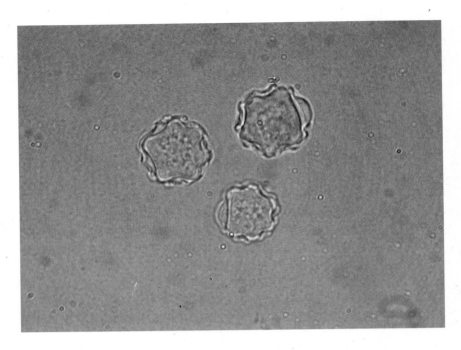

Figure 24. Cysts of *Acanthamoeba* sp. Photo by the author.

bacteria, viruses, protozoa, algae, fungi, and even small invertebrates. Biofilms may contain disease-causing organisms like *Cryptosporidium parvum* (see chapter 3) and serve as a continuing source of contamination in drinking water.

Free-living amoebae are among the larger microorganisms (about one one-thousandth of an inch, or thirty micrometers) living in the biofilm. Bacteria provide a ready food supply, and species like *Acanthamoeba* are resistant to chlorine and other water chemicals. Spiny trophozoites (*acanthamoeba* literally means "spiny amoeba") move about in the biofilm like miniscule aquatic cows, grazing on other life forms. If they run out of food or if conditions become unpleasant, they simply build a tough cyst wall around themselves and wait for things to improve.

In some places the biofilm exists as a dense layer, but in others it forms weird towers and mushroom shapes that bend with the water flow. Blobby chunks occasionally break off and are carried away to stick somewhere else or be flushed out through a tap. Inevitably, trophozoites and cysts of *Acanthamoeba* spp. get swept away as well.

When a cyst or trophozoite of *Acanthamoeba* gets washed into a contact lens case or a lens solution bottle, it may well be able to carry on with its grazing lifestyle. These containers are often contaminated, especially if tap water has been used to rinse lenses or cases or to make solutions. In the 1980s, homemade contact lens solutions were commonplace, and both bacteria and *Acanthamoeba* spp. contaminated them. Amoebae fed on bacteria and multiplied.

Trophozoites of *Acanthamoeba* adhere to plastic surfaces, including the surface of contact lenses. It's a short step from there to the eye when the lens is being worn; if there is the slightest scratch or abrasion on the eye's surface, even corneal cells weakened by frequent lens wear, the amoebae can get through and feed on the eye tissue itself.

When homemade saline solutions were phased out, the first wave of acanthamoeba keratitis subsided, but occasional cases continued to occur in people who didn't follow lens care procedures properly, and in some people who still allowed their lenses to contact tap water at some stage of cleaning. Then researchers discovered that some materials used for making contact lenses allowed the amoebae to stick to the lens better, and prevalence data showed that overnight lens wear increases the risk. Several outbreaks have been associated with commercial contact lens solutions.

A recent decrease in the amount of residual chemicals remaining after water treatment may give *Acanthamoeba* spp. yet another opportunity to invade human eyes. Although the organisms aren't directly affected by these chemicals, their food supply is: a decrease in water treatment chemicals such as chlorine means an increase in water system biofilms, especially in pipes far from the treatment facility, and a corresponding increase in the number of cysts and trophozoites of *Acanthamoeba* spp. issuing from household taps.

The best defense against acanthamoeba keratitis is to prevent tap water from coming in contact with lenses or cases: daily-wear disposable lenses, worn once and then discarded, are the safest option. However, the number of people wearing contact lenses continues to grow, and consumers can sidestep professional care by buying both prescription and cosmetic lenses from vendors who don't warn them about the importance of proper lens care. The incidence of acanthamoeba keratitis continues to increase, if only because the pool of people at risk has grown.

Acanthamoeba spp. have an evil cousin that also finds opportunities in human water resources. Also a free-living amoeba with the ability to become parasitic, it is *Naegleria fowleri*. (Though both are environmental amoebae associated with water, the two are not actually closely related.) *Naegleria* sp. inhabit biofilm like *Acanthamoeba* sp., but *N. fowleri* proliferates in unusually warm water. First discovered in humans in the mid-1960s, it may be on the increase now due to rising global temperatures. Infection caused by *N. fowleri*—primary amoebic meningoencephalitis (PAM)—strikes unexpectedly in healthy individuals, usually children and young adults, and is almost always fatal. Most reported cases have been in Australia, Europe, and the United States. An early case in England followed a patch of unusually hot, dry weather.

—

On a summer day in southwestern England, three young boys splashed happily in a warm puddle left the night before by a passing thunderstorm.[11] The shallow pool, which covered part of a flowerbed, disappeared quickly when the sun returned. During their play, however, at least two of the boys got water up their noses or inhaled airborne droplets created by splashing.

Two days later, the youngest, a two-year-old, developed early symptoms of a cold, which worsened over the following week until he was admitted to hospital with sore throat, irritability, loss of appetite, vomiting, and symptoms of meningitis. He stopped breathing shortly after admission and was comatose on a respirator thereafter.

Two days after hospital admission, a sample of the boy's spinal fluid contained many white blood cells—mostly pus cells, which respond to bacterial infection—and an equal number of amoebic trophozoites. The trophozoites were about the same size as pus cells, and looked very similar, but their nuclei looked distinctly different. They moved slowly across the field of view under a microscope, pushing pseudopods—bulgy extensions of cell contents—ahead of themselves.

The first of these amoebae had traveled from the back of the child's nose, where little separates the nasal tissues from the brain. The amoebae had followed the olfactory nerve, which carries information about odors from the nose to the brain. In the brain, *N. fowleri* found a warm environment and plenty of human tissue for food. The trophozoites began to multiply unchecked, and after nine days they were present in vast numbers.

Meanwhile, the toddler's older brother began complaining of headache and feeling chilly, and he, too, was admitted to hospital. By that evening, he had a fever, sore throat, and neck pains. Both boys were given amphotericin B, which remains the drug of choice for *N. fowleri* forty years later, though treatment is rarely successful.

The younger boy remained comatose, though his temperature came down and a subsequent spinal sample showed fewer amoebae, many of which now appeared to be dead. After sixteen days in hospital, the child's heart stopped and he died. Postmortem examination of his brain revealed that *N. fowleri* had done extensive damage.

His brother's spinal fluid also yielded *N. fowleri* trophozoites, though in lower numbers, and after eighteen days in hospital, during which his symptoms came and went, he went home completely recovered.

The third boy, a neighbor who had played with the brothers in the puddle, also developed a sore throat with headache and vomiting, and he was given amphotericin B, but *N. fowleri* was never identified in his specimens. After two weeks in hospital, he recovered completely, and doctors remained uncertain whether he had actually had PAM or coincidentally suffered from an upper respiratory infection caused by something else.

This tale of *N. fowleri* demonstrates how devastating an encounter with it can be—no wonder it's been called the "brain-eating amoeba"—but the experience of these three young boys is unusual in several ways: the majority of cases occur after the victim has been swimming or participating in water sports; many victims become seriously ill within two or three days of infection; and almost no one survives.

Early cases of PAM were associated with swimming in very warm water, particularly industrial wastewater, where water is used to cool industrial machinery and is then discharged into pools, canals, and rivers. Natural thermal pools are also home to this heat-loving amoeba. In recent years, however, individual cases have followed swimming and water skiing in lakes and play in water parks. Between 1998 and 2007, the United States saw thirty-three cases of PAM, most of them in children, and all but one was fatal.

Not only has warmer water due to industry and global warming caused *N. fowleri* to emerge, but increased human contact with water has also played a role. People in the developed world are engaging in water sports in greater numbers than ever before, and more are coming in contact with the deadly amoebae. Moreover, a few deaths have resulted from *N. fowleri* in bath water, where water in a distribution system came from a holding tank.

Except when a novel parasite evolves to fill a new niche, exposure is a key feature in parasite emergence: people must be exposed to be infected.

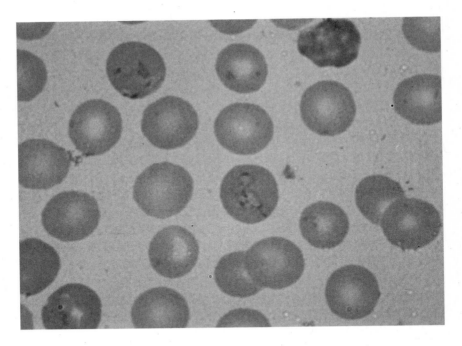

Figure 25. *Babesia* sp. parasites in human blood. Photo by the author.

For parasites like *T. cruzi* and *Acanthamoeba* spp., the steps to increased exposure are fairly simple and easy to understand, at least in retrospect. For others, the mystery is deeper.

One parasite for which a complicated chain of events is fairly well understood is *Babesia microti*, a tiny blood parasite similar to malaria that has been emerging in the northeastern United States for forty years. Its history runs parallel to that of *Borrelia burgdorferi*, the agent of Lyme disease, and is intertwined with the changing fortunes of white-tailed deer, deer ticks, and white-footed mice in coastal New England.

The deer tick, *Ixodes scapularis*, is the tick that transmits *B. microti* to humans, usually the nymph (an immature stage), a tiny creature the size of a poppy seed that often goes unnoticed when it bites. Parasites injected into the bite through the tick's salivary glands invade red blood cells and multiply. The infected human may experience few symptoms, but the unfortunate—usually older victims—develop a flulike illness complete with fever and chills, nausea, vomiting, headache, and aching muscles. Anemia and chronic fatigue are typical, and a small percentage die.

Babesiosis emerged on Nantucket Island, Massachusetts.[12] Like the New England mainland and other islands in the region, Nantucket has a long history of human interference, beginning with native North Americans who kept forests open by burning and hunted white-tailed deer that browsed at the edges of woodland. When European colonists arrived, much of Nantucket was good deer habitat, with lots of low-growing brushy vegetation. But this deer-friendly environment didn't last.

Over the next few hundred years, settlers cut trees for fuel and cleared land for sheep farming and other pursuits. Deer habitat declined, and the animals were hunted until not a single one remained on the island. Though we do not know whether *I. scapularis* lived on Nantucket before the deer were wiped out, the tick could not have survived decades, or even centuries, without its most important host. At the beginning of the twentieth century, Nantucket had neither deer nor deer ticks.

The island likely had white-footed mice, however, or another rodent afflicted by *B. microti*. Ticks, likely *Ixodes muris*, a species that doesn't generally bite humans, passed the parasite from rodent to rodent as they took successive blood meals. Babesiosis was an infection of rodents that didn't cross over into humans.

Meanwhile, the forests were coming back, and on the mainland, the deer came back as well. The animals found plenty of young woodland with abundant undergrowth and miles of forest edges where food was plentiful. With almost no predators to oppose them, they multiplied. In 1922, a buck attempted to swim to Nantucket from the mainland, and the story goes that he was seen by a fisherman and helped to shore, thereafter becoming affectionately known as "Old Buck," the only deer on the island.

In 1926, the islanders brought in two does from Michigan to join Old Buck, and Nantucket's deer population began to grow once more. Today, Nantucket Island, a total land area of about 48 square miles (124 square kilometers), is home to about a thousand white-tailed deer. In 1926, *Ixodes scapularis* had yet to make an appearance: surveys of ticks on the island in the 1930s and 1940s recovered only *I. muris*, whereas *I. scapularis* was identified on Rhode Island and Long Island in the 1960s.

At some point, *I. scapularis* arrived on Nantucket. It may have come with a deer and taken years to multiply to numbers large enough to become an issue for humans, or it may have come in on a migrating bird. By 1974, it had completely replaced *I. muris,* and it was proven to be the tick responsible for maintaining *B. microti* in white-footed mice on the island.[13] By this time, the tick was also common in places that humans favored, and was passing the parasite to them as well. The first case of babesiosis in the northeastern United States occurred on Nantucket Island in 1969. A second case followed in the same location in 1973. By 1981, Nantucket, Martha's Vineyard, Shelter Island, and Long Island were all hot spots for the infection.

Nantucket Island is a relatively small land mass where healthy populations of white-footed mice, deer ticks, white-tailed deer, and humans share the same space—a situation that contributed to *B. microti* emerging there first. The story was similar, however, on many inhabited islands along the New England coast, and predictably, babesiosis began appearing on the mainland during the 1980s. Typically, it emerges in areas where Lyme disease is already present, and some infected people have both diseases, possibly acquired from the same tick bite.

Babesia microti and other *Babesia* spp. are showing up in human infections in many other parts of the world. Though one might assume that these parasites have suddenly changed in some way that allows them to infect humans, their emergence has more to do with human activities, present and past. Increased awareness of babesiosis plays a role: scientists now recognize the tiny parasites in the blood where they missed them before, and epidemiologists are actively looking for the infection. But in the northeastern United States, the return of white-tailed deer, multiplying to higher numbers than ever before and providing abundant food for *I. scapularis* ticks, explains the prevalence of both Lyme disease and babesiosis. Deer are so abundant that they regularly stray into urban areas, denuding flower and vegetable gardens and causing automobile accidents.

The white-tailed deer is not the only wild animal to flourish close to human communities in North America. Our suburban tree-lined streets, with patches of green space and belts of trees, have welcomed raccoons as well. The creatures have benefited from an abundance of food and benevolent treatment from humans, and they've brought a particularly nasty roundworm with them—*Baylisascaris procyonis*.

———

In 1969, parasitologist Paul Beaver described mice that "jump, run, and spin" because of *B. procyonis* larvae in their brains. He noted the potential of *B. procyonis* to cause visceral larva migrans in humans: the larvae could migrate through human tissues, and through the brain as well, if humans were to swallow *B. procyonis* eggs.[14] His words proved prophetic: fifteen years later, the first confirmed human case was reported when an eighteen-month-old boy died with massive numbers of *B. procyonis* larvae in his brain. Today, with cases reported in various regions of the United States and in a few other locations around the world where raccoons live in close proximity to humans, *B. procyonis* is an emerging parasite.

Raccoons acquire *B. procyonis* either by swallowing eggs or by eating infected intermediate hosts.[15] Adult worms live in raccoon intestines, causing few problems and producing more than a hundred thousand eggs per worm every day. Eggs enter the environment in raccoon droppings and mature in moist soil.

A little-known fact about raccoons comes into play in the transmission of the worm: raccoons defecate in communal latrines—favored places such as the tops of stumps, large horizontal branches, and fallen trees. After a raccoon leaves droppings in one of these places, other raccoons visit and make their own deposits, resulting in a concentration of feces and, if the raccoons are infected, a cache of millions of eggs of *B. procyonis*. In two weeks to a month, an egg is infective; however, because latrines are used over an extended period of time, they typically contain eggs in various stages of development.

Small animals such as mice, rabbits, and birds initiate another stage in the life cycle when they forage a raccoon latrine for food and incidentally swallow eggs of *B. procyonis*. In these animals, the infection is deadly. Mature eggs hatch in the intestines but the larvae, instead of maturing to adult worms, migrate through tissues into the bloodstream. Carried through the liver and lungs back to the heart, the larvae leave the bloodstream and move into the tissues again, where they become encysted but remain alive. The majority encyst near the head.

A small percentage of wandering larvae invade the brain, moving about extensively (neural larva migrans), growing and causing significant destruction, both directly by their activities and as a result of inflammation. This activity is what made Beaver's mice "jump, run, and spin." Just one larva in the brain can kill a mouse, but the rodent might swallow thousands of eggs and have many larvae in the brain as a result. Obviously, death or erratic behavior due to brain damage makes these small animals much more likely to fall prey to a hungry raccoon and thus pass the larvae on.

A second little-known fact about raccoons is significant in the next stage: raccoons prefer to eat the head end of animal prey first and may even discard the parts of the body closer to the tail. Thus, concentrating near the head is advantageous for larvae of *B. procyonis* and helps maintain a high level of infection in adult raccoons. Once swallowed, larvae develop to adult worms in the raccoon intestine.

In humans who swallow eggs of *B. procyonis,* the progression is the same, but it's a dead-end road for the larvae because humans are in little danger of being eaten by raccoons. The migration becomes the "aimless wandering of a hapless and frustrated, ill-fated worm having no happier prospect than eventual death after an indefinite period of inflicting damage."[16] Unfortunately, the outcome is often equally bad for the human host.

The people who get caught in the life cycle of *B. procyonis* are almost invariably small children or mentally challenged adults—those most likely to stumble upon a raccoon latrine and transfer eggs from hands to mouths. Immediate preventive treatment with antiparasitic drugs can avert disaster, but by the time the diagnosis is made, it is usually too late. In published cases, the consequences are devastating, with many victims dying and the remainder left with serious permanent brain damage.

Migrating larvae in humans move through various organs and tissues and may cause a rash on the face and trunk, respiratory symptoms, and enlarged liver. In the brain, they grow and wander energetically, causing profound damage. The patient develops a fever, with loss of coordination, sleepiness, and irritability. The illness progresses to seizures and coma.

The majority of reported cases have been in individuals who swallowed a large number of eggs and therefore suffered the most extreme illness. Scientists believe that small numbers of larvae, particularly in adults, cause few symptoms except when they migrate through the eye, causing vision problems. The infection, therefore, may be much more common than we realize.

Why has *B. procyonis* emerged? Part of the explanation is that early cases were not diagnosed or were mistaken for infection with other parasites, but the main reason is that the relationship between raccoons and people has changed. Raccoons have discovered the joys of suburban and city life, enjoying a steady supply of food from vegetable gardens, bird feeders, garbage, treats supplied by people, and even the capture and consumption of household pets. Meanwhile, they multiply, safe from predators, to densities far higher than in the wild.

Raccoon latrines pop up like graffiti in backyards, playgrounds, and parks; there can be dozens of latrines on a single property when raccoon

Figure 26. Young raccoons raiding an urban bird feeder. Photo by the author.

populations are high. In suburban and urban settings, the animals establish latrines directly on the ground or on patios, on the tops of fences and woodpiles, and on roofs, where rain washes eggs down onto adjacent ground. The tough eggs of *B. procyonis,* like those of *Ascaris lumbricoides* (see chapter 1), remain infective for years, making a contaminated yard almost impossible to clean up.

Our unconscious—sometimes conscious—support of the raccoon has resulted in hundreds of the animals per square mile in some suburban environments, and they continue to multiply.[17] Meanwhile, raccoons migrate and are translocated by humans, spreading the parasite to new areas. North American raccoons have been introduced to a number of areas in Europe and Asia, where they thrive and, as usual, their parasites thrive with them. The opportunities for *B. procyonis* to emerge in human health are far from over.

The time-honored way for a human parasite to emerge in a new place is to arrive with a human body. It happened when Europeans colonized the

Americas. It happened when Africans were forcibly brought to the New World. It happens even today when people move, especially when they are displaced by poverty, conflict, or environmental disaster. The emergence of Chagas' disease in the United States is one example. *Taenia solium* neurocysticercosis in developed countries is another (see chapter 5).

One rarely finds a human in North America with a *T. solium* tapeworm living in the intestine these days: pigs are rarely infected here because they lack access to garbage and human feces, and meat inspection procedures screen for infected pork. If a pork tapeworm does show up in a human intestine, that intestine is likely to belong to an immigrant from Central or South America, or to someone who has traveled there.

The Spanish brought pigs to the New World in the 1500s, and the pigs brought *T. solium*. As late as the 1800s, pigs roamed freely in many North American communities, ideal conditions for *T. solium*, but apparently the parasite was not a major health problem everywhere. The incidence of pork tapeworm in humans in the north dropped sharply in the second half of the twentieth century until the parasite was practically nonexistent in North America and most of Europe. The worm flourished, however, in the south.

The persistence of *T. solium* in Latin American pigs may be difficult to understand for a person who has grown up with flush toilets and inspected food. It comes as a shock to Westerners to learn that more than 2 billion of the world's people lack access to decent toilets. In Latin America, 125 million still had no sanitation in 2004.[18] Thus, 125 million people defecate on the ground, or in water, every day.

In many of the same communities where people have to relieve themselves outside, pigs roam freely, scavenging for food, including exposed feces. In other places, fenced pigs are actually fed human feces as a convenient way to dispose of the waste. In this way, people take advantage of both a free source of food for pigs and a means of keeping their environment relatively clean. Unfortunately, this practice plays right into the life cycle of *T. solium* and means lots of infested pigs wherever people have the worms.

Pork for human consumption, in turn, is often not inspected, while pigs that are checked and declared infected are removed from the official pork market and sold privately, sometimes in a different community, or the meat is ground and mixed with meat from uninfected pigs. Lower prices for meat from infected pigs make it more attractive to those with little money. In some areas, raw or undercooked pork sausage, or pork that has been salted and dried in the sun, is often consumed, ensuring lots of infected humans.

The absence of any kind of adequate toilets goes hand in hand with the absence of running water or other means of hand washing. Thus, the person with a pork tapeworm is a danger not only to the local pigs but also to him- or herself and everyone else. Eggs on contaminated hands get transferred to other surfaces, to food items, and even into drinking-water supplies. Estimates suggest that between thirty million and fifty million people in Latin America have been exposed to *T. solium*.[19]

We should not be surprised, then, that travelers to Central and South America sometimes inadvertently swallow *T. solium* eggs and come home with cysticercosis—nor that the surge of Latin Americans moving northward to the United States and even Canada has moved a lot of intestinal tapeworms with it. The problem is not that these worms are infecting pigs in the United States and giving rise to more intestinal tapeworms: the problem is that they are infecting humans and causing neurocysticercosis.

— ·—

In the early 1990s, a mystery illness struck four members of a Jewish community in New York City.[20] The first victim, a sixteen-year-old female, suddenly became unable to speak. A short time later, she suffered a seizure. She had never had a seizure before, and she was promptly taken to the emergency room at a New York hospital, where physicians initially suspected a brain tumor. However, medical tests didn't support that diagnosis.

The tests did show that the young woman had two lesions in her brain. Their origin was a mystery, and nothing provided a satisfactory explanation. The lesions were consistent with the cysticerci of the pork tapeworm, *T. solium,* yet this patient was very unlikely to have that parasite: as an Orthodox Jew, she never ate pork, and she had never traveled to anywhere where she would have been likely to pick up *T. solium.*

You don't have to have a pork tapeworm in your intestine, however, to have tapeworm cysticerci in your brain: you need only swallow the worm eggs produced by someone else's intestinal *T. solium.* And a tapeworm can be in Hong Kong, London, or New York City, without a pig in sight.

Before too long, a six-year-old boy and two adults turned up in New York hospital emergency rooms, having, like the young woman, suffered sudden unexplained seizures. The four patients were unrelated, but they all came from the same Jewish community, and they all had a few lesions typical of *T. solium* cysticerci in their brains. None had a history of seizures or any relevant recent travel history, and none of them had ever eaten pork. None of them, of course, had a *T. solium* tapeworm producing proglottids and expelling eggs in their intestines.

Nonetheless, blood testing turned up antibodies to *T. solium* in three of the four patients and in seven of their family members, meaning that they had indeed had a close encounter with the worm. When tested, two young children of one of the adults had the characteristic brain lesions.

Final confirmation came when the sixteen-year-old girl and the oldest patient, a thirty-nine-year-old man, had brain lesions surgically removed. Indeed, the lesions contained the tiny scolices of *T. solium*. Physicians had to accept that, somehow, the pork tapeworm was making its way around a community where pork was decidedly unwelcome.

Investigators ultimately discovered that pork tapeworms had arrived in the Jewish community in the intestines of housekeepers—immigrants, mostly Mexicans, hired to cook, clean, and look after children for Jewish families. Pork tapeworm flourishes in Mexico: 2 to 4 percent of the population have the worm. Some of the Mexican women who came across the border to the United States unknowingly brought *T. solium* with them and were passing tapeworm eggs in their feces. Despite modern sanitation facilities, the pervasive tendency of humans everywhere to skip a handwash after using the toilet, or before eating, carried the parasite through the next step.

From time to time, and possibly on many occasions, the infected women transferred tapeworm eggs from their feces to their hands and from their hands to objects and food in the homes where they were working. Eggs on doorknobs, bathroom taps, and light switches transferred to other hands and sometimes to mouths. Eggs in uncooked food were swallowed undetected. The Jewish occupants of the houses had pork tapeworm eggs in their intestines and pork tapeworm larvae migrating through their tissues. *T. solium* cysticerci developed in Jewish muscles and brains. For some, seizures followed.

When New York epidemiologists tested Mexican housekeepers, they found that some of them were passing eggs of *T. solium*. Others had antibodies to the parasite in their blood. If even 2 percent of the approximately seven thousand immigrant housekeepers employed in the Orthodox Jewish community harbored pork tapeworms, about 140 worms were pumping out infectious eggs that could potentially cause cysticercosis in others. Indeed, a survey of the Jewish members of the community revealed that 1.3 percent—about 450 people—had antibodies to *T. solium*.[21]

Immigrant housekeepers came and went in the Jewish households, sometimes staying only a short while. After they left, epidemiologists had little hope of finding them to check whether they harbored a tapeworm. Even more perplexing, when told of positive test results, several of the immigrant women simply disappeared. The probable explanation for their behavior is simple: they were more afraid of the backlash than they were of the worm.

When people understand that immigrants might expose them to nasty diseases that they wouldn't otherwise have to worry about, the response is frequently to blame the immigrants. Diseases like neurocysticercosis and Chagas' disease feed intolerance and racism and lead to paranoia about health risks posed by immigration. The risk is small but real: although most American states have not collected data on cases of neurocysticercosis until recently, we know that the number of diagnosed cases began to climb in the 1970s, partly due to better tests to detect the infection but also due to the increasing influx of migrants from the south.

According to the Migration Policy Institute, more than twenty million immigrants from Latin America lived in the United States in 2007.[22] Many of these immigrants came from poverty in areas with minimal health care, hoping for a better future. In their new home, if they're lucky, they have a better standard of living, but their access to good health care is not much better than it was before. If they are in a foreign country "unofficially," the situation is even worse. These people receive no medical screening when they immigrate. Chronic illness goes undiagnosed and untreated. Parasites go undetected. The situation is bad for everyone.

The answer, of course, is not to target the immigrants or to attempt to stop the vast movement of people that has become a feature of twenty-first-century life. The answer is to target the diseases themselves in the places where they are prevalent. The pork tapeworm, surprisingly, is one parasite that we could actually drive to extinction if we set our minds to the task.

NINE

Parasite Extinction

To look into a gallery of parasite faces is to see all the strange beings
we could ever imagine and many we could not. Many of those faces
are gone and we do not even know which ones.

ROB R. DUNN
"On Parasites Lost"

WE HEAR THAT AFRICAN TRYPANOSOMIASIS has reemerged in Africa,
that malaria kills about a million people every year despite decades
of fighting it, that bedbugs are becoming resistant to pesticides, that
all surface waters are now contaminated with cryptosporidium and
giardia. Anyone would think that parasites are the most indestructible
creatures on earth. But parasites are going extinct every day. Why
not ours?

Many parasite species are being lost through coextinction: their hosts
become extinct, and because they can't live anywhere else, they perish too.
Our parasites, especially the ones that live only on humans, are still here
because we are, and because we're still doing all the things they need us
to do to help them spread. Parasites that we share with other species are
even less vulnerable and have good prospects of living on even if humans
become extinct!

The absolute dependence that some parasites have on us represents a
weakness, however: if we were to attempt to eradicate parasites of humans,
these would be the first to fall. *Dracunculus medinensis,* the fiery guinea
worm, is a parasite unique to humans. *Onchocerca volvulus,* the cause of
river blindness, has not been found in any other species. *Taenia solium*
tapeworms live only in human intestines, and the main intermediate host
is the pig. And of the four malaria parasites, only *Plasmodium malariae*

also infects wild animals. These human-dependent parasites are good places to start.

Smallpox is the only human disease ever eradicated through deliberate effort. Dracunculiasis, infection with *D. medinensis*—the fiery serpent we met in chapter 5—is likely to be second. Only twenty-five years ago, the worm infected three and a half million people every year; by early December 2008, only about five thousand cases remained.[1] With any luck on our side of the fight, the worm is doomed.

In reality, *D. medinensis* has been in retreat for most of the past century. Probably spread by nomads, migrants, or translocated prisoners who picked it up at the place where it first emerged, the parasite once afflicted humans in northern and sub-Saharan Africa, the Middle East, India, and even southeastern regions of the former Soviet Union.[2] It disappeared from the former Soviet Union in the 1930s and from Iran in the 1970s but continued to flourish in at least eighteen countries, with 120 million people at risk of infection.[3]

India's initial attempt to wipe out dracunculiasis began in 1980 and coincided neatly with the period that the United Nations dubbed the International Drinking Water Supply and Sanitation Decade (1981 to 1990). Because the guinea worm is acquired by swallowing tiny copepods in water, supplying safe water to everyone in affected areas would wipe out the disease. The coincidence wasn't lost on the Centers for Disease Control (CDC) in the United States, and the idea that the worm could be eradicated took root. In 1984, the World Health Organization (WHO) chose the CDC to head up an eradication effort.

During that decade, India, Pakistan, Ghana, and Nigeria all pursued eradication of *D. medinensis,* but the major turning point in the campaign didn't come until 1986, when two things happened: the World Health Assembly adopted a resolution calling for global eradication, and former U.S. president Jimmy Carter brought the resources of the Carter Center to the effort. Carter was to become the figurehead of dracunculiasis eradication.

Ideally placed to connect with and influence top statesmen in affected countries, Carter first persuaded General Zia al-Haq of Pakistan to accept the help of the Carter Center and the CDC. From there, he proceeded to build a global eradication effort that eventually included all the countries where the worm was endemic. By 1990, he had gained support from other agencies, including the United Nations Development Programme (UNDP) and the United Nations Children's Fund (UNICEF). In 1988,

Figure 27. "Who here has had guinea worm disease?" Former U.S. President Jimmy Carter gets a show of hands in Ghana. Photo by Louise Gubb/The Carter Center.

African ministers of health issued their own resolution to wipe out the worm by 1995. As a result, the parasite faced a common front.

The ultimate program worked because it was developed from the bottom up. Carter, whom many have credited for the program's success, wrote, "The most important partners in the guinea worm eradication ·coalition are the hundreds of village-based health workers in the affected villages. Recruitment of layperson 'village volunteers' at the grass-roots level is the foundation of the campaign."[4] These "village volunteers" watch for and report cases, provide basic first aid, and help prevent victims from contaminating drinking-water supplies. They receive no pay but are given tools such as printed T-shirts, bicycles, and backpacks filled with first aid supplies. Without these individuals, little progress would have been made.

Other facets of the eradication program can indeed be credited to Carter and his knack for getting help from all the right places. For example, he reportedly took his mission to Edgar Bronfman, Sr., a major stakeholder in DuPont, and, over lunch, demonstrated with a damask napkin how tiny infective copepods can be filtered out of drinking water.

Bronfman was impressed, and he was instrumental in DuPont's creation of a fine durable mesh cloth for filtering drinking water, which the company donated for distribution to villagers.[5]

In turn, American Cyanamid Company donated a chemical larvicide for treating ponds. Money came from the governments of both affected and unaffected countries and from many other donors; volunteers came from many countries and organizations, including members of the U.S. Peace Corps; nongovernmental charitable organizations (NGOs) joined the effort; bicycles were donated. In later years, the Bill and Melinda Gates Foundation threw in its financial might as well, pledging $65 million, much of it in the form of challenge grants: the foundation matches, one to one, all other donations to the campaign.

The Carter Center forged on, headed by Carter and associate executive director Donald R. Hopkins, working closely with both the CDC and the WHO. Carter visited affected countries and gained the energetic assistance of two more powerful statesmen whose countries have suffered greatly from the scourge of guinea worm infections: General Amadou Toumani Touré of Mali and General Yakubu Gowon of Nigeria.

From the outset, naysayers gave the effort no chance because of the lack of a drug to treat the infection and of a vaccine to prevent it. Eradication of this disease depends on getting people to change their behavior. People have to stop easing their excruciating lesions in surface water that also serves as drinking water. Everyone has to refrain from potentially contaminated drinking water, even if no other water is available. Everyone has to be told, and has to believe, that the long, thin, veinlike worms erupting through the skin come not as a punishment for bad behavior, and not as a result of eating a dangerous food, but simply from drinking water. Human behavior and belief are notoriously difficult to change.

Nonetheless, the worm failed, country by country. Pakistan was free of guinea worm by 1993; Kenya, by 1994. By 1995, all known endemic countries had joined the campaign (Yemen first discovered cases in 1995), and the total number of reported cases had dropped to about 129,000.[6] But the goal of the African ministers of health to eradicate the worm by that year was not met. Impediments to success included lack of funding, poor reporting of and slow response to cases, refusal of pond treatment by villagers, and armed conflict, particularly in Sudan.

In 1995, Jimmy Carter gave the campaign another boost when he skillfully cut through the furor in Sudan and negotiated the six-month "guinea worm ceasefire," a period when both sides agreed to lay down arms and let volunteers and NGOs enter the region in safety. At the time, this area accounted for half the world's remaining cases of dracunculiasis.

The partners set a new goal: except for Sudan, they predicted, the world would be free of *D. medinensis* by 2000. India achieved eradication in 1996; Yemen, Senegal, and Cameroon followed in 1997. By the end of 1998, the number of reported cases had dropped by 97 percent; fewer than eighty thousand cases existed worldwide.[7] In 2000, the majority of cases were in Sudan as predicted, but the worm was not vanquished elsewhere. Eradication in all of Asia eventually came in 2004. Only a dozen countries in Africa remained.

"We, representing the Governments of Benin, Burkina Faso, Côte d'Ivoire, Ethiopia, Ghana, Mali, Mauritania, Niger, Nigeria, Sudan, Togo, and Uganda, WHO, UNICEF, and The Carter Center, commit ourselves to intensifying implementation of eradication activities to free the world of dracunculiasis by the end of 2009."[8] These words are part of the Geneva Declaration "The Final Push for Dracunculiasis Eradication," signed on May 19, 2004. The signatories pledged greater political involvement in the campaign, better surveillance, funding, provision of safe water, increased personnel, and greater efforts to promote involvement of both leaders and villagers.

Volunteers continued distributing cloth filters and drinking straws containing fine mesh to filter drinking water, ponds were treated with larvicide, reported cases were treated promptly and prevented from contaminating water, and wells were drilled to provide a safe water supply. The Bill and Melinda Gates Foundation made its first challenge grant, resulting in $45 million to keep the program going. And the worm continued to lose ground.

In 2007, only five countries reported cases of dracunculiasis that had been acquired within their borders, and two of these countries appeared to be free of the worm by the end of the year. In 2007, 9,585 cases were reported, 96 percent of which were in Ghana and Sudan.[9] The end of 2008 saw a total for the year of fewer than 5,000 cases, marking a 99 percent reduction from the millions of the 1980s.

The battle isn't over yet, and the 2009 goal is unlikely to be met. In its global surveillance summary for 2007, the WHO points out that

the remaining endemic communities [in Ghana and Sudan] are remote, poor, devoid of infrastructure and present significant challenges. . . . Moreover, residents in endemic areas in both countries are nomadic, moving seasonally with their cattle in pursuit of water and pasture, making it more difficult to determine where and when transmission is occurring.[10]

The partners of the Carter Center will have to stay the course with great determination, perhaps for a number of years, to see their goal finally accomplished—but no one expects them to fail.

The lack of a silver bullet in the form of a drug or vaccine was seen as a weakness at the start of dracunculiasis eradication, but in retrospect, this factor may prove to be a key reason for success. Drugs in particular have a way of letting us down before they finish the job, and both drugs and vaccines can be harder to distribute than knowledge. The attempt to eliminate river blindness (see chapter 7) has soundly proven both points.

———

Because the life cycle of *O. volvulus* requires a black fly host as well as a human one, we have two obvious opportunities to attack the worm: while it's in the human or while it's in the black fly. Early efforts at *O. volvulus* control, begun in the 1940s, targeted black flies and involved spraying insecticides along water courses where the flies breed. Black fly larvae in rivers ingested the chemical, and black fly numbers plummeted, with an accompanying drop in the number of people who acquired the worms.

The insecticide approach is not ideal because one cannot spray everywhere, and where black flies are wiped out, the population is quickly replenished by flies from outside the sprayed area. Though the new arrivals may be uninfected, humans with adult worms, which can live up to fifteen years, are a ready source of infection, and river blindness returns.

In 1987, new hope emerged for elimination of river blindness in the form of a drug that could mass-treat infected people. The drug, ivermectin, was developed by Merck & Co. for use against parasites in animals, but research revealed that it could kill the tiny microfilariae of *O. volvulus* that travel through the skin and cause the terrible itching, drying, and wrinkling, as well as vision loss. Ivermectin doesn't kill adult worms, but it does induce temporary infertility; female worms produce very few microfilariae for up to a year after exposure. Luckily, ivermectin is very safe, and it can be given as a single dose once per year; both are superb features in a drug that needs to be delivered to millions of people, many of whom live in remote villages or practice a nomadic lifestyle. Repeated treatment is thought to enhance the effect of the drug and to kill some adult worms.

In a stunning act of generosity, and in collaboration with the WHO, Merck donated ivermectin, under the trade name Mectizan, to anyone who needed it for as long as is necessary to eliminate onchocerciasis everywhere on earth. With such a magic bullet, eradication of the worm should be possible, and millions upon millions of dollars have been spent on the effort. Annual mass treatment of populations at risk started in large areas of West Africa following Merck's donation and later moved to other parts of the continent, sometimes in conjunction with insecticide spraying to control black flies. Taking a lesson from the dracunculiasis eradication program, organizers eventually anchored distribution of the drug with volunteers in communities, thereby reaching the maximum number of people.

By 1996, the Pan American Health Association (PAHO), the Carter Center, the Bill and Melinda Gates Foundation, Lions Clubs International, and other donors had joined WHO and Merck in the effort to eliminate river blindness. By 2002, experts estimated that eighteen million children had been spared the parasite and that six hundred thousand cases of blindness had been prevented.[11] Much of West Africa was free of the worm. Yet this was the same year that the Carter Center concluded that eradication of onchocerciasis in Africa was impossible.

A handful of obstacles support the Carter Center conclusion. Because treatment doesn't kill the adult worms and worms live ten to fifteen years, mass annual treatments must continue unabated for fifteen years or more; treatment in some areas has still not begun, while new cases still occur in some treated areas. Black flies can travel or coast on the wind for surprisingly large distances, bringing the parasite back to areas where it has been eradicated; the flies have also become resistant to insecticides. Some infected human populations are very difficult to reach because of location or a nomadic lifestyle. Finally, people who are also infected with *Loa loa*, another tissue roundworm, should not be treated with ivermectin because of the possibility of serious side effects.

Though it was only a dreaded possibility in 2002, *O. volvulus* resistance to ivermectin can now be added to the list of obstacles: in some places, female worms that have been exposed repeatedly to the drug resume producing high numbers of microfilariae within a few months of treatment, increasing the chances of passing the parasite on to black flies and, in turn, to more humans. This development is so serious that the scientists who presented the first proof of ivermectin resistance in 2007 wrote, "The lack of attention to the possibility that ivermectin resistance can develop and might spread could, in the long term, threaten all gains that have been achieved through the onchocerciasis control programmes."[12]

In 2006, the African Programme for Onchocerciasis Control (APOC) estimated that thirty-seven million Africans still had the worms and that ninety million more were at risk of infection.[13] Despite considerable gains, sixty-plus years of insecticides and twenty years of ivermectin had hardly made a dent and the available tools were not what they once were.

The situation in Central and South America is not so grim. *Onchocerca volvulus*, introduced by enslaved Africans, was present in thirteen well-defined areas in six countries: Brazil, Colombia, Ecuador, Guatemala, Mexico, and Venezuela, with the vast majority of cases occurring in Guatemala, Mexico, and Venezuela. Many of the black fly species transmitting the parasite were not particularly efficient at doing so, and the Onchocerciasis Elimination Program for the Americas (OEPA) favored treatment twice each year instead of once.

By the end of 2008, four of the original thirteen endemic areas no longer received mass treatments of ivermectin because no new cases had appeared, and Colombia was the first country in the world to free itself of the parasite. In October 2008, OEPA set a goal of interrupting transmission of *O. volvulus* everywhere in the Americas by 2012. If it succeeds and is able to prevent reemergence through people carrying live adult worms, *O. volvulus* will have been eradicated in that part of the world.

Treatment continues in Africa, and though no realistic goal of eradication is possible at this point, the situation isn't hopeless. Hopes rest on either a vaccine or a new antiparasitic drug that can kill adult worms, but even if one of these options were already in our hands, no new drug could pass clinical trials and become available for use before 2015, if then. With luck, the answer or at least a stopgap lies elsewhere.

A curious discovery has exposed an unexpected weakness in *O. volvulus*: a group of bacteria, *Wolbachia* spp., live inside the cells and embryos of *O. volvulus* and other nematodes, passed along through all stages of the worm's life cycle from one generation to the next. This organism is important for two reasons. Research indicates that human disease associated with *O. volvulus* is not caused by the microfilariae themselves but by the body's immune response to *Wolbachia*, which is exposed when microfilariae die. Moreover, the worms can't reproduce—or even live very long—without *Wolbachia*.[14] Thus, we may be able to treat onchocerciasis with antibiotics that are already available—ones that have no effect on worms or microfilariae but kill *Wolbachia.*

Currently, research hasn't revealed an antibiotic that will clear *Wolbachia* bacteria in human cases of onchocerciasis with less than three weeks of treatment, making mass treatment over large areas even more difficult and impractical than single-dose distribution of ivermectin. Nonetheless, it's a hopeful sign. The next magic bullet against river blindness may well be an antibiotic that we already have.

———

Because *O. volvulus* worms characteristically cluster in nodules under the skin—lumps that are obvious to the naked eye—surveillance for onchocerciasis sometimes depends on looking for typical skin nodules. In Africa, APOC has directed mass treatment of communities with ivermectin based on the percentage of people with these nodules.

Using this type of surveillance, scientists conducted a study in four communities in Uganda to determine the effectiveness of twelve years of annual doses of ivermectin.[15] In 1993, two-thirds of the people examined had nodules; in 2005, only about 11 percent had them. The researchers surgically removed twenty-one of the nodules they discovered in 2005 to determine whether the worms were still alive and whether females were producing microfilariae. The results were surprising: a third of the nodules were not *O. volvulus* at all; they were *T. solium* cysticerci.

Aside from raising questions about how the pork tapeworm might be undermining efforts to deal with river blindness, the discovery highlights the fact that *T. solium* is a serious—and seriously ignored—health issue in many parts of the world. That it has become such a serious problem is unfortunate because the life cycle of *T. solium* could be interrupted as easily as that of *D. medinensis.* We need only change human behavior.

The keys to defeating *D. medinensis* were to get people to filter their drinking water and refrain from immersing emerging worms in water sources. The keys to wiping out *T. solium* are to get people to thoroughly cook pork and prevent pigs from gaining access to human feces. But unlike the guinea worm situation, we have other tools for this fight: drugs to treat both infected humans and pigs and vaccines that prevent pigs from becoming infected in the first place. In 1992, the International Task Force for Disease Eradication declared that eradication of cysticercosis—infection in humans with the larval form of the worm—is possible.

It hasn't happened. Today, pork tapeworm infection and cysticercosis are even more common than they were in 1992. According to 2003 estimates, fifty million people are infected with the parasite and fifty thousand people die of cysticercosis every year.[16] The majority of these infections and deaths are in poor countries; poverty has everything to do with the success of the worm.

The power of money to fight *T. solium*—by providing a high standard of living—is evident in the fact that the worm has almost completely disappeared in the West without any large-scale programs to eradicate it. Even before meat inspection, intestinal pork tapeworms were uncommon in developed countries, and so was cysticercosis. Where living standards are high, pigs are kept in fenced areas, people have access to toilets, and meat inspection adds an extra measure of food safety. When Western pig farmers stopped feeding garbage to pigs, the life cycle of the worm was effectively interrupted for good. Today, most industrialized counties do not see cases of pork tapeworm that have been acquired within their borders.

Money—the lack thereof—is also the reason why *T. solium* can't be attacked the way *D. medinensis* was. Eradicating *D. medinensis* cost people nothing because they were provided with filters to make their drinking water safe and needed only to learn not to ease their tortured guinea worm lesions in water. Furthermore, with the disappearance of the guinea worm, productivity increases and the standard of living rises. However, when public-health authorities seek to curb *T. solium* by asking people to corral their pigs, remove infected pigs from the food supply, and prevent pigs from eating human feces—a free source of pig food—they impose direct costs and income loss. People who are already living in poverty cannot afford to take these measures.

A typical poor smallholder farming community in Southeast Asia, Central or South America, Africa, and various other places has packed-earth roads heavily traveled by chickens, pigs, and barefoot children. People living in these communities often don't know which animals are theirs, but the animals know, and the animals also know how to scavenge for much of their own food, clearing up garbage and waste that they find on the ground.

These villages often have no toilets, or they may have one communal toilet, so people frequently defecate outside on the ground. A study done in 1994 and 1995 that looked at whether flies were important in the spread of eggs of *T. solium* concluded that in the study area, pigs consumed "fecal

Figure 28. A Thai mountain village with free-roaming pigs. Photo by the author.

material immediately after defecation, thereby limiting fly contact with *T. solium* eggs."[17] No wonder the villages tend to look relatively clean. As a result, however, individuals passing eggs from intestinal pork tapeworms play a pivotal role in transmitting the parasite to pigs as well as to humans.

The global situation has worsened in recent years because the population of pigs has grown. With the demand for meat rising everywhere, people are raising more pigs both for their own consumption and for sale to others. According to the Food and Agriculture Organization of the United Nations (FAO), Africa had twice as many pigs at the end of the twentieth century as it had in 1970, and this upward trend is likely to continue.[18] Each pig has significant value, so farmers can't afford to have the pork condemned: owners dodge official meat inspection, opt for clandestine slaughter, and sell pork privately.

"Unofficial pig inspection" is carried out by feeling for cysts in pigs' tongues. Although this would appear to be an inefficient method, a study in Huancayo, Peru, found that no pigs slaughtered in the official slaughterhouses had cysticercosis, yet 15 percent of live pigs offered for sale in local markets were infected.[19] In Peru in the 1990s, "slaughtering was performed under clandestine conditions; infested carcasses thus obtained were later introduced into the formal market. . . . Infected pork was sold at cheaper prices and often mixed and disguised with clean meat in order to facilitate its sale to public eating facilities."[20] In the absence of an organized eradication program, not much has changed.

The FAO lists the measures needed to eradicate *T. solium:* meat inspection, animal control, screening of people who have contact with pigs, sewage treatment, control of markets with financial incentives, and farmer and public education. Though a 2005 FAO report lists education last, this element might be better placed first on the list: the guinea worm eradication program proved that once people understand what they have to do and why, they can wipe out the parasite on their own.

In a small Mexican community of about two thousand people, a team of anthropologists and medical specialists demonstrated the value of putting knowledge in the right places in the early 1990s.[21] They first surveyed the local people to identify the risks and transmission factors in the community; then they recruited local leaders and taught them about the worm's life cycle, the diseases it causes, the ways in which local people and pigs were catching it, and measures they could take to stop the spread of disease. The scientists invited religious leaders, teachers, housewives, students, and people already involved in local groups, so that after they left, knowledge would remain in the community. The villagers eventually identified a financial incentive as well: uninfected pigs brought a higher price at slaughter. When epidemiologists returned to the community later, they found no infected pigs.

No infected pigs means, eventually, no infected people, but *T. solium* tapeworms live for years: as long as adult tapeworms lurk in human intestines, a risk remains that the parasite will be reintroduced to local pigs and that new cases of cysticercosis will appear in humans.[22] Thus, any serious eradication effort has to include either mass treatment of people or testing and treatment of those infected.

Global eradication of *T. solium* is certainly possible, and with new vaccines to prevent infection in pigs, it's more feasible today than it was in 1992, when people first began to take the idea seriously. Industrialized countries grow more interested as neurocysticercosis emerges within their borders, but so far eradication isn't happening—perhaps because of the cost of a program or perhaps because *T. solium* is cosmopolitan and eradication would require virtually every country in the world to participate. To date, no organization has stepped forward to spearhead the effort. The FAO has concluded, "Control of neurocysticercosis from *T. solium* infections will require a multidisciplinary and multilevel approach because of the complex nature of its epidemiology. . . . Without this level of preparation, controlling this [disease], which is so dependent upon long-established risky animal rearing and cultural habits, will remain nearly intractable."[23]

The discouraging truth is that, despite untold millions spent in the past, no global effort to eradicate a parasite has been successful to date. The first global attempt to eradicate malaria, in fact, taught us how spectacularly we can fail.

—

Malaria may have originated in Africa, but by 1898, when Ronald Ross, a British physician in the Indian Medical Service, proved that *Anopheles* spp. mosquitoes transmitted the parasites, humans had spread the disease over much of the world. It was a serious health problem in Asia and Continental Europe as far north as Siberia. Malaria was so common in the coastal marshes of Essex, England, that trials of the antimalarial drug quinine were conducted there.[24] European colonization brought the disease to North America. By the 1880s, outbreaks and epidemics were occurring throughout the low-lying regions of the United States and in some parts of southern Canada.

At about the same time that Ross made his discovery, Walter Reed, a U.S. Army physician, proved that *Aedes* spp. mosquitoes spread yellow fever, and the first successful control efforts for yellow fever and malaria went hand in hand: dwellings were screened and water sources where mosquitoes bred were drained. In Havana, Cuba, during the Spanish-American War of 1898 and in Panama during construction of the Panama Canal, these measures proved that mosquito control could drastically lower the number of infections.

In Panama, Surgeon Major William Gorgas of the U.S. Army introduced additional control measures. His program called for adding oil and a chemical mixture toxic to mosquito larvae to ponds, clearing brush and tall grasses, administering quinine to workers to prevent infection, and hand killing adult mosquitoes found in buildings during the day.

Yellow fever disappeared from the region, and malaria deaths fell to about 2.6 per 1,000 people by 1909.[25]

In North America, malaria was already in retreat without the imposition of such control methods.[26] Its demise is a story of people, water, and domestic animals. In the 1800s, development in the United States often meant alteration of water resources: water impoundments in communities provided a reliable water supply; mills needed mill ponds; dams and road construction created artificial lakes. These new bodies of water also created ideal breeding conditions for the mosquito species that transmitted *Plasmodium* spp., allowing the parasite to spread widely.

In time, the ecology of the new ponds and lakes evolved. Water acidity increased, mosquito predators such as fish and amphibians moved in, and aquatic plant growth stabilized. Mosquitoes didn't do so well. At the same time, the number of domestic animals increased, and the mosquitoes, species that prefer biting animals, were diverted from humans. Homes were built better, especially in the north, and admitted fewer mosquitoes to bite human occupants. These changes were enough to drive malaria back to the low-lying wetlands of the southeastern United States.

In England and much of Continental Europe, the story was similar.[27] Tighter homes, drainage of wetlands where mosquitoes bred, an increase in domestic animals, housing of animals in buildings close to human residences, movement of people away from wetlands into industrial cities, and availability of quinine all played a part. Fewer mosquitoes bit infected humans, so there were fewer to pass the parasites on to new human hosts. Transmission was interrupted, and by 1900, malaria was relatively rare. It remained a problem, however, in the countries of Eastern Europe where industrial development didn't proceed as quickly.

Malaria's stronghold in the southeastern United States persisted and sparked occasional epidemics in neighboring regions. In the early years of the twentieth century, individual states tried to control the disease using experience gained in Cuba and Panama. Public education, improved housing, spreading of chemicals to kill mosquito larvae, and control of open water, including hydroelectric projects and irrigation ditches, reduced the incidence of the disease but failed to eradicate it. Then came Malaria Control in War Areas (MCWA).[28]

The office oversaw a program to reduce the impact of malaria in U.S. military bases during World War II, both at home and overseas. Not solely focused on the health of the military, MCWA also sought to prevent malaria from spreading through the country again when soldiers returned home. Relying heavily on mosquito control, MCWA drained mosquito-breeding areas and used larvicides and insecticides—and because the program had the U.S. military behind it, it had more resources to devote to the task than ever before.

By the end of World War II, MCWA had added the insecticide DDT to the antimosquito arsenal and was spraying the interiors of American homes to kill any mosquitoes that might bite troops returning home with communicable diseases. Very effective for malaria control, DDT could be sprayed on walls, where it remained effective for about six months. *Anopheles* spp. mosquitoes tend to land on walls after feeding, so having a persistent and effective pesticide there killed the mosquitoes before they had a chance to pass on malaria or other diseases.

After World War II, the Office of Malaria Control in War Areas became the Communicable Disease Center, whose charter was still to eradicate malaria in the United States. (The Communicable Disease Center later became the Centers for Disease Control and Prevention, or CDC.) From 1945 to 1949, the CDC worked with the health systems of affected states. It sprayed home interiors with DDT twice each year at first, then once a year, and kept track of malaria deaths.

In 1946, the antimalarial drug chloroquine, the first safe alternative to quinine, became available, enabling treatment of Americans who had returned from overseas with relapsing malarial infections as well as infections acquired at home. The multipronged effort succeeded. Transmission of malaria in the United States stopped, probably by 1947.[29] In 1949, the United States was "declared free of malaria as a significant health problem," with the CDC reporting very few cases acquired in the country.[30] By 1952, the CDC turned its attention to surveillance in the United States and eradication in the rest of the world.

Based on the effectiveness of both DDT and chloroquine—but mainly DDT—the World Health Organization teamed with national agencies and governments to eradicate malaria worldwide. In every location afflicted by malaria, homes would be sprayed for three years, after which any human cases could be treated along with limited spraying to prevent further outbreaks; once eradication was achieved, continuous surveillance would ensure the disease didn't recur or get reintroduced. Malaria would die out. Even without chloroquine, planners thought, five years of dedicated spraying in each malarious area should do the job. The Global Eradication of Malaria Program, begun in 1955, took just fourteen years to fail.

Not all *Anopheles* mosquitoes pause after feeding to rest on the wall; not all homes in malaria-endemic areas have walls to rest on. In addition, the widespread use of DDT in agriculture at the same time had two devastating effects: mosquitoes became resistant to the insecticide, and scientists began to see the serious adverse effects that DDT had on the environment, particularly on birds of prey. At the same time, malaria parasites, particularly the dangerous *P. falciparum*, developed resistance to chloroquine.[31]

Add the difficulties of reaching remote areas, cultural misunderstandings and miscommunications, and resource shortfalls, and the parasite had the conditions it needed to persist despite untold millions spent to wipe it out. By 1969, the word *eradication* was changed to *control.* In some regions, particularly developed countries like the United States, malaria was wiped out, and a few countries eliminated it after 1969. However, in much of the world, it began to rebound where some success had been achieved. Elsewhere, notably equatorial Africa, there had never been much progress to begin with.

Plasmodium spp. are in no immediate danger of becoming extinct. In 2006, half the world's people lived in areas where they were at risk of catching malaria from a mosquito bite. That year saw some 247 million cases, the vast majority caused by *P. falciparum*, and close to a million deaths. As always, Africa was hardest hit, accounting for nine of every ten deaths, mostly of children under the age of five.[32]

These numbers, often referred to as the "burden of malaria," conjure an image of a monstrous mosquito with its legs tightly wrapped around the planet. But despite that challenge, we are once again in pursuit of this troublemaker. The Roll Back Malaria Partnership (RBM), founded in 1998, is trying to break malaria's hold on us, this time by setting long-term goals and taking incremental steps toward eradication. The partnership's vision is that "by 2015 the malaria-specific Millennium Development Goal is achieved and malaria is no longer a major cause of mortality and no longer a barrier to social and economic development and growth anywhere in the world."[33]

The phrase "roll back malaria" is actually a brief but accurate description of the plan. Elimination efforts focus on the edges, rolling those edges back and leaving malaria–free territory behind. Away from the edges, the focus is on control: no country can realistically aim for elimination if it can't even control the disease, or if its neighbors are unable to achieve control. Controlling infection effectively in people has an immediate impact on transmission; fewer infected people means fewer infected mosquitoes and a decreased chance that any one mosquito bite will transmit *Plasmodium* sp.

The tools for eradication this time are the same but different and complement each other. The program emphasizes control of mosquitoes, using insecticide-treated bed nets to protect sleepers against mosquito bites at night and recommending twelve possible insecticides for spraying on the interior walls of buildings. Prompt treatment of cases is important too, using a combination of antimalarial drugs to lower the risk of treatment failure due to drug resistance. Finally, in high-risk areas, preventive drug treatment of pregnant women is recommended.[34]

The RBM guidelines are flexible but suggest that a country aim for elimination of malaria only if it has the political will and financial resources, has the disease under control within its borders and has low transmission rates, and can prevent reintroduction from neighboring countries. The ability to detect and treat cases immediately is imperative. When a country has had no cases of malaria transmitted within its borders for three years, it can be declared malaria free.[35]

Countries at the edge of malaria risk areas have an inherently better situation because at least some of their borders are malaria free, and transmission is likely already less intense. The hope is that these countries will gradually move from control to elimination, shrinking the range of *Plasmodium* spp. parasites in a stepwise fashion until, one day, the world sees the last case of malaria.

Still, not all mosquitoes bite indoors at night when people are protected by bed nets; mosquito resistance to insecticides and *Plasmodium* resistance to drugs continue to evolve, and some highly malarious areas are remote, hostile, or embroiled in political conflicts. Infected people can harbor the less dangerous *P. vivax* for years, reinfecting mosquitoes and setting off a new cycle of transmission. On RBM's wish list are new ways of controlling mosquitoes, ways to avoid drug resistance, a practical means to find and treat carriers of *P. vivax*,. and a vaccine that works, among other things. And all of these solutions must work well and be readily available, affordable, and easy to use. If we achieve the World Health Assembly goal of reducing the burden of malaria by 75 percent by 2015, we will be very lucky.[36]

On the prospects for global eradication, the WHO has written, "While the sequence of events leading to elimination is logically clear, there is no evidence yet to show that malaria elimination can be achieved and maintained in areas that currently have high transmission."[37] The extinction of the *Plasmodium* species that infect humans is a goal we can't see yet, and only time will reveal whether we have the resources and the tools to get there.

——

Another serious attempt at parasite elimination targets *Trypanosoma cruzi*, that denizen of poor housing and the international blood supply that we met in the previous chapter. The cynic might notice that developed countries had little concern about this mass killer of the south until immigrants started bringing it north and threatening blood transfusion and organ-donation recipients. In fact, its eradication was so far down the list of priorities for international health organizations, pharmaceutical companies, and even governments in endemic areas that it is commonly referred to as a "neglected parasitic disease." The realist knows that this neglect is because the majority of victims are poor.

But things have changed. The World Health Organization now refers to Chagas' disease as a global problem,[38] and, in 1991, Latin American countries partnered with the Pan American Health Organization to create the Southern Cone Initiative, an effort to stop transmission of Chagas' by controlling the kissing bug *Triatoma infestans* and screening the blood supply.

Trypanosoma cruzi seems an unlikely candidate for elimination because it exists so widely in nature. More than a hundred wild mammals carry the parasite, and all species of triatomine bugs are potential vectors. The network of life that supports *T. cruzi* covers Central and most of South America like a web.

The web does have a weak spot, however—the same feature that allowed *T. cruzi* to emerge in humans in the first place. The vast majority of infections are initiated by domesticated kissing bugs, the most significant of which is *T. infestans*. The Southern Cone Initiative launched a two-pronged attack: screening of blood donors has all but halted transmission by blood transfusion in many places, and bug control has halted transmission by kissing bugs. Millions of homes have been sprayed with insecticide, painted with insecticidal paint, and upgraded to remove thatch or tile roofing and cracks in walls and floors, and they no longer harbor the bugs.

Southern Cone Initiative countries included Argentina, Bolivia, Brazil, Chile, Paraguay, and Uruguay, with Peru joining in 1997. By 2001, the incidence of Chagas' disease in these seven countries had dropped by about 94 percent, deaths were down by half, and a similar eradication effort was under way in Central America. In 2007, the World Health Organization announced that it was "expanding the global effort to eliminate Chagas," and that Bayer HC had pledged funds and free drugs to treat thirty thousand patients.[39] The recipients of these pledges were presumably victims infected outside of Central and South America by blood transfusion or through mother-to-child prenatal spread.

The success of the Southern Cone Initiative is encouraging, but the fact that the conversation is always about elimination of Chagas' rather than extinction of *T. cruzi* is significant. We're trying to send the parasite back to the woods, and that's all: because *T. cruzi* is so prevalent in nature, we cannot hope to wipe it out completely, and we can expect it to continue to make sporadic appearances like other diseases that lurk in animal reservoirs.

Trypanosoma cruzi will be with us for the foreseeable future for a handful of reasons. First, *T. infestans* will not be extinct even if we kill every bug in every infested house. The species lives in the wild in Bolivia, and contrary to prior belief, studies indicate that feral populations live in other countries as well. These bugs, and other domesticated species, will reinfest homes if inhabitants and health systems aren't watchful.

In some areas, infestation of houses has never been the problem. Instead, kissing bugs—nondomesticated species—live outside the home in woodpiles and in vegetation, particularly in palm trees. In areas where people are encroaching on forest, clearing land to raise crops and domestic animals, scattered palm trees are the only things left standing, and surveys have shown that these palms harbor many triatomids in every stage of development. While sparing the palms has left the bugs a place to live, land clearing has removed most of the mammals that provide their usual food supply, so hungry bugs feed on humans, flying to lighted dwellings at night. Such conditions can maintain a steady level of trypanosomiasis in humans, even where the area has no domestic kissing bugs. Similarly, people who venture into the forest to harvest palm leaves, palm fiber, and other natural products are at risk of infection and will remain so.

Finally, if today we were to see the last incidence of *T. cruzi* infection of a human being, we would not be able to declare the parasite extinct in humans for a century or more. Some of those who progress to chronic infection suffer serious disease later in life, but many do not, and these people can pass the parasite on if they are bitten by a kissing bug, give blood, or give birth.

——

Most human parasites and those of our domestic animals are at least as safe from extinction as we are. They won't be easily swept away, as these brief vignettes of eradication efforts illustrate. Though we can see a path forward in a few cases, the more people we have, the more contaminated the water and soil become, the more parasitic infections take hold, the bigger the challenge becomes.

Eradicate *Ascaris lumbricoides?* Everyone—6.7 billion of us—must use a toilet connected to a sewage treatment system and scrupulously wash hands after passing stool. Eggs of *A. lumbricoides* can remain viable for ten years or more, so even if environmental contamination were to stop now, more than a decade would pass before we could see the last new case acquired from the eggs presently out there. All sewage would have to be treated with temperatures or chemicals lethal to *A. lumbricoides:* treated sewage used as fertilizer has been known to actually increase the level of infection in communities near the treatment plant.[40]

Eradicate *Schistosoma hematobium?* Never allow urine to contaminate freshwater, control snail populations, treat all infected people, and find a vaccine. The other common schistosomes, *S. mansoni* and *S. japonicum,* also infect animal species; therefore, they would be a lot harder to conquer.

Drive *Giardia lamblia, Cryptosporidium parvum,* or *Toxoplasma gondii* to extinction? Forget it. These protozoa are everywhere on earth, too widespread in the environment and in other species to yield to the knowledge, technology, and resources we have now. We may succeed in reducing human infections with better sanitation or vaccines, but even those possibilities lie far in our future.

Epilogue

OUR CULTURAL BIAS MAINTAINS THAT parasites are inherently bad. If we could eradicate them one by one, where would we stop? At disease-causing parasites of humans? At parasites that afflict humans and domestic animals? Perhaps at those that cause significant disease as a result of our activities, our interference with the environment? How would the extinction of a few—or many—parasitic species affect populations and ecosystems, and should we weigh these effects against the expected benefits of their demise? These questions plunge us into a moral-ethical tangle.

This dilemma isn't new. An old idea with a somewhat narrower focus—and one fraught with ethical quicksand—is the "parasitologist's dilemma": This idea basically states that if we succeed in halting the loss of human life due to parasitic disease, we may inadvertently create another problem—overpopulation.[1] In 1973, economist Edwin J. Cohn illustrated the dilemma with his analysis of India's economy after the first global malaria eradication program. He concluded, "On the basis of the evidence at hand, the reduction of mortality brought about by the anti-malaria program may be said to have substantial social or welfare benefits, but to have exerted a decelerating effect on economic development."[2] He argued, among other things, that reduced mortality in infants increases the number of people who are dependent on others, whereas reduced mortality in adults increases the healthy work force in countries that already have "large amounts of surplus labor."[3]

Cohn's work has been paraphrased as "better dead than alive and riotously reproducing," which illustrates the dangers of wrestling with the parasitologist's dilemma: it's an interesting theoretical idea, but to use it as an argument against fighting parasitic disease would be profoundly unethical.[4] A sociologist might also argue that the idea is wrong in any case. Parasitic diseases disproportionately affect the poor, whereas wealthy people have relatively few parasites and, usually, a low birthrate. Lowering the global burden of parasites requires an attack on poverty, which in turn will ultimately give the world's poor countries the ability to control population.

Nonetheless, a dilemma does exist, and it becomes clear when we acknowledge just how many parasites there are. Roberts and Janovy have written, "Few people realize that there are far more kinds of parasitic than nonparasitic organisms in the world. Even if we exclude the viruses and rickettsias, which are all parasitic, and the many kinds of parasitic bacteria and fungi, the parasites are still in the majority."[5] Given this reality, we need to rethink our negative attitude toward parasites and ponder the role these organisms play in the complex web of life on earth before we attempt to expunge them wholesale.

We still have a lot to learn. New scientific discoveries, such as evidence that intestinal worms may moderate our immune systems and protect against allergies and autoimmune diseases, should give us pause as we plan the next assault. Perhaps parasitic infection brings other health benefits that we don't yet know about. Good things *have* come of parasites: *Trichinella spiralis* inspired the first drafts of meat inspection guidelines, and malaria laid the foundations of the world-renowned U.S. Centers for Disease Control and Prevention. Screwworm brought political foes together in the spirit of cooperation, and African trypanosomiasis probably saved equatorial Africa from the environmental damage suffered in much of the world. What might we lose—physically, socially, and environmentally—if we permanently evict our unwelcome guests?

Parasites don't just make hosts sick; they are an important part of life on earth. Scientists are realizing that "parasitism is a process that through multiple agencies contributes to within and between species diversity, community structure and diversity, and therefore to the ability of organisms to respond to change," and the ability to change is as important as it has ever been in a world of species movement, climate change, and environmental damage.[6] Much the same can be said from a cultural perspective. Our relationship with parasites is a long conversation in which humans and parasites each react and adapt in countless ways in response to the other. Here, too, parasites are doing something important. Throughout history, they have not just caused disease; they have had other wide-ranging impacts on our lives, both good and bad, and will continue to do so.

We're making progress against parasitic diseases, and we must continue to reduce both the chronic illness and mortality that they cause. But we should proceed with curiosity, learning as much about these fascinating creatures as we can. And we should proceed with caution. In many instances, a compromise may be necessary—a level of cultural and emotional tolerance, a manageable balance between devastating disease on one hand and species extinction on the other. We must remember the law of unintended consequences.

NOTES

INTRODUCTION

1. In standard textbook definitions, a *parasite* benefits while harming its host, a *commensal* benefits but does no harm to the host, and a *mutualist* benefits while the host also receives some benefit.

ONE. AMBUSH

1. Some of the parasites that infest humans today evolved with us and go back millions of years. Others crossed from animals to humans after the hunter-gatherer lifestyle was abandoned and humans domesticated animals.

2. The transmission of intestinal parasites would have been aided in hunter-gatherers in at least two ways. First, the use of latrine sites—places where people habitually go to relieve themselves—repeatedly exposes people to worm eggs and larvae. In turn, viable plant seeds passed in feces would have resulted in the growth of edible plants at latrine sites and, subsequently, consumption of plants contaminated with human feces. For a discussion of how latrine sites contributed to the domestication of plants, see Diamond 1994, 101–5.

3. Hunter-gatherer lifestyles differed, of course, and groups would have stayed in some locations for extended periods. See Burenhult 1993. Nonetheless, each time they moved, the transmission of parasites that spend part of their lives in the environment, or in another host, was interrupted.

4. For a detailed discussion of how permanent settlements, increasing human populations, and the domestication of animals aided human diseases, including parasites, see Diamond 1997, particularly chapter 11; and Porter 1996, 16–30.

5. Many parasitic organisms do not significantly harm their hosts and would not benefit from doing so. Humans, too, host parasites that don't cause disease. For the most part, this book is not about them.

6. Hulse 1971 explores the evidence that supports a theory of schistosomiasis in Jericho—biblical, archaeological, and medical. This is the main source for the evidence of schistosomiasis I describe below.

7. Adult pairs of *S. hematobium* migrate from the liver to the bladder through the blood vessels, moving *against* the blood flow.

8. Biggs 1960 identified *B. truncatus* from about 1650 B.C. recovered during excavation at Jericho.

9. Opinions are divided about the walls of Jericho, which so famously fell in the biblical account. Jericho was a walled community at several times during its long history; archaeology reveals that at least some of these walls were destroyed by either fire or earthquake. Some scholars maintain that Jericho had no walls in Joshua's time (the biblical account may combine two separate destructive events), whereas others suggest that the population, worn down by chronic disease, would likely have let any walls fall into disrepair. See, for example, Hulse 1971.

10. The Volta was dammed to produce hydroelectric power for industry. Lake Volta's surface area is some 3,283 square miles (8,502 sq km).

11. For statistics on the schistosomiasis problem arising from the Akosombo and Kpong dams, see Hunter et al. 1993.

12. Zakhary 1997, 100.

13. Sleeping sickness may have been present in the lower Congo, but if so, it was rare and people did not associate it with the tsetse. See McKelvey 1973.

14. *Trypanosoma brucei* evades destruction by the immune system: as soon as antibodies are produced against it, the organism changes the antigenic molecules on its surface, making itself unrecognizable to the immune system again—and continues to multiply.

15. Both male and female tsetse flies suck blood. During her life span of about three months, a female tsetse produces between eight and twenty larval young, one at a time.

16. "Tens of Thousands Killed by a Tiny Fly," *New York Times,* March 20, 1904.

17. Ibid.

18. McKelvey 1973, 207.

19. See Moore and Galloway 1992.

20. Beadle and Hoffman 1993.

21. In war, casualties are the people taken out of action for any reason: injury, death, disease, capture, and so on.

22. *Artemisia annua* is the source of the traditional Chinese medicine *qinghao*, used to treat malaria for over a thousand years. In the late 1960s, the China Academy of Traditional Chinese Medicine began looking for a "new" antimalarial among the traditional herbs and subsequently rediscovered *qinghao*. The remarkable circumstances that brought about this "discovery" are discussed in Hsu 2006.

23. Gonçalves, Araújo, and Ferreira 2003 list more than fifty published reports of *A. lumbricoides* in archaeological sites and human mummies. Most are from present-day Europe.

24. Watt 1979, 154–55.

25. See, in particular, various works by John C. Beaglehole. Beaglehole devoted much of his career to studying the life and voyages of Captain James Cook, and he published edited volumes of Cook's journals as well as a biography.

26. *Bilious colic* is an archaic medical term referring to severe abdominal pain, often accompanied by vomiting of yellowish green fluid (bile).

27. For an overview of current medical knowledge about the effect of *A. lumbricoides* and other helminths (parasitic worms) on learning and childhood development, see Crompton et al. 2003, particularly "Part 1: Public Health Significance."

TWO. MARKET OF PERIL

1. This account comes from a Canadian legal case, the details of which were presumably recorded because of its potential to create precedent. I have used pseudonyms to protect the privacy of the family involved.

2. Ironically, *T. spiralis* was probably introduced to North America in pigs imported from Europe. See Rosenthal et al. 2008.

3. Pigs on both sides of the Atlantic were infested with *T. spiralis*. In this dispute, the worm was a cover for a protectionist agenda to keep American pork out of Europe. See Gignilliat 1961.

4. *Yachetti et al. v. John Duff & Sons Limited and Paolini* [1942], O.R. 682, 688–89.

5. Other diseases of swine also prompted laws against feeding raw garbage to pigs, notably vesicular exanthema and hog cholera.

6. Not every farmer had pigs, of course: disposal of dead animals was also an old and widespread problem.

7. Estimates indicate that the annual global burden of hydatid disease is more than a million DALYs (disability adjusted life years, which indicate the

years of healthy life lost) and place the economic loss at more than $4 billion; see C. Budke, P. Deplazes, and P. R. Torgerson, "Global Socioeconomic Impact of Cystic Echinococcus," *Emerging Infectious Diseases* (February 2006) [online serial], www.cdc.gov/ncidod/EID/vol12no02/05-0499.htm (accessed August 24, 2009).

8. Initially, suspicion fell on strawberries from California, causing California berry growers to lose some $40 million; Institute of Food Science & Technology, "*Cyclospora,*" Institute of Food Science and Technology Information Statement, May 2008, www.ifst.org/science_technology_resources/for_food_professionals/information_statements (accessed September 2, 2009).

9. For a detailed history of the Guatemalan raspberry industry's struggle with *Cyclospora,* see Calvin, Flores, and Foster 2003.

10. For details of the investigation that linked this outbreak to Guatemalan raspberries, see A. Y. Ho, A. S. Lopez, M. G. Eberhart, R. Levenson, B. S. Finkel, and A. J. da Silva, "Outbreak of Cyclosporiasis Associated with Imported Raspberries, Philadelphia, Pennsylvania," *Emerging Infectious Diseases* [online serial] 8 (8), www.cdc.gov/ncidod/EID/vol8no8/02-0012.htm (accessed August 26, 2009).

11. Calvin, Flores, and Foster 2003.

12. Centers for Disease Control 2004a.

13. See National Institute for Public Health Surveillance 2002 for an account of the epidemic in Nord-Pas-de-Calais.

14. Plath et al. 2001. Dieter Jansen is a pseudonym used to protect the patient's confidentiality.

15. See Berland 2003 for a discussion of shifting approaches to international importation of fish infested with anisakid larvae.

16. The remaining cases were attributed to pork consumed outside the country, meat from wild game, or unknown sources (Centers for Disease Control 2003).

17. The story was told to me by a pathologist who had some connection to the event, but it apparently was not documented.

18. For a review of the inspection procedures at the time, see Dewhirst, Cramer, and Sheldon 1967.

19. This incident was reported in Moskowitz 1995.

20. A copy of the Notice of Violation and an account of the event are posted on the Internet: "Rocco, There's a Fly in My Zuppa: Star of 'The Restaurant' Hit with Health Violations," *Smoking Gun,* www.thesmokinggun.com/archive/roccoinspect1.html (accessed August 28, 2009).

21. For a fascinating discussion of insects and their potential to spread protozoan parasites, see Graczyk, Knight, and Tamang 2005.

1. *Toxoplasma gondii* was first discovered in the gundi, a desert rodent, and can infect any warm-blooded vertebrate. Only cats harbor the sexually reproductive stage of the parasite and pass oocysts. For the life cycle of *T. gondii* in cats, see chapter 5 in this book.

2. Bowie et al. 1997.

3. Health Canada 1995.

4. Laing 2002.

5. A 1991 study (LeChefallier, Norton, and Lee) of sixty-six watersheds in North America detected *Cryptosporidium* spp. oocysts in 87 percent of samples.

6. Graczyk et al. 1998 found oocysts of *Cryptosporidium* sp. in the feces of Canada geese at seven out of nine sampling sites near Chesapeake Bay, Maryland.

7. For a full account of the source, cause, events, and outcomes of the 2001 cryptosporidiosis outbreak in North Battleford, see Laing 2002.

8. U.S. Department of Justice press releases provide an official account of the legal dispute over the Croton water supply. See "United States Sues New York City for Failing to Filter Croton Water Supply" (April 24, 1997), www .usdoj.gov/opa/pr/1997/April97/171enr.htm; and "New York City Agrees to Filter Croton Drinking Water System" (May 20, 1998), www.usdoj.gov/opa/ pr/1998/May/226enr.htm.html (both accessed September 9, 2009).

9. Isaac-Renton et al. 1993 investigated and documented this outbreak.

10. Ibid.

11. For details of the Milwaukee case, see MacKenzie et al. 1994.

12. Though lawsuits named General Chemical Corporation, there was nothing wrong with the water treatment chemicals the company supplied, and it was not found to be at fault. The company settled out of court.

13. Corso et al. 2003.

14. Though generally underplayed as a source of *G. lamblia,* grazing domesticated animals are often the major contributor of *G. lamblia* cysts to surface waters. See Alberta Agriculture and Rural Development, "Relationship between Beef Production and Waterborne Parasites (*Cryptosporidium* spp. and *Giardia* spp.) in the North Saskatchewan River Basin" (2002), www1.agric.gov.ab .ca/$department/deptdocs.nsf/all/wat6400 (accessed August 24, 2009).

15. Winiecka-Krusnell and Kettis 2003 discuss the global distribution and transmission of *G. lamblia* (103–4).

16. For an excellent summary of the history of the domestic cat, see Serpell 2000.

17. Rochlitz 2000, 208.

18. MacDonald, Yamaguchi, and Kerby 2000, 109.

19. A 1991 survey found *Cryptosporidium parvum* in 65 percent of dairy herds and 80 percent of feedlots. See Roberts and Janovy 2000, 136.

20. *Cryptosporidium* spp., *Giardia lamblia,* and *Toxoplasma gondii* are far from the only parasites transmitted by contaminated drinking water. Many other parasitic protozoa and worms can infect their hosts by this route.

FOUR. ILLEGAL ALIENS

Epigraph: R. Desowitz, *Who Gave Pinta to the Santa Maria?* (New York: Norton, 1997).

1. For more on microfilariae, read about *Onchocerca volvulus* in chapter 7 in this book.

2. Several ingenious and dedicated parasitologists have carried live parasites safely over long distances and across international borders. Both *S. hematobium* and *Diphyllobothrium latum,* the freshwater fish tapeworm, have been "imported" into the United States by scientists who deliberately infected themselves for research purposes. See Mayberry 1996.

3. Clark 1968, 24. Quoted by permission of Oxford University Press, Inc.

4. For a lengthy discussion of Andersonville and the conditions there, see D. F. Cross, "Why Did the Vermonters Die at Andersonville? The Deadly Hookworm" (2003), www.weldonrailroad.com (accessed August 25, 2009).

5. Quoted in ibid.

6. See chapter 1 for more on *T. gambiense.* Slavers were familiar with Winterbottom's sign, the swollen lymph nodes characteristic of advancing African sleeping sickness, and avoided taking Africans who had this symptom. See McKelvey 1973.

7. See Mann 2007 for a discussion of the early years of Jamestown, Virginia.

8. Ibid. Colonists imported the bees for honey, unwittingly providing themselves with pollinators for imported crops as well. North America has native bee species and other pollinators, but none match the crop-pollinating abilities of the European honeybee.

9. See, for example, H. A. Denmark, L. Cromroy, and M. T. Sanford, "Honey Bee Tracheal Mite," Featured Creatures, University of Florida EENY-172, November 2000, http://creatures.ifas.ufl.edu/misc/bees/tracheal_mite.htm (accessed August 25, 2009).

10. Matheson 2000 discusses the various ways that bees and bee parasites move around the world.

11. For more on the effects of *V. destructor,* see M. T. Sanford and H. A. Denmark, "Varroa Mite," Featured Creatures, University of Florida EENY-37, May 2007, http://creatures.ifas.ufl.edu/misc/bees/varroa_mite.htm (accessed August 27, 2009).

12. No one knows exactly when or where *V. destructor* entered the United States; however, most experts think that infected bees were smuggled into Florida and spread from there. See Wenner and Bushing 1996.

13. One of the first confirmations of *V. destructor* in Canada came from Peace River, Alberta, some 425 miles (680 kilometers) from the Canada-U.S. border as the bee flies. See National Farmers Union 2004.

14. In addition to crossing borders through the deliberate transport of hives and illegal smuggling, the mite could move between relatively close land-masses—such as Australia and Papua New Guinea—if swarming bees were to "stow away" undetected on cargo ships.

15. It's unclear whether all of the reindeer were delivered to northern Newfoundland. A 1910 article in the *New York Times*, which quotes Grenfell, mentions both Newfoundland and Labrador and reports that the animals were released onto the ice and made their own way to land ("Reindeer to Save Labrador's Future," May 30). The Vashti Bartlett Photograph Collection in the Alan Mason Chesney Medical Archives, Newfoundland, includes a brief account of Grenfell's life in Newfoundland as well as photographs of both Grenfell and the *Anita;* www.medicalarchives.jhmi.edu/vbartlett/phnewfound .htm (accessed August 31, 2009).

16. Centers for Disease Control and Prevention, "Alveolar Echinococcosis" (2008), www.cdc.gov/ncidod/dpd/parasites/alveolarechinococcosis/factsht_alveola rechinococcosis.htm (accessed August 25, 2009).

17. The results of this testing are reported by Davidson et al. 1992. The authors conclude that translocating foxes for fox enclosures is hazardous to people and wildlife.

18. Southeastern Cooperative Wildlife Disease Study 1991.

19. Southeastern Cooperative Wildlife Disease Study 1994c.

20. This fictional account of a screwworm fly in Libya is based on the documented events of the Libyan screwworm outbreak.

21. Gabaj et al. 1989, 347.

22. Wyss and Galvin 1996 write that the annual economic producer benefits of screwworm eradication were estimated at $500 million in the United States and $275 million in Mexico. They predict an annual economic benefit for producers and consumers in Central America of $588 million.

23. For a detailed account of the Libyan screwworm eradication effort, see Food and Agriculture Organization of the United Nations 1992.

FIVE. PARASITES IN CONTROL

Epigraph: J. Moore, *Parasites and the Behavior of Animals* (New York: Oxford University Press, 2002), 47. By permission of Oxford University Press.

1. The guinea worm can emerge almost anywhere on the body, but the most common sites are the extremities, particularly the feet and ankles.

2. The stepwells of India and Pakistan, which have stairs leading down into the water, and the large cisterns in the Middle East make it easy for people to walk and even swim in water supplies, thus aiding the guinea worm.

3. In some recipes for chocolate-covered ants, the insects are added to hot melted chocolate at nearly 100°F. This temperature may be sufficient to kill *D. dendriticum;* however, if gourmets simply dip infected ants in liquid chocolate, the parasite probably survives.

4. The life cycle of *D. dendriticum* is similar to that of *S. hematobium,* which I describe in chapter 1.

5. One study of *L. aequispina* in the Portland Inlet System found that Alice Arm had four times the number of crabs that neighboring Hastings Arm had. Overall, 41 percent of the crabs were infected with *B. callosus.* See Sloan 1985.

6. Coumans 2002, 12, discusses Canadian legislation governing disposal of mine tailings in marine waters.

7. Berdoy, Webster, and Macdonald 2000 report the effect that toxoplasmosis has on rat behavior.

8. Toxoplasmosis becomes a chronic infection: the parasite remains in the tissues, held in check by host immunity. People who carry the parasite are identified by the presence of antibodies in the blood.

9. Jaroslav Flegr (2007, 757) provides an excellent summary of the observed effects of toxoplasmosis on humans to date.

10. Webster et al. 2006.

11. Kean 1990.

12. Navratilova (1985) calculated that her bout with *T. gondii* had cost her $1 million in potential winnings. See Kean 1990, 239–62, on the "steak tartare defense."

13. "Navratilova Accused," *New York Times,* September 18, 1986.

14. Kean describes Navratilova knocking the photographer down and ripping out the film (1990, 241). In her autobiography, however, Navratilova plays down the confrontation but vividly describes her physical and mental exhaustion and her disappointment at losing to Shriver (1985, 229–43).

15. The *New York Times* story "Doctor Was Not Surprised" (September 8, 1982) describes the match and provides the comments of both Navratilova and Wadler immediately afterward.

16. "Navratilova Accused." Two other *New York Times* articles, "Navratilova Testifies" (September 23, 1986) and "Photographer Testifies" (September 19, 1986), also provide accounts of the dispute.

17. These figures, like most data on *T. gondii* prevalence, come from screening tests on pregnant women. See Lafferty 2006, 2751.

18. Ibid., 2752.

19. Singh et al. 2004, 1522.

20. Mahajan et al. 2004, 663.

21. For an objective account of the details of Keogh's death in hindsight, see P. Rubin, "Jump Street," *Phoenix New Times*, December 13, 2006, www.phoenixnewtimes.com/2006-12-14/news/jump-street. For an alternate viewpoint, see J. Dougherty, "The Mystery Deepens," *Phoenix New Times*, September 29, 2005, www.phoenixnewtimes.com/2005-09-29/news/the-mystery-deepens (both accessed August 25, 2009).

22. G. D. Richardson, H. Johnson, and K. Fehr-Snyder, "Official's Bizarre Death Has Equally Odd Explanation," *Arizona Republic,* December 9, 2004; C. McClain, "Worm in Brain a Rare and Horrifying Affliction," *Arizona Daily Star,* December 31, 2004, www.azstarnet.com/sn/health/54959.php (accessed August 27, 2009).

23. Diagnosis and treatment of neurocysticercosis can be difficult: light infections are not always identified by standard testing, and some patients require more than one course of antiparasitic drugs to kill the parasites. Even then, dead cysts remain and can cause further problems.

SIX. IN THE HOUSE OF MIRRORS

1. See chapter 1 for more on *Ascaris lumbricoides.* On early Chinese medical uses for the worm, see Hoeppli 1959, 168–72.

2. Ibid., 107–8.

3. Ibid., 432.

4. The life and afterlife of Tsafendas's infamous tapeworm is chronicled in Van Woerden 2000.

5. Tsafendas lived in South Africa illegally for several extended periods. Though an illegal immigrant, at the time of the assassination he was working as a parliamentary messenger.

6. Blair Higgins is not the patient's real name, and I have inferred minor details of events and individual experience based on the published account of his case. See Monk and Rao 1994.

7. Delusional parasitosis, also known as Ekbom's syndrome or Morgellons disease, has evolved in recent years as a direct result of the Internet. Sufferers who were once isolated now find each other and compare experiences, often reinforcing the delusion and wasting time and energy chasing unproven and unlikely theories about the cause of their trouble. See Koblenzer 2006.

8. Physical explanations for delusional parasitosis have been suggested. One blames springtails, tiny six-legged creatures common in damp, decaying organic material that have occasionally been found on the skin. Another theory blames toxic dental sealants. Though these explanations might account for some cases

of delusional parasitosis, they cannot explain all cases, and they do not explain *folie à deux.*

9. Bourgeois, Duhamel, and Verdoux 1992. The names used in this account are fictitious, and I have inferred minor details of events and individual experience.

10. The skin mites of other animals can infect humans; however, the most common mite species in cats is *Notoedres cati,* a mite that doesn't persist on human skin. An epidemic in humans caused by *N. cati* is very unlikely, if not impossible.

11. Thibierge 1894 is the first published report of delusional parasitosis.

12. The story of Victoria Climbié, as it emerged in the inquiry after her death, is chronicled in "The Victoria Climbié Inquiry," 2003, www.victoria-climbie-inquiry.org.uk/index.htm (accessed August 28, 2009).

13. In the psychiatric condition Munchausen's syndrome by proxy, a caregiver fabricates symptoms of illness, or actually induces illness in another person (usually a child), to get attention. Using this syndrome as a model, delusional parasitosis by proxy would be a caregiver who holds on to the false belief that another person is infested with parasites and acts on that belief.

14. On eighteenth-century beliefs about lice, see Zinsser 1965, 138–39. On the British idea of lice as a sign of health, see Drew 1950, 158.

15. Most likely head lice do transmit disease; however, most of the scientific research to date has focused on body lice. In disease outbreaks involving lice, both head and body lice are typically common.

16. For a translation of Edward Grim's eyewitness account of Becket's murder, see Medieval Sourcebook, "Edward Grim: The Murder of Thomas Becket," translated by Dawn Marie Hayes, www.fordham.edu/halsall/source/grim-becket.html; and EyeWitness to History.com, "The Murder of Thomas Becket, 1170" (1997), www.eyewitnesstohistory.com/becket.htm (both accessed August 25, 2009).

17. Quoted in Zinsser 1965, 138, author given as "MacArthur."

18. Bottomley 1915, 41–45.

19. The myriad ways in which lice have interacted with man and influenced events would fill several books. For lice from a historical perspective, see Zinsser 1965. For benefits, culinary and medicinal uses, and misconceptions, see Hoeppli 1959.

20. Buckman 2003, 31.

21. The story of "the punishment of the boats" and Plutarch's account of the death of Mithridates are in Hoeppli 1959, 198–99.

22. The barber-surgeon of the late Middle Ages had the combined roles of shaving the face and head and performing minor surgery and first aid.

23. For more information on recent research and theory on how parasitic worms may protect us from disease, see Weiss 2000; Elliott, Summers, and Weinstock 2005; and Rook 2009.

24. Rook 2009, 5. In this theory, "old friends" also include common fungi and bacteria.

SEVEN. THE PARASITE FELONIES

1. Adult insects as well as other stages, and discarded pupal coverings, are found in and under decomposing remains. They can tell forensic entomologists how long the remains have been there and whether the remains have been moved from another location. For more on this subject, see Goff 2000.

2. Prichard et al. 1986. Some descriptive details have been inferred in this true account.

3. Jones 1878.

4. A French Army physician, Charles Louis Alphonse Laveran, was the first to see *Plasmodium* sp. parasites inside red blood cells and realize what he was looking at. He reported his discovery in November 1880.

5. Jones 1878, 151. The hyaline mass Jones described was probably the parasite itself.

6. Ibid.

7. For an in-depth account of the activities of Ahmed Ressam (alias Benni Antoine Noris) from the time he left Algeria until September 11, 2001, see H. Bernton, M. Carter, D. Heath, and J. Neff, "The Terrorist Within: The Story behind One Man's Holy War against America," *Seattle Times,* June 23–July 7, 2002, http://seattletimes.nwsource.com/news/nation-world/terroristwithin/about .html (accessed August 24, 2009).

8. The possible significance of Ressam's malaria is explored in S. Miletich and M. Carter, "Malaria May Have Unmasked Ressam," *Seattle Times*, June 1, 2001, http://community.seattletimes.nwsource.com/archive/?date=20010601 &slug=ressam01 (accessed September 6, 2009).

9. Both the Japanese and the Americans have researched agents of biological warfare and considered spreading plague. The Japanese apparently tried to start plague epidemics in several Chinese communities in 1940 and 1941; see Regis 1999, 10–21, 112. The account of the attack on Chuhsien and the epidemic that followed is on 17–19.

10. Today, if caught in time, plague can be treated with antibiotics.

11. Regis 1999, 12.

12. Reproduced in Gunaratna 1987, 51–52.

13. The medical perspective of this case is given in Phills et al. 1972.

14. In the 1920s, researcher Sui Koino reputedly enlisted his brother in an experiment. He swallowed *A. lumbricoides* eggs and had his brother swallow *A.*

suum eggs. Both men had symptoms, with Sui Koino apparently suffering the worst. Robson may or may not have known of the experiment, which was reported in a Japanese journal in 1922.

EIGHT. EMERGING PARASITES

Epigraph: I. J. Loefler 1996, "Microbes, Chemotherapy, Evolution, and Folly," *Lancet,* 348 (9043): 1704. Reprinted with permission from Elsevier.

1. In their recent DNA analysis of head and body lice from different geographic regions, Kittler, Kayser, and Stoneking (2003) determined that the two species diverged between 30,000 and 114,000 thousand years ago.

2. Epidemic typhus, caused by *Rickettsia prowazekii,* is a bacterial disease characterized by severe flulike symptoms and rash. It is typically associated with poor hygiene and crowded conditions.

3. A sociological concept developed by Robert K. Merton, the law of unintended consequences says that all human actions have both intended and unintended consequences. Unintended consequences are frequently negative.

4. Darwin 1884, 330. Although Darwin described the bugs as wingless, adult kissing bugs have wings.

5. Ibid.

6. Using molecular methods, Guhl et al. (1997) found DNA of *Trypanosoma cruzi* in skeletal and visceral tissues from twenty-seven mummies representing different cultures and spanning four thousand years.

7. Carlos Chagas, "Resume of the Etiology and Clinical Aspects of American Trypanosomiasis" (1920), http://carloschagas.ibict.br/traj/trajtext/pdf/pi.51-237 .pdf (accessed August 25, 2009), 2.

8. Hanford et al. 2007.

9. Zayas et al. 2002 described this case in the first published report of Chagas' disease following organ transplantation in the United States.

10. Treatment of acanthamoeba keratitis is still difficult and usually requires a combination of drugs. The risk of permanent vision loss remains high.

11. This was the first reported case of PAM in the United Kingdom. Apley et al. 1970.

12. A few scattered cases of babesiosis were known before 1969 in Europe and North America; they involved either different *Babesia* sp. or different tick species, or both.

13. White-tailed deer don't suffer from babesiosis, even when they are continually bitten by infected ticks. Deer are important in the life cycle of *B. microti* and *I. scapularis* because they are the major food source for adult ticks and because they carry ticks into areas frequented by humans.

14. Beaver 1969, 5. Visceral larva migrans in humans is better known from the wanderings of larvae of *Toxocara canis,* the intestinal roundworm of the domestic dog.

15. Scientists believe that, in nature, most young raccoons initially become infected when they eat eggs passed by adults. In raccoons, the larvae develop to adults without leaving the intestine.

16. Beaver 1969, 3.

17. Wildlife managers predict that uncontrolled raccoon populations can double in a ten-year period. See Kenyon, Southwick, and Wynne 1999, 3.

18. See World Health Organization and UNICEF 2006.

19. Schantz 2002.

20. Schantz et al. 1992 describes this unusual epidemic.

21. Ibid.

22. This estimate includes foreign-born individuals residing in the United States for any reason, including illegal immigrants. Migration Policy Institute, Washington, DC, www.migrationinformation.org/DataHub/state.cfm?ID=US (accessed September 7, 2009).

NINE. PARASITE EXTINCTION

Epigraph: R. Dunn, North Carolina State University, "On Parasites Lost," *Wild Earth,* Spring 2002.

1. Carter Center, "Guinea Worm Cases Hit All-Time Low: Carter Center, WHO, Gates Foundation, and U.K. Government Commit $55 Million Toward Ultimate Eradication Goal," December 5, 2008, press release, www .cartercenter.org/news/pr/gates_120508.html (accessed September 7, 2009).

2. One possible source of guinea worm in Asia was the removal of Assyrian prisoners from Egypt to Assyria in the seventh century B.C. See Adamson 1988.

3. Centers for Disease Control and Prevention 2005.

4. Carter 1999, 143.

5. Ibid. More than two million square yards of the fabric was donated by E. I. Du Pont de Nemours Company and Precision Fabrics Group.

6. Ibid.

7. Ibid.

8. Reproduced in Centers for Disease Control and Prevention 2004b.

9. World Health Organization 2008a.

10. Ibid.

11. Basáñez et al. 2006.

12. Osei-Atweneboana et al. 2007, 2028.

13. Basáñez et al. 2006.

14. Scientists think that *Wolbachia* produce certain nutrients that tissue nematodes need to survive and reproduce, which the nematodes cannot produce for themselves. Killing *Wolbachia* bacteria may be the key to treating other tissue nematodes as well, including those that cause elephantiasis. See Pfarr and Hoerauf 2005.

15. Katabarwa et al. 2008.

16. Eddi, Nari, and Amanfu 2003.

17. Martinez, de Aluja, and Gemmell 2000, 489.

18. Eddi, Nari, and Amanfu 2003.

19. Gonzalez, Wilkins, and Lopez 2002.

20. Garcia et al. 2002, 79.

21. For a discussion of the ways that the pork tapeworm spreads and of preventive measures that have been tried, see Flisser et al. 2003.

22. No one knows the average life span of a *T. solium* adult worm, but recent evidence indicates that it is shorter than that of *T. saginata,* perhaps three to five years. See Garcia et al. 2006.

23. Murrell and Pawlowski 2005, 44.

24. Reiter 2000.

25. Centers for Disease Control and Prevention, "The Panama Canal" (2004), www.cdc.gov/malaria/history/panama_canal.htm (accessed August 25, 2009).

26. Williams 1963.

27. Reiter 2000.

28. Centers for Disease Control and Prevention, "The History of Malaria, an Ancient Disease" (2004), www.cdc.gov/malaria/history/index.htm (accessed August 25, 2009).

29. Williams 1963.

30. Centers for Disease Control and Prevention, "Eradication of Malaria in the United States (1947–1951)" (2004), www.cdc.gov/malaria/history/eradication_us.htm (accessed August 25, 2009).

31. Intensive use of a drug or chemical tends to make resistance appear more quickly because all the sensitive individuals are killed off quickly, leaving only those able to withstand the attack to reproduce. If their resistance is passed on to their offspring, a resistant population multiplies to fill the void left by the sensitive population that has died. This happened with both DDT and mosquitoes, and chloroquine and *Plasmodium* spp.

In relation to the effect on birds, DDT (1,1,1-trichloro-2,2-bis(p-chlorophenyl)ethane), an organic pesticide, breaks down to DDE (1,1-dichloro-2,2-bis(chlorophenyl) ethylene). DDE compromises the eggshells of birds, particularly birds of prey, which build up high levels of the chemical in their tissues. Eggshells become thin and fragile, and few chicks hatch. In 1972, DDT was banned in the United States.

32. World Health Organization 2008b, vii.

33. Roll Back Malaria Partnership, "RBM Vision," www.rollbackmalaria.org/rbmvision.html (accessed September 8, 2009). The Millennium Development Goals are ten international goals adopted by the United Nations General Assembly, including to "combat HIV/AIDS, malaria and other diseases"; see www.un.org/millenniumgoals (accessed September 8, 2009).

34. World Health Organization 2008b, 3–8.

35. Roll Back Malaria Partnership, "Global Malaria Action Plan for a Malaria-Free World," www.rollbackmalaria.org/gmap/2-3.html (accessed August 27, 2009).

36. World Health Organization 2008b, viii.

37. Ibid., 31.

38. World Health Organization, 2007, "WHO Expands Fight against Chagas Disease with Support from Bayer," www.who.int/mediacentre/news/notes/2007/np16/en/index.html (accessed August 31, 2009).

39. Ibid.

40. Sadighian et al. 1976.

EPILOGUE

1. The origin of the idea of the parasitologist's dilemma is unknown; see Roberts and Janovy 2000, 3.

2. Cohn 1973, 1093.

3. Ibid., 1094.

4. Robert Desowitz offered this summation of Cohn's idea in *The Malaria Capers* (1991, 217).

5. Roberts and Janovy 2000, 1.

6. Quote from Horwitz and Wilcox 2005, 728–29.

Adamson, P. B. 1988. "Dracontiasis in Antiquity." *Medical History* 32 (2): 204–9.

Akuffo, H., E. Linder, I. Ljungström, and M. Wahlgren, eds. 2003. *Parasites of the Colder Climates.* London: Taylor and Francis.

Amin, O. M. 2004. "On the Course of Neurocutaneous Syndrome (NCS) and Its Pseudo-Diagnosis by Medical Professionals." *Explore* 13: 4–9.

Apley, J., S. K. R. Clarke, A. P. C. H. Roome, S. A. Sandry, G. Saygi, B. Silk, and D. C. Warhurst. 1970. "Primary Amoebic Meningoencephalitis in Britain." *British Medical Journal* 1 (5696): 596–99.

Barry, M. 2007. "The Tail End of Guinea Worm—Global Eradication Without a Drug or a Vaccine." *New England Journal of Medicine* 356 (25): 2561–64.

Basáñez, M., S. D. S. Pion, T. S. Churcher, L. P. Breitling, M. P. Little, and M. Boussinesq. 2006. "River Blindness: A Success Story under Threat?" *PLoS Medicine* 3 (9): 1454–60.

Beadle, C., and S. L. Hoffman. 1993. "History of Malaria in the United States Naval Forces at War: World War I through the Vietnam Conflict." *Clinical Infectious Diseases* 16 (2): 320–29.

Beaglehole, J. C. 1974. *The Life of Captain James Cook.* London: Hakluyt Society.

Beaver, P. 1969. "The Nature of Visceral Larva Migrans." *Journal of Parasitology* 55 (1): 3–12.

Beaver, P.C., R.C. Jung, and E.W. Cupp. 1984. *Clinical Parasitology,* 9th ed. Philadelphia: Lea and Febiger.

Beesley, W.N. 1991. "North Africa." *Annals of Tropical Medicine & Parasitology* 85 (1): 173–79.

Berdoy, M., J.P. Webster, and D.W. Macdonald. 2000. "Fatal Attraction in Rats Infected With *Toxoplasma gondii.*" *Proceedings of the Royal Society of London* B 267 (1452): 1591–94.

Berland, B. "*Anisakis* spp." 2003. In Akuffo et al., *Parasites of the Colder Climates,* 161–68.

Bernstein, R.E. 1984. "Darwin's Illness: Chagas' Disease Resurgens." *Journal of the Royal Society of Medicine* 77 (7): 608–9.

Biggs, H.E.J. 1960. "Molluscs from Prehistoric Jericho." *Journal of Conchology* 24: 379–87.

Boni, S. 2005. "Blending the Rules." *Grist Magazine*, March 10. www.grist.org/article/boni-sewage/ (accessed August 24, 2009).

Bottomley, G. 1915. *King Lear's Wife.* In *Georgian Poetry 1913–1915.* New York: G.P. Putnam's Sons. Pp. 41–47.

Bourgeois, M.L., P. Duhamel, and H. Verdoux. 1992. "Delusional Parasitosis: *Folie à deux* and Attempted Murder of a Family Doctor." *British Journal of Psychiatry* 161: 709–11.

Bowie, W.R., A.S. King, D.H. Werker, J.L. Isaac-Renton, A. Bell, S.B. Eng, and S.A. Marion. 1997. "Outbreak of Toxoplasmosis Associated with Municipal Drinking Water." *Lancet* 350 (9072): 173–77.

Buckman, R. 2003. *Human Wildlife: The Life That Lives on Us.* Baltimore: Johns Hopkins University Press.

Burenhult, G. 1993. *People of the Stone Age.* New York: HarperCollins.

Calvin, L., L. Flores, and W. Foster. 2003. "Food Safety in Food Security and Food Trade. Case Study: Guatemalan Raspberries and *Cyclospora.* 2020 Vision for Food, Agriculture, and the Environment." Focus 10, Brief 7 of 17 (September). www.ifpri.org/sites/default/files/publications/focus10_07.pdf (accessed August 24, 2009).

Carter, J. 1999. "The Power of Partnership: The Eradication of Guinea Worm Disease." *Cooperation South Journal* (2): 140–47.

Center for Global Development. "Controlling Chagas Disease in the Southern Cone of South America." www.cgdev.org/doc/millions/MS_case_12.pdf (accessed August 25, 2009).

Centers for Disease Control and Prevention. 2007. "Blood Donor Screening for Chagas Disease—United States, 2006–2007." *Morbidity and Mortality Weekly Report* 56 (7): 141–43.

———. 2005. "Progress toward Global Eradication of Dracunculiasis, January 2004–July 2005." *Morbidity and Mortality Weekly Report* 54 (42): 1075–77.

———. 2004a. "Outbreak of Cyclosporiasis Associated with Snow Peas—Pennsylvania, 2004." *Morbidity and Mortality Weekly Report* 53 (37): 876–78.

———. 2004b. Guinea Worm Wrap-Up #143. WHO Collaborating Center for Research, Training and Eradication of Dracunculiasis. May 28. www.cdc.gov/ncidod/dpd/parasites/dracunculiasis/wrapup/word143.pdf (accessed September 7, 2009).

———. 2003. "Trichinellosis Surveillance—United States, 1997–2001." *Morbidity and Mortality Weekly Report Surveillance Summaries* 52 (SS06): 1–8.

———. 1998. "Outbreak of Cyclosporiasis—Ontario, May 1998." *Morbidity and Mortality Weekly Report* 47 (38): 806–9.

———. 1997. "Update: Outbreaks of Cyclosporiasis—United States, 1997." *Morbidity and Mortality Weekly Report* 46 (21): 461–62.

Chernin, E. 1986. "Joseph Jones: Idiosyncratic Student of Malaria." *Perspectives in Biology and Medicine* 29 (2): 260–71.

Clark, T. D. 1968. *The Emerging South*, 2nd ed. New York: Oxford University Press.

Cohn, E. J. 1973. "Assessing the Costs and Benefits of Anti-Malaria Programs: The Indian Experience." *American Journal of Public Health* 63 (12): 1086–96.

Colp, R., Jr. 1977. *To Be an Invalid*. Chicago: University of Chicago Press. Pp. 126–31.

Cook, J. 1967. *The Journals of Captain James Cook on His Voyages of Discovery: The Voyage of the Resolution and Discovery 1776–1780, Part One and Part Two.* Edited by J. C. Beaglehole. Cambridge: Cambridge University Press.

Corso, P. S., M. H. Kramer, K. A. Blair, D. G. Addiss, J. P. Davis, and A. C. Haddix. 2003. "Cost of Illness in the 1993 Waterborne *Cryptosporidium* Outbreak, Milwaukee, Wisconsin." *Emerging Infectious Diseases* 9 (4): 426–31.

Coumans, Catherine. 2002. "Canadian Legislation on Submarine Tailings Disposal." In the introduction to *Submarine Tailings Disposal Toolkit.* Ottawa: MiningWatch Canada.

Crompton, D. W. T., A. Montresor, M. C. Nesheim, and L. Savioli. 2003. *Controlling Diseases Due to Helminth Infections.* Geneva: World Health Organization.

Daniel, E., and T. N. Srinivasan. 2004. "*Folie à Famille:* Delusional Parasitosis Affecting All the Members of a Family." *Indian Journal of Dermatology, Venereology and Leprology* 70 (5): 296–97.

Darwin, C. 1884. *A Naturalist's Voyage: Journal of Researches into the Natural History and Geology of the Countries Visited During the Voyage of H. M. S. 'Beagle' Round the World.* London: John Murray.

Davidson W. R., M. J. Appel, G. L. Doster, O. E. Baker, and J. F. Brown. 1992. "Diseases and Parasites of Red Foxes, Gray Foxes, and Coyotes from Commercial Sources Selling to Fox-Chasing Enclosures." *Journal of Wildlife Diseases* 28 (4): 581–89.

De Jonckheere, J. F. 2002. "A Century of Research on the Amoeboflagellate Genus *Naegleria*." *Acta Protozoologica* 41: 309–42.

Desowitz, R. S. 1997. *Who Gave Pinta to the Santa Maria?* New York: Norton.

———. 1991. *The Malaria Capers: Tales of Parasites and People.* New York: Norton.

———. 1987. *New Guinea Tapeworms and Jewish Grandmothers: Tales of Parasites and People.* New York: Norton.

Dewhirst, L. W., J. D. Cramer, and J. J. Sheldon. 1967. "An Analysis of Current Inspection Procedures for Detecting Bovine Cysticercosis." *Journal of the American Veterinary Association* 150 (4). 412–17.

Diamond, J. 1997. *Guns, Germs, and Steel.* New York: Norton.

———. 1994. "How to Tame a Wild Plant." *Discover,* September.

Drew, J. 1950. *Man, Microbe and Malady.* Harmondsworth: Penguin Books.

Dreyfuss, G., P. Vignoles, and D. Rondelaud, 2005. "*Fasciola hepatica*: Epidemiological Surveillane of Natural Watercress Beds in Central France." *Parasitology Research* 95 (4): 278–82.

Dugard, M. 2003. *Into Africa: The Epic Adventures of Stanley & Livingstone.* New York: Doubleday.

Eddi, C., A. Nari, and W. Amanfu. 2003. "*Taenia solium* cysticercosis / taeniosis: Potential Linkage with FAO Activities; FAO Support Possibilities." *Acta Tropica* 87 (1): 145–48.

el-Azazy, O. M. 1989. "Wound Myiasis Caused by *Cochliomyia hominivorax* in Libya." *Veterinary Record* 124: 103.

Elliott, D. E., R. W. Summers, and J. V. Weinstock. 2005. "Helminths and the Modulation of Mucosal Inflammation." *Current Opinion in Gastroenterology* 21 (1): 51–58.

Elliott, D. E., J. F. Urban, Jr., C. K. Argo, and J. V. Weinstock. 2000. "Does the Failure to Acquire Helminthic Parasites Predispose to Crohn's Disease?" *FASEB Journal* 14 (September): 1848–55.

Esch, G. W. 2007. *Parasites and Infectious Disease: Discovery by Serendipity, and Otherwise.* Cambridge: Cambridge University Press.

———. 2004. *Parasites, People, and Places: Essays on Field Parasitology.* Cambridge: Cambridge University Press.

Flegr, J. 2007. "Effects of *Toxoplasma* on Human Behavior." *Schizophrenia Bulletin* 33 (3): 757–60.

Flegr, J., P. Kodym, and V. Tolarová. 2000. "Correlation of Duration of Latent *Toxoplasma gondii* Infection with Personality Changes in Women." *Biological Psychology* 53 (1): 57–68.

Flegr, J., M. Preiss, J. Klose, J. Havlíček, M. Vitáková, and P. Kodym. 2003. "Decreased Level of Psychobiological Factor Novelty Seeking and Lower Intelligence in Men Latently Infected with the Protozoan Parasite *Toxoplasma gondii* Dopamine, a Missing Link between Schizophrenia and Toxoplasmosis?" *Biological Psychology* 63 (3): 253–68.

Flegr, J., Š. Zitková, P. Kodym, and D. Frynta. 1996. "Induction of Changes in Human Behavior by the Parasitic Protozoan *Toxoplasma gondii*." *Parasitology* 113 (Part 1): 49–54.

Flisser, A., E. Sarti, M. Lightowlers, and D. Schantz. 2003. "Neurocysticercosis: Regional Status, Epidemiology, Impact and Control Measures in the Americas." *Acta Tropica* 87 (1): 43–51.

Food and Agriculture Organization of the United Nations. 1992. *The New World Screwworm Eradication Programme: North Africa 1988–1992.* Rome: Food and Agriculture Organization.

Ford, E. B., D. P. Calfee, and R. D. Pearson. 2001. "Delusions of Intestinal Parasitosis." *Southern Medical Journal* 94 (5): 545–47.

Forlenza, O. V., A. H. Filho, J. P. Nobrega, L. dos Ramos Machado, N. G. de Barros, C. H. de Camargo, and M. F. da Silva. 1997. "Psychiatric Manifestations of Neurocysticercosis: A Study of 38 Patients from a Neurology Clinic in Brazil." *Journal of Neurology, Neurosurgery, and Psychiatry* 62 (6): 612–16.

Foulks, G. N. 2007. "*Acanthamoeba* Keratitis and Contact Lens Wear: Static or Increasing Problem?" *Eye and Contact Lens* 33 (6, part 2): 412–14.

Gabaj, M. M., N. P. Wyatt, A. C. Pont, W. N. Beesley, M. A. Awan, A. M. Gusbi, and K. M. Benhaj. 1989. "The Screwworm Fly in Libya: A Threat to the Livestock Industry of the Old World." *Veterinary Record* 125 (13): 347–49.

Garcia, H. H., R. H. Gilman, A. E. Gonzalez, M. Verastegui, V. C. W. Tsang, and the Cysticercosis Working Group in Peru. 2002. "What Have We Learnt from Epidemiological Studies of *Taenia solium* Cysticercosis in Peru?" In Singh and Prabhakar, Taenia solium *Cysticercosis*, 75–81.

Garcia, H. H., A. E. Gonzalez, R. H. Gilman, L. H. Moulton, M. Verastegui, S. Rodriguez, C. Gavidia, V. C. W. Tsang, and the Cysticercosis Working Group in Peru. 2006. "Combined Human and Porcine Mass Chemotherapy for the Control of *T. solium*." *American Journal of Tropical Medicine and Hygiene* 74 (5): 850–55.

Garcia, L. S., and D. A. Bruckner. 1997. *Diagnostic Medical Parasitology,* 3rd ed. Washington, DC: ASM Press.

Gavin, P. J., K. R. Kazacos, and S. T. Shulman. 2005. "Baylisascariasis." *Clinical Microbiology Reviews* 18 (4): 703–18.

Ghannoum, M., and G. A. O'Toole, eds. 2004. *Microbial Biofilms.* Washington, DC: ASM Press.

Gignilliat, J. L. 1961. "Pigs, Politics, and Protection: The European Boycott of American Pork, 1879–1891." *Agricultural History* 35 (1): 3–12.

Goff, M. L. 2000. *A Fly for the Prosecution*. Cambridge, MA: Harvard University Press.

Gonçalves, M. L. C., A. Araújo, and L. F. Ferreira. 2003. "Human Intestinal Parasites in the Past: New Findings and a Review." *Memórias do Instituto Oswaldo Cruz, Rio de Janeiro*, 98 (supplement I): 103–18.

Gonzalez, A. E., C. G. Gauci, D. Barber, R. H. Gilman, V. C. W. Tsang, H. H. Garcia, M. Verastegui, and M. W. Lightowlers. 2005. "Short Report: Vaccination of Pigs to Control Human Neurocysticercosis." *American Journal of Tropical Medicine and Hygiene* 72 (6): 837–39.

Gonzalez, A. E., P. P. Wilkins, and T. Lopez. 2002. "Porcine Cysticercosis." In Singh and Prabhakar, Taenia solium *Cysticercosis*, 145–56.

Gostin, L. O., Z. Lazzarini, V. S. Neslund, and M. T. Osterholm. 2000. "Water Quality Laws and Waterborne Diseases: *Cryptosporidium* and Other Emerging Pathogens." *American Journal of Public Health* 90 (6): 847–53.

Graczyk, T. K., R. Fayer, J. M. Trout, E. J. Lewis, C. A. Farley, I. Sulaiman, and A. A. Lal. 1998. "*Giardia* sp. Cysts and Infectious *Cryptosporidium parvum* Oocysts in the Feces of Migratory Canada Geese *(Branta Canadensis)*." *Applied and Environmental Microbiology* 64 (7): 2736–38.

Graczyk, T. K., R. Knight, and L. Tamang. 2005. "Mechanical Transmission of Human Protozoan Parasites by Insects." *Clinical Microbiology Reviews* 18 (1): 128–32.

Guhl, F., C. Jaramillo, R. Yockteng, G. A. Vallejo, and F. Cárdenas-Arroyo. 1997. "*Trypanosoma cruzi* DNA in Human Mummies." *Lancet* 349 (9062): 1370.

Gunaratna, R. 1987. *War and Peace in Sri Lanka*. Sri Lanka: Institute of Fundamental Studies.

Hanford, E. J., F. B. Zhan, Y. Lu, and A. Giordano. 2007. "Chagas Disease in Texas: Recognizing the Significance and Implications of Evidence in the Literature." *Social Science & Medicine* 65 (1): 60–79.

Havlíček, J., Z. Gašová, A. P. Smith, K. Zvara, and J. Flegr. 2001. "Decrease of Psychomotor Performance in Subjects with Latent 'Asymptomatic' Toxoplasmosis." *Parasitology* 122 (Part 5): 515–20.

Health Canada. 2008. Guidelines for Canadian Drinking Water Quality Summary Table. Federal-Provincial-Territorial Committee on Drinking Water of the Federal-Provincial-Territorial Committee on Health and the Environment. May.

———. 1995. "Outbreak of Toxoplasmosis Associated with Municipal Drinking Water—British Columbia." *Canada Communicable Disease Report* 21–18 (September 30): 161–64.

Hoeppli, R. 1959. *Parasites and Parasitic Infections in Early Medicine and Science*. Singapore: University of Malaya Press.

Holliman, R. E. 1997. "Toxoplasmosis, Behavior and Personality." *Journal of Infection* 35 (2): 105–10.

· Horwitz, P., and B. A. Wilcox. 2005. "Parasites, Ecosystems and Sustainability: An Ecological and Complex Systems Perspective." *International Journal for Parasitology* 35: 725–32.

Hough, R. 1995. *Captain James Cook.* New York: Norton.

Hsu, E. 2006. "Reflections on the 'Discovery' of the Antimalarial *Qinghao.*" *British Journal of Clinical Pharmacology* 61 (6): 666–70.

Hulse, E. V. 1971. "Joshua's Curse and the Abandonment of Ancient Jericho: Schistosomiasis as a Possible Medical Explanation." *Medical History* 15 (4): 376–86.

Hunter, J. M., L. Rey, K. Y. Chu, E. O. Adekolu-John, and K. E. Mott. 1993 *Parasitic Diseases in Water Resources Development: The Need for Intersectorial Negotiation.* Geneva: World Health Organization.

Isaac-Renton, J. L., C. Cordeiro, K. Sarafis, and H. Shahriari. 1993. "Characterization of *Giardia duodenalis* Isolates from a Waterborne Outbreak." *Journal of Infectious Diseases* 167 (2): 431–40.

Jones, J. 1878. "Medico-Legal Evidence Relating to the Detection of Human Blood, Presenting the Alterations Characteristic of Malarial Fever, on the Clothing of a Man, Accused of the Murder of Narcisse Arrieux, December 27th, 1876, near Donaldsonville." *New Orleans Medical and Surgical Journal* 6 (August): 139–56.

Katabarwa, M., T. Lakwo, P. Habumogisha, F. Richards, and M. Eberhard. 2008. "Short Report: Could Neurocysticercosis Be the Cause of 'Onchocerciasis-Associated' Epileptic Seizures?" *American Journal of Tropical Medicine and Hygiene* 78 (3): 400–401.

Kean, B. H., with T. Dahlby. 1990. "The Steak Tartare Defense." In *M.D.,* 239–62. New York: Ballantine.

Kenyon, S., R. Southwick, and C. Wynne. 1999. "Bears in the Backyard, Deer in the Driveway." International Association of Fish and Wildlife Agencies. Washington, DC.

Kittler, R., M. Kayser, and M. Stoneking. 2003. "Molecular Evolution of *Pediculus humanus* and the Origin of Clothing." *Current Biology* 13 (16): 1414–17.

Knutson, R. M. 1992. *Furtive Fauna: A Field Guide to the Creatures Who Live on You.* New York: Penguin Books.

Kober, A. S. 2005. "Big Bipartisan Victories for Clean Water." *American Rivers,* May 19.

Koblenzer, C. S. 2006. "The Challenge of Morgellons Disease." *Journal of the American Academy of Dermatology* 55 (5): 920–22.

Kouba, V. 2004. "History of the Screwworm (*Cochliomyia hominivorax*) Eradication in the Eastern Hemisphere." *Historia Medicinae Veterinariae* 29 (2): 43–53.

Krause, P. J., K. McKay, J. Gadbaw, D. Christianson, L. Closter, T. Lepore, S. R. Telford III et al. 2003. "Increasing Health Burden of Human Babesiosis in Endemic Sites." *American Journal of Tropical Medicine and Hygiene* 68 (4): 431–36.

Krause, R. M. 1998. "Introduction to Emerging Infectious Diseases: Stemming the Tide." In *Emerging Infections*, edited by R. M. Krause, 1–22. San Diego: Academic Press.

Lafferty, K. D. 2006. "Can the Common Brain Parasite, *Toxoplasma gondii*, Influence Human Culture?" *Proceedings of the Royal Society B* 273 (1602): 2749–55.

Laing, R. D. 2002. "Report of the Commission of Inquiry into Matters Relating to the Safety of the Public Drinking Water in the City of North Battleford, Sasketchewan." Office of the Queen's Printer, Regina.

Lashley, F. R., and J. D. Durham, eds. 2002. *Emerging Infectious Diseases: Trends and Issues*. New York: Springer Publishing Company.

LeChevallier, M. W., W. D. Norton, and R. G. Lee. 1991. "Occurrence of *Giardia* and *Cryptosporidium* spp. in Surface Water Supplies." *Applied and Environmental Microbiology* 57 (9): 2610–16.

Lee, G. W., K. A. Lee, and W. R. Davidson. 1993. "Evaluation of Fox-Chasing Enclosures as Sites of Potential Introduction and Establishment of *Echinococcus multilocularis*." *Journal of Wildlife Diseases* 29 (3): 498–501.

Lindsay, R. G., G. Watters, R. Johnson, S. E. Ormonde, and G. R. Snibson. 2007. "Acanthamoeba Keratitis and Contact Lens Wear." *Clinical and Experimental Optometry* 90 (5): 351–60.

Loefler, I. J. P. 1996. "Microbes, Chemotherapy, Evolution, and Folly." *Lancet* 348 (9043): 1703–4.

MacDonald, D. W., N. Yamaguchi, and G. Kerby. 2000. "Group-Living in the Domestic Cat: Its Sociobiology and Epidemiology." In Turner and Bateson, *The Domestic Cat*, 95–118.

MacKenzie, W. R., N. J. Hoxie, M. E. Proctor, M. S. Gradus, K. A. Blair, D. E. Peterson, J. J. Kazmierczak et al. 1994. "A Massive Outbreak in Milwaukee of *Cryptosporidium* Infection Transmitted through the Public Water Supply." *New England Journal of Medicine* 331 (3): 161–67.

Macpherson, C. N. L. 2005. "Human Behavior and the Epidemiology of Parasitic Zoonoses." *International Journal for Parasitology* 35 (11–12): 1319–31.

Mahajan, S. K., P. C. Machhan, B. R. Sood, S. Kumar, D. D. Sharma, J. Mokta, and L. S. Pal. 2004. "Neurocysticercosis Presenting with Psychosis." *Journal of the Association of Physicians of India* 52: 663–65.

Mann, C. C. 2007. "America, Found and Lost." *National Geographic*. May.

Manning, O. 1985. *The Remarkable Expedition: The Story of Stanley's Rescue of Emin Pasha from Equatorial Africa*. New York: Atheneum.

Martinez, M. J., A. S. de Aluja, and M. Gemmell. 2000. "Failure to Incriminate Domestic Flies (Diptera: Muscidae) as Mechanical Vectors of *Taenia* eggs (Cyclophyllidea: Taeniidae) in Rural Mexico." *Journal of Medical Entomology* 37 (4):489–91.

Matheson, A. 2000. "Managing Risks in World Trade in Bees and Bee Products." *Apiacta* 35 (1): 1–12.

Mayberry, L. F. 1996. "The Infectious Nature of Parasitology." *Journal of Parasitology* 82 (6): 855–64.

McClelland, R. 1997. "*Cyclospora cayetanensis*—Biography of an Unfamiliar Intestinal Parasite." *Canadian Journal of Medical Laboratory Science* 59: 23–29.

McKelvey, J. J., Jr. 1973. *Man against Tsetse: Struggle for Africa.* Ithaca, NY: Cornell University Press.

McKenna, T. 2001. "Trail of a Terrorist." *Frontline*, PBS. www.pbs.org/wgbh/pages/frontline/shows/trail/etc/script.html (accessed August 27, 2009).

Miller, J., S. Engelberg, and W. Broad. 2001. "The Attack." In *Germs: Biological Weapons and America's Secret War*, 15–33. New York: Simon & Schuster.

Moncayo, A. 1999. "Progress towards Interruption of Transmission of Chagas Disease." *Memórias do Instituto* Oswaldo Cruz, *Rio de Janeiro*, 94 (Supplement 1): 401–4.

Monk, B. E., and Y. J. Rao. 1994. "Delusions of Parasitosis with Fatal Outcome." *Clinical and Experimental Dermatology* 19 (4): 341–42.

Monteiro, F. A., R. Pérez, F. Panzera, J-P Dujardin, C. Galvão, D. Rocha, F. Noireau, C. Schofield, and C. B. Beard. 1999. "Mitochondrial DNA Variation of *Triatoma infestans* Populations and Its Implication in the Specific Status of *T. melanosoma.*" *Memórias do Instituto* Oswaldo Cruz, *Rio de Janeiro*, 94 (Supplement 1): 229–38.

Moore, H. G., and J. L. Galloway. 1992. *We Were Soldiers Once . . . and Young: Ia Drang—The Battle That Changed the War in Vietnam.* New York: Random House.

Moore, J. 2002. *Parasites and the Behavior of Animals.* New York: Oxford University Press.

Moskowitz, M. R. 1995. "Kentucky Fried Chicken." *Business & Society Review* (1974) 95: 69.

Mumcuoglu, K. Y., N. Gallili, A. Reshef, P. Brauner, and H. Grant. 2004. "Use of Human Lice in Forensic Entomology." *Journal of Medical Entomology* 41 (4): 803–6.

Murrell, K. D., and Z. Pawlowski. 2005. "Capacity Building for Surveillance and Control of *Taenia solium*/cysticercosis." In *Capacity Building for Surveillance and Control of Zoonotic Diseases,* Food and Agriculture Organization of the United Nations, Appendix 3: Expert Consultation, 37–45.

Narang, S. K., and M. E. Degrugillier. 1995. "Genetic Fingerprinting of the Screwworm (Diptera: Calliphoridae) Infestation in North Africa by Mitochondrial DNA Markers." *Florida Entomologist* 78 (2): 294–304.

National Farmers Union. 2004. Submission to the Canadian Food Inspection Agency (CFIA): A Response to Notice of Changes to the Honeybee Importation Prohibition Regulations 2004." May. www.nfu.ca/Releases/NFU_Res ponse_to_notice_of_changes_to_Honeybee_Importation.rel.pdf (accessed August 27, 2009).

National Institute for Public Health Surveillance (France). 2002. "Fascioliasis from Eating Cultivated Watercress: An Epidemic in Nord-Pas-de-Calais." *Annual Report 2000*, 63–65.

Navratilova, M., with G. Vecsey. 1985. *Martina*. New York: Alfred A. Knopf.

Newman, J. L. 2004. *Imperial Footprints: Henry Morton Stanley's African Journeys*. Washington, DC: Brassey's.

Newman, R., and D. Shepperd. 2006. *Bury Us Upside Down: The Misty Pilots and the Secret Battle for the Ho Chi Minh Trail*. New York: Ballantine.

Noireau, F., M. G. Rojas Cortez, F. A. Monteiro, A. M. Jansen, and F. Torrico. 2005. "Can Wild *Triatome infestans* Foci in Bolivia Jeopardize Chagas Disease Control Efforts?" *Trends in Parasitology* 21 (1): 7–10.

Osei-Atweneboana, M. Y., J. K. L. Eng, D. A. Boakye, J. O. Gyapong, and R. K. Prichard. 2007. "Prevalence and Intensity of *Onchocerca volvulus* Infection and Efficacy of Ivermectin in Endemic Communities in Ghana: A Two-Phase Epidemiological Study." *Lancet* 369 (9578): 2021–29.

Overstreet, R. M. 2003. "Flavor Buds and Other Delights." *Journal of Parasitology* 89 (6): 1093–1107.

Pfarr, K., and A. Hoerauf. 2005. "The Annotated Genome of *Wolbachia* from the Filarial Nematode *Brugis malayi*: What It Means for Progress on Antifilarial Medicine." *PLoS Medicine* 2 (4): e110.

Phills, J. A., A. J. Harrold, G. V. Whiteman, and L. Perelmutter. 1972. "Pulmonary Infiltrates, Asthma and Eosinophilia Due to *Ascaris suum* Infestation in Man." *New England Journal of Medicine* 286 (18): 965–70.

Plath, F., A. Holle, D. Zendeh, F. W. Möller, M. Barten, E. C. Reisinger, and S. Leibe. 2001. "Anisakiasis of the Stomach—A Case Report from Germany." *Zeitschrift für Gastroenterologie* 39 (2): 177–80 (article in German).

Porter, R., ed. 1996. *Cambridge Illustrated History of Medicine*. Cambridge: Cambridge University Press.

Prichard, J. G., P. D. Kossoris, R. A. Leibovitch, L. D. Robertson, and F. W. Lovell. 1986. "Implications of Trombiculid Mite Bites: Report of a Case and Submission of Evidence in a Murder Trial." *Journal of Forensic Sciences* 31 (1): 301–6.

Ramsay, H. 2004–05. "Ghost Town Worth Millions—in Cash and Memories." *Northword Magazine.* Winter. www.niho.com/Press/Press97.asp (accessed August 27, 2009).

Rasmussen, E. 1959. "Behavior of Sacculinized Shore Crabs (*Carcinus maenas* Pennant)." *Nature* 183: 479–80.

Reed, D. L., J. E. Light, J. M. Allen, and J. J. Kirchman. 2007. "Pair of Lice Lost or Parasites Regained: The Evolutionary History of Anthropoid Primate Lice." *BioMed Central Biology* 5 (7). www.biomedcentral.com/1741-7007/5/7 (accessed August 27, 2009).

Regis, E. 1999. *The Biology of Doom: The History of America's Secret Germ Warfare Project.* New York: Henry Holt.

Reichard, R. E., M. Vargas-Terán, and M. Abu Sowa. 1992. "Myiasis: The Battle Continues against Screwworm Infestation." *World Health Forum* 13 (2–3): 130–38.

Reiter, P. 2000. "From Shakespeare to Defoe: Malaria in England in the Little Ice Age." *Emerging Infectious Diseases* 6 (1): 1–11.

Roberts, L. S., and J. Janovy, Jr. 2000. *Foundations of Parasitology,* 6th ed. Boston: McGraw Hill.

Rochlitz, I. 2000. "Feline Welfare Issues." In Turner and Bateson, *The Domestic Cat,* 207–26.

Rook, G. A. 2009. "Review Series on Helminths, Immune Modulation and the Hygiene Hypothesis: The Broader Implications of the Hygiene Hypothesis." *Immunology* 126 (1): 3–11.

Rosenthal, B. M., G. LaRosa, D. Zarlenga, D. Dunams, Y. Chunyu, L. Mingyuan, and E. Pozio. 2008. "Human Disposal of *Trichinella spiralis* in Domesticated Pigs." *Infection, Genetics and Evolution* 8 (6): 799–805.

Ruebush, T. K., II, D. D. Juranek, A. Spielman, J. Piesman, and G. R. Healy. 1981. "Epidemiology of Babesiosis on Nantucket Island." *American Journal of Tropical Medicine and Hygiene* 30 (5): 937–41.

Sadighian, A., F. Arfaa, E. Ghadirian, and K. Movafagh. 1976. "Contamination with Helminth Eggs of Various Processing Stages of the Sewage Treatment Plant in Isfahan, Central Iran." *Iranian Journal of Public Health* 5 (4): 180–87.

Schantz, P. M. 2002. "*Taenia solium* Cysticercosis: An Overview of Global Distribution and Transmission." In Singh and Prabhakar, Taenia solium Cysticercosis, 63–73.

Schantz, P. M., A. C. Moore, J. L. Muñoz, B. J. Hartman, J. A. Schaefer, A. M. Aron, D. Persaud, E. Sarti, M. Wilson, and A. Flisser. 1992. "Neurocysticercosis in an Orthodox Jewish Community in New York City." *New England Journal of Medicine* 327 (10): 692–95.

Scheld, W. M., D. Armstrong, and J. M. Hughes, eds. 1998. *Emerging Infections 1.* Washington, DC: ASM Press.

Scheld, W. M., W. A. Craig, and J. M. Hughes, eds. 2000. *Emerging Infections 4*. Washington, DC: ASM Press.

———, eds. 1999. *Emerging Infections 3*. Washington, DC: ASM Press.

———, eds. 1998. *Emerging Infections 2*. Washington, DC: ASM Press.

Scheld, W. M., B. E. Murray, and J. M. Hughes, eds. 2004. *Emerging Infections 6*. Washington, DC: ASM Press.

Schmunis, G. A. 1999. "Prevention of Transfusional *Trypanosoma cruzi* Infection in Latin America." *Memórias do Instituto* Oswaldo Cruz, *Rio de Janeiro*, 94 (Supplement I): 93–101.

Serpell, J. A. 2000. "Domestication and History of the Cat." In Turner and Bateson, *The Domestic Cat*, 179–92.

Singh, G., and S. Prabhakar, eds. 2002. Taenia solium *Cysticercosis*. Wallingford, UK: CABI Publishing.

Singh, S., V. Dhikav, N. Agarwal, and K. S. Anand. 2004. "An Unusual Cause of Psychosis." *Lancet* 363 (9420): 1522.

Sloan, N. A. 1985. "Life History Characteristics of Fjord-Dwelling Golden King Crabs *Lithodes aequispina*." *Marine Ecology Progress Series* 22 (3): 219–28.

Smith, J. W., ed. 1976a. Photographic slide no. 40: Hookworm: *N. americanus*, buccal capsule (scanning electron photomicrograph). *Diagnostic Medical Parasitology: Helminths*. Chicago: American Society of Clinical Pathologists.

——— 1976b. Photographic slide no. 87: *Toxoplasma gondii*, cyst in mouse brain (H&E stain). *Diagnostic Medical Parasitology: Blood and Tissue Parasites*. Chicago: American Society of Clinical Pathologists.

Southeastern Cooperative Wildlife Disease Study (SCWDS). *SCWDS Briefs:*

———. 1995. "Animals Examined from a Florida Foxpen." April.

———. 1994a. "Advisory on *Echinococcus multilocularis.*" July.

———. 1994b. "Dangerous Tapeworm." April.

———. 1994c. "More Translocated Foxes." April.

———. 1992. "Fox Hunting Enclosures Surveyed for Dangerous Parasite." July.

———. 1991. "Fox Sales Numerous and Widespread." October.

———. 1990. "Operation 'Fox Trot' Yields More Than Foxes." January.

———. 1986. "Translocated Foxes and Public Health." July.

Spielman, A. 1994. "The Emergence of Lyme Disease and Human Babesiosis in a Changing Environment." *Annals of the New York Academy of Sciences* 740: 146–56.

———. 1976. "Human Babesiosis on Nantucket Island: Transmission by Nymphal *Ixodes* Ticks." *American Journal of Tropical Medicine and Hygiene* 25 (6): 784–87.

Stephenson, L. S., M. C. Latham, and E. A. Ottesen. 2000. "Malnutrition and Parasitic Helminth Infections." *Parasitology* 121: S23–S38 (supplement).

Taylor, D. B., A. L. Szalanski, and R. D. Peterson, II. 1996. "Mitochondrial DNA Variation in Screwworm." *Medical and Veterinary Entomology* 10: 161–69.

Teixeira, A. R. L., P. S. Monteiro, J. M. Rebelo, E. R. Argañaraz, D. Vieira, L. Lauria-Pires, R. Nascimento et al. 2001. "Emerging Chagas Disease: Trophic Network and Cycle of Transmission of Trypanosoma cruzi from Palm Trees in the Amazon." *Emerging Infectious Diseases* 7 (1): 100–12.

Thebpatiphat, N., K. M. Hammersmith, F. N. Rocha, C. J. Rapuano, B. D. Ayres, P. R. Laibson, R. C. Eagle Jr., and E. J. Cohen. 2007. "*Acanthamoeba* Keratitis: A Parasite on the Rise." *Cornea* 26 (6): 701–6.

Thibierge, G. 1894. "Les acarophobes." *Revue générale de clinique et de therapeutique* 8: 373–76.

Thylefors, B., and M. Alleman. 2006. "Towards the Elimination of Onchocerciasis." *Annals of Tropical Medicine & Parasitology* 100 (8): 733–46.

Torrey, E. F., and R. H. Yolken. 2003. "*Toxoplasma gondii* and Schizophrenia." *Emerging Infectious Diseases* 9 (11): 1375–80.

Townson, S., S. Tagboto, H. F. McGarry, G. I. Egerton, and M. J. Taylor. 2006. "Onchocerca Parasites and *Wolbachia* Endosymbionts: Evaluation of a Spectrum of Antibiotic Types for Activity against *Onchocerca gutturosa in vitro*." *Filaria Journal* 5 (4): 9 pages.

Turner, D. C., and P. Bateson, eds. 2000. *The Domestic Cat: The Biology of Its Behavior.* Cambridge: Cambridge University Press.

U.S. Environmental Protection Agency. 2004. *Safe Drinking Water Act 30th Anniversary: Understanding the Safe Drinking Water Act.* www.epa.gov/safewater/sdwa/pdfs/fs-30ann_sdwa_web.pdf (accessed August 25, 2009).

———. Office of Ground Water and Drinking Water Standards and Risk Management Division. 2002. "Health Risks from Microbial Growth and Biofilms in Drinking Water Distribution Systems." June 17. White paper. Washington, DC.

Van Woerden, H. 2000. *The Assassin.* New York: Metropolitan.

Wallin, M. T., and J. F. Kurtzke. 2004. "Neurocysticercosis in the United States." *Neurology* 63 (9): 1559–64.

Watt, J. 1979. "Medical Aspects and Consequences of Cook's Travels." In *Captain James Cook and His Times*, edited by R. Fisher and H. Johnson, 129–57. Vancouver: Douglas and McIntyre.

Webster, J. P., P. H. L. Lamberton, C. A. Donnelly, and E. F. Torrey. 2006. "Parasites as Causative Agents of Human Affective Disorders? The Impact of Anti-Psychotic, Mood Stabilizer and Anti-Parasite Medication on *Toxoplasma gondii*'s Ability to Alter Host Behavior." *Proceedings of the Royal Society B Biological Sciences* 273 (1589): 1023–30.

Weiss, S. T. 2000. "Parasites and Asthma/Allergy: What Is the Relationship?" *Journal of Allergy and Clinical Immunology* 105 (2 part 1): 205–10.

Wenner, A. M., and W. W. Bushing. 1996. "*Varroa* Mite Spread in the United States." *Bee Culture* (June): 341–43.

Williams, L. L. 1963. "Malaria Eradication in the United States." *American Journal of Public Health* 53 (1): 17–21.

Wilson, J. F., R. L. Rausch, and F. R. Wilson. 1995. "Alveolar Hydatid Disease: Review of the Surgical Experience in 42 Cases of Active Disease among Alaskan Eskimos." *Annals of Surgery* 221 (3): 315–23.

Winiecka-Krusnell, J., and A. A. Kettis. 2003. *"Giardia intestinalis."* In Akuffo et al., *Parasites of the Colder Climates*, 102–7.

World Health Organization. 2008a. "Dracunculiasis Eradication." *Weekly Epidemiological Record* 83 (18): 159–67.

———. 2008b. *World Malaria Report 2008.* Geneva: WHO Press.

World Health Organization and UNICEF. 2006. *Meeting the MDG Drinking Water and Sanitation Targets: The Urban and Rural Challenge of the Decade.* WHO/UNICEF Joint Monitoring Programme, Geneva and New York. Geneva: WHO Press.

Wykoff, R. F. 1987. "Delusions of Parasitosis: A Review." *Reviews of Infectious Diseases* 9 (3): 433–37.

Wyss, J. H., and T. J. Galvin. 1996. "Central America Regional Screwworm Eradication Program (Benefit/Cost Study)." *Annals of the New York Academy of Sciences* 791 (July 23): 241–47.

Zakhary, K. 1997. "Factors Affecting the Prevalence of Schistosomiasis in the Volta Region of Ghana." *McGill Journal of Medicine* 3 (2): 93–101.

Zayas, C. F, C. Perlino, A. Caliendo, D. Jackson, E. J. Martinez, P. Tso, T. G. Heffron et al. 2002. "Chagas Disease after Organ Transplantation—United States, 2001." *Morbidity and Mortality Weekly Report* 51 (10): 210–12.

Zimmer, C. 2000. *Parasite Rex.* New York: Free Press.

Zinsser, H. 1965. *Rats, Lice and History.* New York: Bantam Books.

Zomer, S. F., R. F. DeWit, J. E. Van Bronswijk, G. Nabarro, and W. A. Van Vloten. 1998. "Delusions of Parasitosis: A Psychiatric Disorder to Be Treated by Dermatologists? An Analysis of 33 Patients." *British Journal of Dermatology* 138 (6): 1030–32.

INDEX

Page numbers in italics indicate illustrations.

Canada geese, 67
Capital Regional District Health
  Department (British Columbia), 62,
  64
caribou, 92–93
Carter, Jimmy, 197–201, *198*
Carter Center, 197–201, 202
cats: mites and, 228n10; toxoplasmosis
  and, 57, 62, 64, 113–15, 117
cattle: *Cryptosporidium* and, 66; *Taenia
  saginata* and, 52–55; *Toxoplasma
  gondii* and, 116–19. *See also* livestock
CDC. *See* U.S. Centers for Disease
  Control and Prevention
cerebrospinal elaphostrongylosis (CSE),
  93, 94
Chagas, Carlos, 178–79
Chagas' disease. *See* *Trypanosoma cruzi*
Chaucer, Geoffrey, 143
chlorination: *Acanthamoeba* and, 182;
  protozoa and, 68, 69, 70, 72, 73
chloroquine, 23–24, 210, 232n31
Cimex lectularius (bedbug), *144*, 144–49
Clark, Thomas D., 84–86
Clerke, Charles, 31
Climbié, Victoria, 136–40, 228n12
clothing, 141–43, 173, 174
Cochliomyia hominivorax (screwworm fly),
  98–104, 217, 225nn22,23, 226n2
Cohn, Edwin J., 216–17
colonialism, 13–19
conditions for infestations: emerging
  parasites and, 174; eradication and,
  214–15; malaria and, 5–6, 24;
  schistosomiasis and, 7–9; tapeworm
  and, 41–42, 53–54; trichinosis and,
  40–41; trypanosomiasis and, 15.
  See also clothing; emerging parasites;
  water resources development
contact lenses, 180–84
Cook, Captain James, 27–32, 169
Coughenour, John, 161
Creston (British Columbia), 70–72
crime involving parasites: arrest of
  terrorist, 158–62; murder evidence,
  150–58, 167–72; "parasite killer,"
  167–72. *See also* "punishment of the
  boats"

Croton watershed (New York City),
  69–70
Cryptosporidium spp. (cryptosporidiosis),
  62, 182, 215; *C. parvum*, 58; chlorine
  and, 69, 73; life cycle of, 75; oocysts
  of, 58, 65–67; public water supply
  contamination and, 72–78. *See also*
  oocysts
CSE. *See* cerebrospinal elaphostrongylosis
Cuba, 208
cultural attitudes: fear of parasites, 3, 138;
  toward lice, 140, 141–43; toward
  tapeworms, 125–28; toxoplasmosis
  and, 119. *See also* behavior change;
  beliefs about parasites; human brain;
  usefulness of parasites
Cyclospora cayetanensis (cyclosporiasis),
  45–47, 62
cyclosporiasis. *See* *Cyclospora cayetanensis*
Cyrus the Younger (Persian prince),
  145–46
cysticercosis. *See* *Taenia* spp. (tapeworm)

Dahoumane, Abdelmajid, 159
Darwin, Charles, 175–76, 180
DDT, 210, 211, 232n31
deer ticks, 186–88, 230n13
delusional parasitosis (Ekbom's syndrome;
  folie à deux; Morgellons disease),
  128–35, 138–40, 227n7, 228n13
Demodex folliculorum (face mite), 131, *132*
Denny, Henry, 175
Dicrocoelium dendriticum (lancet fluke),
  107–9, 226n3
Diphyllobothrium spp. (fish tapeworm), 31
DiSpirito, Rocco, 55–56
DNA profiling: bedbugs and, 145;
  lice and, 143
dogs, 41–42, 43, 97
domestication of animals, 6; Chagas'
  disease and, 178; hydatid disease and,
  41–44; trichinosis and, 40–41, 43–44.
  See also cats; cattle; dogs; guinea pigs;
  livestock; pigs; sheep; *Triatoma
  infestans* (kissing bug)
Donaldsonville (LA), murder in, 154–58
Dracunculus medinensis (guinea worm),
  105–7, *108*, 197–201, 205, 226n1

drinking water, 224n20; in Canada, 62–65, 70–72, 75–78; contamination of, 59–61, 68–70; cryptosporidiosis and, 73–78; giardiasis and, 70–72; in India/Pakistan, 226n2; toxoplasmosis and, 62–65, 70; treatment of, 61–62, 63, 64, 68–70; in U.S., 73–75; watershed protection and, 64–65, 69. See also *Cryptosporidium* spp. (cryptosporidiosis); *Giardia lamblia* (giardiasis); *Toxoplasma gondii* (toxoplasmosis); water resources development; water treatment systems

drugs, 201. *See also* resistance

DuPont, 198–99

Duval, Marie (pseud.), 133–35

Echinococcus spp. (hydatid tapeworm): *E. granulosus* and, 41–44, 47, 57, 221n7; *E. multilocularis* and, 95–98

Egypt, Aswan High Dam in, 164

Ekbom's syndrome. *See* delusional parasitosis

Elaphostrongylus spp. (roundworm), 92–95; *E. cervi* and, 94–95; *E. rangiferi* and, 92–94, 94

emerging parasites: amoebic parasites, 180–85; *Babesia microti*, 186–88; *Baylisascaris procyonis*, 188–91; body lice, 173–74; Chagas' disease, 175–80; definition of, 173–75; *Taenia solium* neurocysticercosis, 191–93

England: beliefs about lice in, 140, 141–43; malaria in, 209; PAM in, 184–85; "scabies" case in, 136–40

Enterobius vermicularis (pinworm), 26

eosinophils, 168

EPA. *See* U.S. Environmental Protection Agency

eradication projects, 196–215; *Dracunculus medinensis* and, 197–201, 205; human dependence and, 196–97; malaria and, 208–13; *Onchocerca volvulus* and, 201–4; screwworm in American South and, 101; screwworm in Central America and, 103; screwworm in Libya and, 100–4; *Taenia solium* and, 204–8; *Trypanosoma cruzi* and, 213–15

Eutrombicula belkini (chigger mites), 150–54

externa, 110. See also *Briarosaccus callosus* (barnacle)

face mite *(Demodex folliculorum)*, 131, *132*

FAO. *See* United Nations Food and Agriculture Organization

farmer's markets, 44–45

farming practices: *Echinococcus granulosus* and, 41–44; eradication efforts and, 205–6; tapeworm and, 52–53; trichinsosis and, 40–41, 43–44

Fasciola hepatica (liver fluke), 47–49, *48*

FDA. *See* U.S. Food and Drug Administration

feces. *See* human waste

fish parasites, 49–52

fleas. See *Xenopsylla cheopis* (rat flea)

Flegr, Jaroslav, 115

floc (in water treatment), 68–69, 74

flukes. See *Dicrocoelium dendriticum* (lancet fluke); *Fasciola hepatica* (liver fluke); *Schistosoma* spp. (blood fluke)

fly, 55–58; medical use of maggots and, 147–48; "punishment of the boats" and, 145–47; screwworm fly and, 98–104. See also black fly; tsetse fly

folie à deux, 133–35, 138–40

foodborne illness, 33, 34–58; beef and, 52–54; cyclosporiasis and, 45–47; fish and, 49–52; flies and, 55–58; fresh produce and, 44–49; pork and, 36–44; regulation and, 34–35, 37, 54, 55

food inspection, 44, 52; beef, 54, 55; pork, 37, 40, 192–93

Fox, Leon A., 162

foxhunting, 96–98

freezing: fish parasites and, 50–52; pork and, 44

Galvin, T. J., 225n22

Gambian sleeping sickness (trypanosomiasis), 13, 14–19

General Chemical Corporation, 74, 223n12

Geneva Declaration, 200

Ghana, 11–14

Giardia lamblia (giardiasis), 215, 223n14; beaver and, 70–72; cysts of, 65, *66*, 68, 70, 71, 72; filtration and, 69, 70, 72; water contamination and, 65, 68–69, 70–72

Global Eradication of Malaria Program, 210

Glossina spp. (tsetse flies), 13, 14

Gorgas, William, 208–9

Grenfell, Wilfred, 92, 225n15

Guatemala, 45–47

guinea pigs, 178

guinea worm. See *Dracunculus medinensis*

al-Haq, Zia, 197

head lice *(Pediculus humanus capitis)*, 140–41, 228n15

health inspection, 55–56. *See also* regulation

herring worm *(Anisakis simplex)*, 49–51

Higgins, Blair (pseud.), 128–29, *130*, 227n6

Ho Chi Minh Trail, 20–24, *21*

hookworm. See *Necator americanus*

Hopkins, Donald R., 199

host control: *Briarosaccus callosus* and, 109–12; *Dicrocoelium dendriticum* and, 107–9; *Dracunculus medinensis* and, 105–6, 107; *Taenia solium* and, 120–24; *Toxoplasma gondii* and, 112–20

Hsu, Rebecca, 123

human affairs, impacts of parasites on, 5; costs of cryptosomiasis outbreaks, 74, 77–78; guinea worm, 107; hookworm, 84; hydatid disease, 221n7; intestinal worms, 32–33; malaria, 19; screwworm, 100–2, 225n22; sleeping sickness, 18–19. *See also* warfare

human brain: *Baylisascaris procyonis* and, 188–91; *Echinococcus multilocularis* and, 98; *Taenia solium* and, 120, 121–24, *122; Toxoplasma gondii* and, 115–20; trypanosomiasis and, 17–18

human dwelling places, 6, 178, 190–91, 213–14

human immune system: benefits of parasites on, 148–49; river blindness and, 203–4; *T. brucei* and, 220n14; toxoplasmosis and, 63, 226n8

human inventions. *See* clothing; domestication of animals; foxhunting; human dwelling places; law of unintended consequences; medical advances; slavery; warfare; water resources development; water sports; water treatment systems

human waste, 57, 60–61; absence of sanitation and, 26, 59–61, 205–6, *206;* contamination of water supplies and, 7, 11, 12; eradication of parasites and, 204, 205–6, 215; hookworm disease and, 83–86; as manure, 6, 52–53; pork tapeworm and, 192–93, 204, 205–6. *See also* sewage treatment

Humpback Reservoir (Victoria, British Columbia), 62–65

hunter-gatherers, 5–6, 219n2

hydatid tapeworm. See *Echinococcus* spp.

immigration, 195

imported foods, 45–47

imported parasites: bee mites, 87–91; *Echinococcus multilocularis* tapeworm, 95–98; *Elaphostrongylus* spp. roundworm, 92–94; hookworm, 83–86; New World screwworm in Libya, 98–104

India, 55, 197, 226n2

intermediate hosts, 25, 82–83; *Anisakis simplex* and, 51; babesiosis and, 186–88; *Baylisascaris procyonis* and, 189–91; *Dicrocoelium dendriticum* and, 107–9; *Echinococcus granulosus* and, 41–42; *E. multilocularis* and, 95; *Elaphostrongylus rangiferi* and, 92–92; fascioliasis and, 47–49; guinea worm and, 106; *Onchocerca volvulus* and, 165–66; schistosomiasis and, 8, 10, 13; tapeworms and, 41–42, 53, 55; toxoplasmosis and, 64; *Trypanosoma brucei* and, 13–14; *Trypanosoma cruzi* and, 175–76, 213–14. *See also* black fly; mosquitoes; snails; tsetse fly

Merck & Co., 201–2
merozoites, 22, 23, 75
Merton, Robert K., 230n3
Mexico, 143, 194–95, 207
microfilariae, 166, *167*, 201, 203–4. *See also*
   life cycles of parasites
Migration Policy Institute, 195
"millennium bomber." *See* Ressam,
   Ahmed (alias Benni Antoine Noris)
Millennium Development Goals, 211,
   233n33
Milwaukee (WI), 73–75
mites. See *Acarapis woodi* (tracheal
   bee mite); *Demodex folliculorum*
   (face mite); *Eutrombicula belkini*
   (chigger mites); *Notoedres cati*
   (cat mite); *Sarcoptes scabiei* (scabies
   mite); *Varroa destructor* (bee mite)
Mithridates, 146–47
Morgellons disease. *See* delusional
   parasitosis
mosquitoes: control of, 210–11, 212;
   insecticide resistance and, 211, 232n31;
   malaria and, 13, 20, 21, 208, 209–10

Naegleria fowleri ("brain-eating amoeba"),
   183–86
nagana *(Trypanosoma b. brucei)*, 13–14
Nantucket Island (MA), 187–88
nauplius, 110
Navratilova, Martina, 116–19, 226n14
Necator americanus (hookworm), 57,
   83–86, *85*, 148, 174–75
Netherlands, 49–51
neurocysticercosis, 121–24, 126, 192–93;
   diagnosis and treatment of, 227n23;
   eradication efforts and, 207–8. See
   also *Taenia* spp. (tapeworm)
Newfoundland, 92–94, 225n15
New York City: health inspection in,
   55–56; pork tapeworm outbreak in,
   193–95; water supply for, 69–70
New York Times, sleeping sickness covered
   in, 18
NGOs. *See* nongovernmental
   organizations
nongovernmental organizations (NGOs),
   199, 200

Noris, Benni Antoine (pseud.). *See*
   Ressam, Ahmed
North America: bees in, 87–91, 224n8;
   exported parasites and, 98–104;
   imported parasites and, 83–86, 87–98;
   malaria in, 209–10; pork tapeworm
   and, 192. *See also* Canada; United
   States
North Battleford. *See* North Saskatchewan
   River
North Saskatchewan River
   (Saskatchewan), 61–68, 75;
   cryptosporidiosis outbreak in, 75–78
Notoedres cati (cat mite), 228n10

OEPA. *See* Onchocerciasis Elimination
   Program for the Americas
Onchocerca volvulus (river blindness), 13,
   165–67, *167;* as biological weapon,
   165–67; eradication efforts and,
   201–4; in South America, 86
Onchocerciasis Elimination Program for
   the Americas (OEPA), 203
onchospheres, 120–21
oocysts: *Cryptosporidium* spp. and, 58,
   65–67, 74–75; *Cyclospora cayetanensis*
   and, 45–47; imaginary journey of,
   65–66, 68–69, 73, 75; *Toxoplasma
   gondii* and, 63, 117. *See also* life cycles
   of parasites
organ donation, 177, 179–80, 213

PAHO. *See* Pan American Health
   Organization
Pakistan, 197, 199, 226n2
PAM. *See* primary amoebic
   meningoencephalitis
Panama, 208–9
Pan American Health Organization
   (PAHO), 202, 213
"parasitologist's dilemma," 216–17
Paré, Ambroise, 147
Pediculus humanus (lice), 140–43, 175
pickled herring, 49–51
pigs: *Taenia solium* (tapeworm) and,
   120–24, 191–93, 204–8; *Trichinella
   spiralis* and, 35–41, 43–44; *Trichuris
   suis* (whipworm) and, 148

Text:	11.25/13.5 Adobe Garamond
Display:	Adobe Garamond
Indexer:	Marcia Carlson
Cartographer:	Bill Nelson
Compositor:	Toppan Best-set Premedia Limited
Printer and Binder:	Maple-Vail Book Manufacturing Group